A HISTORY OF THE
NEW AVIATION

THE DEVELOPMENT OF
HANG-GLIDING,
PARAGLIDING,
MICROLIGHTING
AND PARAMOTORING

BRIAN MILTON

AIR WORLD

AIR WORLD

A HISTORY OF THE NEW AVIATION
The Development of Hang-gliding, Paragliding, Microlighting and Paramotoring

First published in Great Britain in 2024 by
Air World
An imprint of
Pen & Sword Books Ltd
Yorkshire – Philadelphia

ISBN 978 1 39904 858 3

Typeset by SJmagic DESIGN SERVICES, India.

Printed and bound in the UK by CPI Group (UK) Ltd.

Pen & Sword Books Limited incorporates the imprints of Atlas, Archaeology, Aviation, Discovery, Family History, Fiction, History, Maritime, After the Battle, Military, Military Classics, Politics, Select, Transport, True Crime, Air World, Frontline Publishing, Leo Cooper, Remember When, Seaforth Publishing, The Praetorian Press, Wharncliffe Local History, Wharncliffe Transport, Wharncliffe True Crime and White Owl.

For a complete list of Pen & Sword titles please contact

PEN & SWORD BOOKS LIMITED
George House, Units 12 & 13, Beevor Street, Off Pontefract Road,
Barnsley, South Yorkshire, S71 1HN, England
E-mail: enquiries@pen-and-sword.co.uk
Website: www.pen-and-sword.co.uk

or
PEN AND SWORD BOOKS
1950 Lawrence Rd, Havertown, PA 19083, USA
E-mail: uspen-and-sword@casematepublishers.com
Website: www.penandswordbooks.com

Contents

Introduction

The new aviation has the same early roots as the mainstream: Icarus and Daedalus, King Bladud, Leonardo da Vinci, Sir George Cayley, as far as the great nineteenth-century German pioneer Otto Lilienthal, the first man truly to fly. Then, when mainstream aviation went on after 1903 to develop flight through the American Wright brothers, the French giants Louis Blériot, Hubert Latham, Roland Garros, the Atlantic flyers Alcock and Brown, America's towering ocean-beater Charles Lindbergh and the other trail-breakers. This was followed by space flights in the 1960s leaving a small group behind. This group was dissatisfied by the parameters of an aviation science that led to the Jumbo Jet, Concorde and the way NASA and the Russians tackled space travel. The more as a human species we knew about how to fly, the less we enjoyed the simple existential experience of actually doing it. We lost that wind in the face feeling, we ceased to be something aesthetic, and became mechanical, mundane, hedged in by rules. Inside mainstream aviation, that small left-behind group was caricatured – and still is – as lunatics, though among them were a group I call the 'Holy Lunatics'. You may have seen moving pictures of their efforts to fly, cycling along madly on a bike with wings that collapse around them, running off hills flapping their home-made wings, plummeting out of the sky in a vain effort to find another way to fly. Sane people waited for experts to build them safe machines, and then were content to be sealed up inside the resulting silver tubes, to breathe second-hand air for hours, listen to crying babies and sit lined up like packed sardines … and call the experience *flying*. But of course, it is merely using the air to get from one place to another, as quickly as possible.

Despite sharing early roots, the new aviation marks a distinct change from the mainstream. It has an exact beginning, 23 May 1971, what would have been the 123rd birthday of Otto Lilienthal had he not been killed in 1896; that new aviation birth occurred three quarters of a century, seventy-five years after Lilienthal's death. This second history mirrors the risks taken by the pioneering mainstream, but sets off in a different direction. Where the mainstream, on the one hand, aims to be bigger and go higher, faster, and further, on the other hand it is weighed down with regulation. When it began, the new aviation when it began was a return to man's original dreams of flight, virtually naked into the wind, and crucially, foot launched. Fourteen young men were on the southern California sand dune that day of the first Lilienthal meet, where hang gliding was born in what *Reader's Digest* called 'the flyingest flying there is'. The women who were there that day supported their menfolk, nursed them, took photographs of them, even fed them but did not do any of the flying until later that year. Modern women's liberation was in its early youth in 1971.

Now the descendants of the wings flown that day are called hang gliders and paragliders, and those with motors attached are called microlights and ultralights. They make up one fifth of all the registered aircraft in advanced countries, including Great Britain.

We are the future. One day, in a hang glider or a paraglider, we will learn how to migrate, to go south with the birds in the autumn, and fly from northern Europe to central Africa, or North to South America, entirely unsupported by anything but our own efforts and the powers of nature. In microlighting, we are paving the way in the not too distant future to fly around the world, powered by the sun without it costing more than $40 million from wealthy commercial sponsors.

I think the idea of a second history of aviation is true and potent. It is a noble story, worth telling, of courage, daring, stoicism and sacrifice. When I completed the first draft of this book, all the new aviation pioneers were either still alive, or, if dead, there are recordings on video, film and sound recordings of their achievements. I know ATV in the British Midlands made a fifteen-minute profile of my friend Alvin Russell in the middle of 1976, the year he was killed. The first superstar of our branch of aviation, the great American Bob Wills, did all the stunt work in the James Coburn film *Sky Riders* before being killed by a helicopter flown by the same pilot involved in that Hollywood movie. Francis Rogallo, another American, who with his wife Gertrude created the flying designs that launched the new aviation, died only in 2009. He left a priceless archive of NASA films, some of which he showed me personally, of the bizarre and fascinating results of the US government throwing $50 million at his simple design in the late 1950s to see where Rogallo wings could go. Most of us in the new aviation do not know our own past. This is a comprehensive attempt to come to terms with it.

In the new aviation there is still much to do. Young people who are told that there is no adventure left in the world, because the *wrinklies* – that includes me – have had all the adventures there are, can take heart. Forget that subliminal message to shove something exotic up your nose, or to fiddle with virtual reality machines if you want to experience the heights of adventure that were achieved in the early days of mainstream aviation. There are real, not virtual adventures, left to do. The act of erecting a wing on a hill and walking into the air unassisted, well, the OFT will have an impossible job killing our spirit. Unlike mainstream aviation, which on its thirtieth anniversary in 1933 – dramatised by Robert Redford in the Hollywood film *The Great Waldo Pepper* – had been tied down, kicking and screaming, every new development in the new aviation makes us more independent of the instruments by which those who went before us in the air are controlled. The key to our type of flying is foot launching.

There are still records to be won, history books to be ransacked to see just where in the original mainstream aviation we can match their achievements with our own wings, and imaginative things to do in flight. And you do not even have to be young to do it. At one time all the best hang gliding records in the world were held by one man, a 60-year-old American called George Worthington, who fought like a battered but wily lion against any attempt by younger men to wrest those records from him. And he had taken up hang gliding only seven years earlier.

I have provided the linkage and context for individual stories inside our history, but nearly half the text has been buried in hundreds of individual articles in magazines for decades. There is a freshness to the experiences of this form of flying that reaches across the pages, and which has long been missing from mainstream aviation. Anyone else can read the thousands of stories that mark our progress, and tell the same history in a different way. But I was intimately involved in parts of that history, and I have not written a disinterested account of what happened. I am still a player in the game in my own field, in microlights; for a while I was a player in world competition hang gliding, and was honoured by the Queen of England for my contribution. But I believe I have made vital connections to link Lilienthal to today's top pilots and designers, so this is also a personal history. I am not ashamed of the fire and the passion of some of the passages, however unfashionable that might be in our modern 'cool' world.

My son James, who did three tours of Iraq as a captain with the British Army, once asked me to stop having any more adventures, because there would be nothing left for him and his generation to do. There are still great adventures to be had, James. I hope that you find here the inspiration for them.

Chapter 1

Life, work and death of Alvin Russell, my best friend and the first flying and training officer of the British Hang Gliding Association (BHGA). He laid down the regulations for safe teaching in Britain. He was killed on a hill in Ireland on Christmas Eve, 1976, flying a prototype that he had rigged wrongly, and which, except for sheer chance, I should have flown; it would have killed me instead.

Chapter 2

History of aviation from Icarus and Daedalus, through King Bladud and Leonardo da Vinci, to the great German pioneer Otto Lilienthal, our last common ancestor with mainstream aviation. Includes an account of an expedition to Crete to see if Daedalus could have flown from there in 1500 BC. Could that flight be repeated today? The English apprentice who, 500 years after Leonardo da Vinci conceived a working flying wing in 1493, built and flew a hang glider designed by the Italian genius. Some comments on mainstream aviation since the Wright brothers, and the death of Tom Wolfe's 'right stuff' by 1970.

Chapter 3

Francis Rogallo and the 'Holy Lunatics', two streams of research, one Australian, one Californian, which led to the first Lilienthal meet on 23 May 1971. It was seventy-five years after Lilienthal's death, and would have been his 123rd birthday, which led to the official birth of the new aviation. Includes links through Francis Rogallo, John Dickenson, Bill Moyes and Bill Bennett in Australia, plus US characters via Richard Miller and Jack Lambie. Those I dub 'Holy Lunatics' include man-powered flight pioneer Paul MacCready. Bill Liscomb's account, one of fourteen men who flew that day; where the longest distance flown was 196ft and the longest time in the air was eleven seconds.

Chapter 4

British pioneers Geoff McBroom, Len Gabriels, the Haynes brothers and Nick Regan. Ken Messenger jumps off Mount Snowdon. Brian Wood's eight-hour flight including in-air feeding, formation of the BHGA, 'clubbiness' and excitement of early flying, the first World Championships, Brian Wood's spectacular accident and how Americans became demi-gods of the sport.

Chapter 5

Learning how to fly cross-country (XC). Graham Hobson's innocent 'What is a thermal?'. Early 'wave' flight, a mile high over Snowdon, Bob Calvert leaves a hill in a thunderstorm, 1977 League cross-country flights (XCs), Nigel Milnes' 22-mile record, different regional XC styles, Robert Bailey's 50-mile flight compared to Hemingway's 'Big Two-Hearted River', American go-for-it flying in Owens Valley and US pilot Jim Lee flies 168 miles.

Chapter 6

Gliding and hang gliding, the organised campaign by some British conventional gliding clubs to remove hang gliders from 'their' hills and 'their' air, advantages and disadvantages of both flying disciplines and yearnings from sailplanes to capture the huge energy and excitement of the new aviation.

Chapter 7

Competitions evolve from spot landings to cross-country. Foundation and early problems of the ground-breaking British League, and movement of Britain from nowhere to edge of world domination in competitions. Challenge to Americans, reverse of yachting's America's Cup, 'watershed' wins by Britain and the American fight-back with the 'Comet Revolution' in 1980.

Chapter 8

Power, evolution of successful man-powered flight, winning the Kremer prizes, sun-powered flight, first petrol engines, Soarmaster Arab units start *Intifada,* James Bond and the John Long 'Moonraker', birth of the trike, early experiences, record flights, to Africa, Australia, across the Atlantic and microlights 20 per cent of UK registration.

Chapter 1

Alvin Russell, My Best Friend

When he was a young man, Alvin Russell set a British hill climbing record. So far as I know, it still stands. I met him on the Long Mynd in Shropshire, a distinctive 10-mile hill running north-south with west-facing slopes already claimed by conventional sailplanes. It looked the perfect hill for me to make an attempt at the British hang gliding duration record, then set at eight and a half hours, but in the event I never tried. Alvin was the founder of the Long Mynd Hang Gliding Club, and lived in an Elizabethan cottage, with black wooden beams and leaning white plaster walls, at the foot of the hill.

He was bearded, heavily spectacled and had an accent I thought came from Birmingham, but then I am a southerner. He owned a garage in Montgomery, a market town in Wales that persisted in voting Liberal decades after the death of the great Liberal statesman David Lloyd George; the rest of the principality has long gone on to vote Labour or Welsh Nationalist. The Mynd seemed to cut off the region from the rest of Britain and produce quiet but determined individualists. Alvin was one.

It was early 1975, and in Britain we were moving from standard Rogallo hang gliders, so-called bog-rogs – bog-standard Rogallos – on to wings where it was not always necessary to fly to the bottom of the hill. If we ran off and turned close to the hill, it was possible to maintain height, even increase it, but at the risk of incurring the anger of the gliding club, which looked upon us with alarm and contempt. They were contemptuous because they could soar high and it appeared we could not. They were alarmed because we were learning quickly, and if we started to soar high, as Alvin did and the rest of us were beginning to, we would get into *their* airspace. They thought it was *their* air to dispose of as they wished.

I was a BBC radio reporter at the time, and almost every weekend I drove to the Long Mynd from my home in St Albans, a Roman city just north of London, to stay at Alvin's house. If the wind blew from the west, as it often did, we would drive to the top and walk over Eddie Bowen's land

1

to set up our wings to fly. Eddie, a kindly farmer, lived at the base of the Mynd, and was the president of Alvin's club. We used his fields to land in if we could not land back on top. Eddie was not open to blandishments from the local gliding club to ban our flying.

Alvin was a complicated man, with skills he never boasted about and which were a surprise to learn. He played the cello to a high enough standard to belong to an orchestra. He was a noted rally driver and drove brilliantly. During the seven months he took hang gliding by the scruff of its neck in Britain and shook it into safety he also studied and qualified as a Royal Automobile Club car rally scrutineer. He collected porcelain of high quality, which was scattered around his house. He had not the intellectual capacity or education of John le Carré's George Smiley, but there was that quality about him; from time to time you learned something new and startling on which he was an expert.

Alvin was the driving force behind the small group of hang glider pilots who used the Long Mynd. He was so self-effacing about his talent that, when we totted up the experts on the hill we forgot to include his name, though he had taught most of them to fly. He was curious about the air, not reading about it or learning from books, but being in it to find out for himself how it behaved.

That winter, 1975–76, he broke his leg on a heavy landing and had to stand and watch while the rest of us flew. It was too much. He persuaded two other pilots, Tony Jones and Graham Driscoll, to go out on to the Mynd on a moonlit night to rig in the cold rushing air and launch him gloriously, like a huge paper dart, hopping into the sky in a seated harness, his plaster cast a white ghost in the smooth lift. After half an hour of sublime flight Alvin swooped into Eddie's field and hopped breathlessly down for a safe landing. I would love to have been with him then.

We flew a lot together because I had done a number of soaring flights, but he was always a better pilot than me. He was there the day I launched into a high wind, trying to tape-record a flight for the BBC, and being blown backwards, helplessly, over the hill. I apologised to the tape recorder because I had to concentrate on staying alive and Alvin caught me as I landed, running backwards, before I hit a stone wall and was sent tumbling.

In the evenings we dreamed of where we were going, and what we might do. Neither of us, each in our early thirties, was in the first flush of youth. But hang gliding was fulfilling atavistic dreams of flight. We wondered where we would take this new form of flight, and what wonders we would see. After a visit to the club by Martin Hunt, first chairman of the newly formed British Hang Gliding Association (BHGA), we decided

2

to get more involved in the national organisation. Martin let slip he was pushing for a hang gliding world championships in Apartheid-era South Africa. As he did not fly at all during his weekend with us, despite perfect conditions, and instead spoke movingly about a system he had developed for stowing his hang glider in a garage, we took against him. Who was he, we thought, to get us into a political row over the racial politics of South Africa? He doesn't even fly! No man's view was separate from his flying skills, and because Hunt was a bureaucrat rather than a real flyer, we were not impressed by his opinions. It mattered more to me than others, because a few years earlier I had been one of the six journalists in 1969 expelled by the South African government annually under Apartheid. I knew nothing about politics and little about racism at the time; the expulsion gave me some forceful opinions.

The club agreed to back Alvin against Martin Hunt for the chairmanship of the BHGA the following year. I would try to support him by getting on to the governing council. It was not a popular move. Most people at the AGM were flyers; who cared about politics? All flyers want is to fly. We played down the South African issue, but it rumbled along underneath. Alvin lost convincingly to Martin, but I was elected to council; the votes of the club were enough for me to scrape in. I could see that those in charge thought that on my own, without allies, I would be containable. They waited, aggressively, for me to raise the South African issue so they could squash me. I waited, too.

In the spring of 1976, Bill Bennett, an Australian living in America and one of the giants of the sport, came out with a new hang glider wing called the Phoenix 6B. Alvin became the British agent to sell the Bennett wonder-kites in England. I needed to change my glider and there were a number on offer, including a British Cobra and the new American SST, Super Swallowtail.

'Don't touch the others, Brian,' Alvin told me on the phone. 'This 6B is a magic machine, and you must have one.'

'Is it better than the McBroom Cobra?' I asked, dubiously. I was not happy about buying an American wing, though it was hard to say why, because they dominated the sport internationally. Hardly any of us had actually *met* an American hang glider pilot.

'It's in another world,' said Alvin. 'I am going to fly one, and you won't live with me unless you do too.'

My first flight on the 6B was from a tall hill called Cornden. The wing was so delicate and responsive that I was as curious as anyone else to discover where I was going to land. Its performance was far beyond my ability to judge it in the minutes I had going to the bottom, and I aimed for the biggest field and just hoped it would deposit me safely there. It did, to my relief. Alvin, back on the hill where the wind had risen, showed me how to soar like a bird.

That year's British National Championships were held in the Hole of Horcum in Pickering, Yorkshire, sponsored by Embassy cigarettes and covered by the BBC's *Grandstand* (sports programme). To compete, I had to accumulate five hours flying to get my pilot rating, in a sport where a five-minute flight was considered good. The week before the championships I cruised up and down the Long Mynd on my Phoenix 6B, putting in the minutes and then the hours, flying seated rather than prone because I was nervous. In the competition itself, bedevilled by rain, Alvin and I survived through to the final, our gliders showing up well against the others. To everyone's surprise, including my own, the Phoenix 6B carted me to equal first place with a pilot from the south, Bob Wiseley on a Wills Super Swallowtail, an SST, the main American rival to my Phoenix 6B. Bob Wisely became British champion because he was in the air a shorter time than I was. My performance, in second place, was almost entirely due to my wing. Alvin placed tenth ahead of names like Keith Cockroft and Bob Calvert, pilots who were later to be legends in world hang gliding.

That hang gliding competition was so arbitrary and unfair that I resolved to make them better, and I persuaded the BHGA council to make me competitions chairman to shake everything up. The job was considered a nest of thorns anyway, so no one else volunteered. At the same time, that summer saw two early deaths in the sport, Guy Twiss and Barbara Jones, and a British member of parliament, Colonel Marcus Lipton, was persuaded by the media to attack us for being dangerous. Lipton was a member of the Old Farts Tendency, nice enough in himself, but an old-fashioned rent-a-quote parliamentarian. He was not particular about the effects of his attack, and obviously knew nothing about hang gliding, but he was happy to be quoted in the best-selling tabloid newspaper, *The Sun,* which labelled us 'poisonous butterflies'. Lord Boyd-Carpenter, then air minister, whom I met in the House of Lords, actually talked to me about the drain we were on the National Health Service, all two deaths and various unspecified injuries. In the political kerfuffle, it was easy to forget about the tragedy of the two deaths, Guy Twiss in a downwind stall and Barbara Jones who put on her harness incorrectly and could not in consequence control her machine. We were in danger of being strangled at birth.

The governing council of British hang gliding, on which I sat, had to meet this threat, but was not sure how. Something had to be done and be seen to be done. Alvin, at this time, had sold his garage in Montgomery and was restless, thinking of going to America to fly. We talked over the media attacks and decided a public investigation had to be made into how the sport was taught. Two years earlier, I had learned by being told how to control the kite – 'simple really, just push, pull, left and right' – and then I was thrown off a big hill, the 500ft Devil's Dyke near Brighton. I was expected to learn how to fly the wing during the two minutes in the air before I hit the ground. At least I had been 'coached' by experts that day. Alvin had just bought a kit, read the instructions, rigged the wing, lined up and ran off. We had both lived and thought little of it. But it was a less than ideal way of learning. Perhaps an investigation into training would stop the media witch-hunt?

Alvin was chairman of the Hang Gliding Instructors Association (HIA), at the time a loose collection of people banded together to look after their own interests, but who had not agreed a common standard. The BHGA council agreed the princely salary of £19.23 a week (about $30 at the current exchange rate), at a time when £100 per week was good money, to send Alvin around the schools and report back on training methods. We told the media and Colonel Lipton what Alvin was doing, both of whom subsided and looked for other stories to talk about, but we realised then that we were just holding them off for a while. The next hang gliding death would have them howling for our heads again.

Alvin toured every school in the country, and then borrowed a typewriter, learning to type as he put the report together. It was full of spelling and grammatical mistakes, causing snobbish sniffs among council members who saw the early draft, but it was full of insight and good sense. He not only pulled together the various methods of teaching, but laid down a standard, in equipment as well as teaching methods, for schools to adhere to. The BHGA council agreed to endorse his recommendations in a hurried fifteen minutes at the end of a seven-hour meeting. Journalists and Colonel Lipton appeared happy that we had come up with something to show willing, and looked for someone else to harass.

It took a few tough hours of debate to get the BHGA council to agree that we needed a permanent training officer. I proposed that he should be paid a living wage of £3,500 a year, and that Alvin had won the right to the job because of the work he had done on the miserly £19.23 a week. Probably the main case against Alvin was that he and I both acted together, virtually as brothers, backing each other in anything. This can be a dangerous relationship between a paid officer and an elected council member. But it was, with grumbling, accepted.

In the autumn of 1976, Alvin was one of ten pilots who laid down the rules for the National League of Hang Gliding, a series of six competitions I had proposed as a substitute for sending British teams to South Africa. In passing, that world cup competition was cancelled, partly because of my public opposition to it. I had won that vote on the council, with those originally opposed to 'bringing politics into sport' going off to find out more about Apartheid to put up a case against me. They decided there wasn't a decent case, and they did not wish – on this issue – to press the case to the point of my resignation. I would, of course, have had to resign if we had sent a team there. I hoped that by founding the League I would produce a worthy British champion, better than Wisely and myself, and be the means whereby decent teams could be chosen to fly in foreign countries. In general, and again with Alvin as an ally, this was accepted, though I heard later there were always cabals being formed to find out what I was doing, and then see if there were ways to stop it (whatever it was).

Alvin was rated one of the best pilots in the country by those who saw him fly. The only way we would find out how good he actually was would be in the League, due to start the following year. But he had already been chosen as one of the group of elite pilots to fly in a meeting called by one manufacturer, Ken Messenger's Birdman company, to see which had the best glider. The Birdman was the best hang gliding competition run in Britain up to then, testing flying skills and not the landing skills that dominated competition. Alvin flew for Birdman itself, and had a narrow escape when, coming out of his prone harness and banked over into a tight landing area, his foot stirrup wound around the back rigging and he could not recover from the turn. His glider smashed into trees and was wrecked. Alvin was unhurt. We learned to put stiff plastic tubing over our stirrups to stop the same thing happening to the rest of us. Accidents were often the way we were taught how not to fly. Alvin was lucky he did not pay a fatal price for that lesson.

His reputation had been enhanced before he started flying the American Phoenix 6B by a published account of a flight he made on the Long Mynd in the middle of battles with the gliding club to be allowed to use *their* ridge and *their* air:

> Saturday night came with an air of expectancy. The wind was west, 6 to 8 mph, smack on the ridge. Tomorrow was the big day, the end of four months' negotiating. We were to be able to soar the big ridge at the south end of the Long Mynd again. After a restless night, Sunday dawned, wind still west, but had

it freshened? By mid-day it had. This was it, 26mph straight on, first time in our new second-generation kites.

Most of the other lads had gone for lunch so I was first in the air. My flying rival Graham Driscoll with his 21/20 American Swallowtail had yet to arrive so I decided to get as high as possible and rub it in as he walked the hill. At about 500–800 feet above the ridge [Alvin had no flying instruments, nor a parachute], the lift stopped, so I wandered around doing 360 degree turns and passing the time. Where the hell is he? I thought. I had been tweaking my Cobra so I wanted to fly it against Graham's American Swallowtail, as in the past Graham had always had that 50ft or 100ft edge over me.

After what seemed ages he arrived. I could see by the frantic way he was climbing the hill that he wanted to be up here with me. I flew over his head, holding station, making rude gestures to spur him on. Eventually he rigged up and was airborne. Well, this is it. I was high, I knew where the lift was, having had an hour or so feeling my way around, so I made capital and went for height. Slowly, ever so slowly, Graham kept coming. He couldn't make the last 100ft or so – I was delighted. For the first time I was 'standing on his head'.

I circled twice, dropping below him, climbed up above him again and then did it again to prove it wasn't a fluke. Graham was furious. Off he went, sniffing for lift. He found some, he was with me and then, while making my way back to my known source of lift, it happened. I started climbing, higher, higher, higher (my God, will it ever stop?) and still I kept climbing. I looked down. Graham was just a small white kite hundreds of feet below. I could see him coming after whatever it was that I had found, and still I was climbing. I was beginning to get worried now. The Long Mynd was three quarters of a mile behind me. It looked so small it wasn't true. I could see ant-like figures in a cluster on the take-off area. All the other kites had landed except Graham, who was gaining height 500ft or so below and behind me.

The clouds were beginning to whisk by, the lift stopped and I began to get used to the height. Gradually I felt my way around, but the lift seemed to be everywhere. No matter what I did, 360s, figure eights or whatever, I could still climb back up to cloud base. I could circle and lose nothing. I could climb, downwind! In fact, gravity was lost. I was free. I could do anything I wanted – Oh boy, Oh boy!

I now turned my attention to Graham only to find that he had entered the latter stages of top landing. I could see him eating height with consecutive 360s, and then he landed. So here I was, all alone save for a couple of conventional gliders 500ft or so below me. A very gratifying feeling indeed.

I can well imagine the looks of utter disbelief and dismay when the glider pilot had to admit to being 'sat on' by a hang glider.

My feet and legs were getting cold now so I decided to land. A series of consecutive side-slipping 360s lost me 1,000ft or so, then a quick beat up the hill, three or four more 360s over the top and I was down.

I had been airborne for 90 minutes, prone, and what height had I reached? We telephoned the glider station. They confirmed cloud base 1,500ft above the 700 foot ridge, and there it was, 2,200ft above the valley. What a day, what a feeling and what a memory to cherish! It makes me feel very humble that God chose me to place His magic upon. I shall always be grateful.

There is one small close-up picture of Alvin that I have been able to track down. It was difficult to find, despite looking for years at all the obvious sources. But thanks to the wonders of You Tube, nearly fifty years later, I have found poor-quality moving pictures showing brave but daft attempts at flying hang gliders off the Long Mynd in Shropshire. Find it by Googling Alvin Russell + British + hang glider + Long Mynd.

In 1976 my wife Fiona Campbell and I resolved to spend Christmas with my parents, Tom and Eileen. After thirty years in the Royal Air Force, my dad decided to retire to their birthplace, Dublin. We drove there in an old VW combi-van with our 16-month old son James, and of course, my Phoenix 6B. Alvin had a son of his own, 6 years old and mortally ill from leukaemia, but his wife had left him and taken his son with her. Fiona and I were not sure how Alvin was spending Christmas, so we invited him with us. At first, he said yes, but when we passed through Shrewsbury and he was not at the rendezvous, we phoned him and learned his red setter dog had torn open its leg on barbed wire and he had decided to stay with it. I dearly wanted Alvin to fly with me, and dangled visions of the flying in Ireland in front of him in an attempt to persuade him to leave his dog with his neighbour. In the end Alvin said yes, but he would meet us at the ferry in Holyhead, on the northwestern tip of Wales, to cross the Irish Sea. Alvin got there in his little Alfa sports car with just minutes to spare and walked on to the ship carrying his luggage and hang glider on his shoulder.

Alvin had moved on from the Phoenix 6B. He did not blame that summer's tree accident on the aircraft he was flying, and Ken Messenger was keen to get such a good flyer on his new Birdman wing. Ken was one of the pioneers of the sport in Britain, and like other British manufacturers was trying to stay level with leading developments in the USA and Australia. The Phoenix had been outshone by a new Australian wing made by the legendary Bill Moyes, which had thrashed all-comers at the 1976 British Open, and like other British manufacturers, Ken had copied much of what Moyes invented. The key new idea was a keel pocket, lifting the sail off the keel of the wing and allowing easier control and performance with a tighter sail. But while Moyes had a keel-pocket holding down only the back part of the sail, Messenger's new prototype, called a Moonraker, had a pocket all the way through the sail. Alvin was flying the Moonraker prototype, which had all sorts of adjustments to allow him to change the billow of the sail and so on. It was this kite he took to Ireland.

My parents lived in Howth Head, north of Dublin itself. We were only a mile away from the east-facing cliffs that look over the Irish Sea and an island called 'Ireland's Eye'. Howth is where the Irish Republicans, when Ireland was still part of Great Britain, received their shipload of rifles before the First World War, and is a famous little port in Irish history. But until now, no one had soared the Howth cliffs, which lay 2,000ft under the airway leading into Dublin airport.

On 23 December 1976, Alvin and I trekked to the cliffs with our wings, rigged them, and walked around trying to summon up the nerve to fly. The wind was on the cliffs, a rare easterly, but there was no bottom landing. The cliffs just fell into the sea, and if we lost the lift band, that is what would happen to us, too. But the sea breeze was smooth so we had good conditions to test the Moonraker against my Phoenix, which we both agreed was that rare glider in a production run that is just better, no one knows why, than all the other gliders in the run. Seagulls were soaring, we reasoned, so why should we go down into the sea? Prudently, I let Alvin take off first. When he went up, I joined him.

We had more than an hour each in the air, trying to get higher than the other, pulling speed to see how fast we could go without losing height, 360ing back over the top of the cliffs when we were too far forward. It was smooth easy flying, and the Moonraker showed up well against my Phoenix

6B. But it was late in the afternoon when we came down safely, and I had no chance to test the Moonraker myself. Next time, we thought.

That evening we sat, weary and content, in my parents' sitting room, while Alvin told my father how lucky we both were to be living through such an era. Like me, Alvin would have wanted to have been alive when mainstream aviation started in the heroic period before the First World War, when no one knew that flying was now probable, and magical deeds were done. But as we were alive now, hang gliding fulfilled us, gave us more than we could have expected from modern flight, put us in the air next to birds flying at the same speed as us, and the same height. Like all young men with a sense of adventure, we wanted to be heroes. What other aspiration should a man have? We thought our new form of flying was how we could reach that state.

A group of Irish hang glider pilots picked us up the following day, Christmas Eve. Flying conditions were poor, with little wind, a slight mist and about 800ft cloud base. We were both sated with the previous day's flying, but the Irish were happy to have someone as famous as Alvin with them and wanted to hear our stories of Howth Head. We took our wings with us, went out for lunch, and just to pass the time of day, we went looking for a hill to fly together.

We were guided to the Sugarloaf Mountain, south and east of Dublin, a distinctive outline I look for whenever I am around Dublin Bay. It looks like a volcano from the distance, just a cone, but its peak was under cloud when we arrived at the landing area and I looked up at the 600ft climb to a small ledge for take-off. Alvin took his glider and gear and, hill-climbing champion that he was, virtually ran up the mountain. At that time I smoked heavily, twenty a day, so I 'died' six or seven times struggling up the slope. I was wheezing when I arrived at take-off to find Alvin talking to a group of Irish pilots while rigging his wing.

When I came to rig my own wing I found, for the first and only time in my life, that I had lost a wing nut on the way up. The wing nut was to secure the ring-bolt holding the bottom rigging to the front keel of the wing; without it I could not fly. I was contemplating de-rigging to walk down again when Alvin came over.

'I've lost my wing nut. I'm going to walk down,' I said.

'Don't do that. I have about twenty wing nuts on my wing. You can have one,' he said, and sure enough, he had wing nuts everywhere.

'Don't you need it?' I asked.

'No, it's belt and braces. Ken Messenger put wing nuts on the top and bottom of everything, and the kite doesn't need them. Anyway, why don't you fly my machine and I fly yours? You said you wanted to have a go.'

But I felt that even though the wing nut he gave me fitted, I was flying a wing that wasn't standard. It would not have been fair to let Alvin fly it, though he was effectively a test pilot to the prototype Moonraker. If he had pressed me I would probably have said yes, but he didn't and I said no, I would stick to my own machine, and completed rigging. That is how I lived to tell this story.

We agreed, as always, a competition, closest landing to the centre of a football pitch would win a beer from the loser. I watched Alvin line up to take-off, fly off to the left, get into his prone harness, and cruise along the mountain losing little height. At the end of his beat he made a 180 degree turn to the right and came back towards us, still at the same height, about 400ft above the ground, and looking regularly at the landing field to judge how he would approach it. He was keen on winning, however often he had beaten me in these competitions. As he started to turn left a small cloud came through, obscuring my view. I turned, ran back to pick up my wing, clipped in and took off. I went much further to the left than he did, thinking I would crow about, that's when I saw him on the ground, but on the way back, looking at the landing field, I found I could not see him at all. He was not lining up on the landing as he should have been, and he was not at the same height I was. It was only when I looked vertically down that I saw him and his glider, one wing completely broken, smashed up against the side of the mountain.

I shouted and shouted and threw my wing out of the sky, seeing an Irish pilot scrambling up the mountain to where Alvin lay as I lined up to land. I jumped out of my harness and ran up too, but the Irishman was on the way down.

'I'm going to phone for an ambulance,' he said.

'How did it happen?'

'When he turned left he seemed to lock into the turn. He just spiralled down, about six turns, and cracked into the mountain.'

Full of dread, I asked, 'How is he?'

'He's gone.'

I did not believe him (we had been joking together just ten minutes before!) and I ran up to where Alvin lay. He was still. I eased his false teeth out, thinking he might choke, but I also got a handful of clotted blood. I sat there, rocking, trying to cradle his head in my bloody hands, until someone else arrived. Then I walked back down the hill and waited until the ambulance arrived. When they took Alvin's body away a group of pilots started to build a cairn on the hill where he had crashed, a classical Irish response. Then someone else shouted 'no, no!' and they dismantled it.

I phoned my parents' home to tell them what had happened, and cried on the way home. At midnight mass that evening I looked at all the shiny Irish faces and the eagerness to be gone to celebrate Christmas Day, and left in the middle of the service. My wife Fiona and I made love that night. In my mind it was for Alvin, my lost and best friend. Fiona and I had to keep a surface cheeriness for James's first real Christmas, but Fiona had lost our first unnamed baby on Christmas Eve in Ireland three years earlier, and Alvin's death confirmed her dislike of the place. I have only attended a Catholic church service since for funerals or weddings.

Johnny Carr, who went on to be one of the best pilots in the world, said 'all the other deaths, you think, I could have got out of that situation or I wouldn't have got into it. But Alvin ...'

We came to the conclusion, a month later, that Alvin was distracted in rigging his wing, because he was talking to the Irish pilots. There were three holes on each cross-boom, which held the leading edges of the sail apart. A pilot could choose to have the sail taut or floppy, as he wished. But Alvin missed his count of the holes, and made one sail floppy, and the other taut. As he offered to let me fly his wing, it was already set up to kill whoever flew it. It was, in fact, my turn to have a go, but the loss of that wing nut as I crawled up the hill, wheezing, made me stick with my own wing. Smoking saved my life.

Alvin Russell was buried in a little country graveyard on the outskirts of Montgomery, within sight of Cornden Hill, masking the Long Mynd from his view. I was not a pallbearer, a job taken by regular members of his local club whom he had taught to fly. I went back to visit the grave seventeen years later; though I looked for half an hour, I could not find it. I do not know why.

When the British National League of Hang Gliding started the following year and did all those things for British hang gliding that, together, Alvin and I had dreamed about, I was able to name the trophy the pilots flew for, and still fly for, the Alvin Russell Trophy. It is awarded to the best hang glider pilot in Britain. Only the eternally young Johnny Carr of the current League pilots knows why, or even who he was.

Alvin is not just a few lines in a newspaper, or an unfound grave in Wales. Had he lived he could have been a contender, first for the British title, later for the title of world champion. He was one of hundreds of people who dreamed the new aviation into life and flew in the same way as the real pioneer of flight, the German Otto Lilienthal. We flew as he did, foot launched and weight shifting to control the wing and took a different route to that laid down by the Wright brothers and all who followed them.

Hang gliding and the children of the wind that it spawned, in microlighting and paragliding, are normally seen in terms of the deaths of some of us who try to fly in such a simple way. In the public's mind, hang gliding is about death first and then perhaps about flying. That is the wrong way round. Hang gliding is about flying, face-in-the-air, wind-on-the-cheek, smell-the-woodsmoke flying. Death is the price some of us paid, and will continue to pay, to experience it. But, contrary to popular belief, it is not absolutely necessary.

Pilot's Creed – Mike Collis

Why do I leap and try
These wild rides through the sky?
Does not the pounding of my heart
Before the start,
The terror of Death's fall
Me appal?
It does, it does, but then
Safe home on lovely Earth again
After that fragile dive
I'm twice as glad to be alive.

Chapter 2

History of Aviation to Lilienthal in 1896

Lazy thinkers, especially in America, believe that aviation began in 1903 with the American Wright brothers. Orville and Wilbur Wright, raised in Ohio, made the first successful powered flights on 17 December that year at Kittyhawk in North Carolina. It was a vital breakthrough, and for some time the French, then leading the quest to achieve flight, could not believe the Americans had got there first. But in flying terms the Wrights should not be seen as a beginning but as part of a stream of experiments about flight that has a much longer history. They did not succeed in a vacuum. Had they not been men of their time, at the end of a long, evolutionary line of pioneers, they are likely not to have made the vital breakthrough.

The quest to fly is old, and cuts across all cultures and generations. In Asia, the earliest stories of flight are of eighteen hundred years before Christ, when Ki-Kung-Shi is said to have made a flying chariot without the use of birds in the reign of the Chinese Emperor Ch'eng T'ang.

To Westerners, the first flyers were Icarus and his father Daedalus. In Greek mythology, both men lived fifteen hundred years before Christ, but the first written sources we have of their flight are from nearly a thousand years after the event. It was inevitably corrupted, as the oral tradition of historical narrative is, by the needs of each speaker, passing the story on, to find a reasonable explanation for what happened. Daedalus was employed on the island of Crete by King Minos to build the great labyrinth as a prison for the Minotaur, a half-bull, half-man that had the rather antisocial habit of eating young virgins. King Minos, who had lost a son in Athens in a battle on mainland Greece, had a powerful fleet of ships, and dominated the seas around Athens. In revenge for his son's death, he threatened to destroy the city unless it paid him fourteen young Athenian hostages a year. These hostages he sent in to the labyrinth to be killed and eaten by the Minotaur, who was kept inside, and from which they were not expected to escape.

14

When the labyrinth was completed, the king decided to detain Daedalus on Crete because, having designed it, he knew the way out, and might tell someone. Icarus was also kept on the island.

In Athens, King Aegeus had a brave son, Theseus, who volunteered to pose as a sacrifice in order to slay the Minotaur. He promised his father that he would put up a white sail on his journey back home if he was successful, but the boat would carry a black sail if he was killed. In Crete, Minos' daughter Ariadne fell madly in love with Theseus. She helped him navigate the labyrinth by giving him a ball of string allowing him to retrace his path. Theseus killed the Minotaur with his father's sword and led the other Athenians back out of the labyrinth. On the way home, Theseus abandoned Ariadne on the island of Naxos and continued on home. He neglected, however, to put up the white sail. King Aegeus, from his lookout on Cape Sounion, saw the black-sailed ship approach and, presuming his son dead, committed suicide by throwing himself into the sea that was then named after him. This act secured the throne for Theseus.

However caddishly Theseus behaved towards the unfortunate Ariadne, her father, King Minos was so upset at the loss of his daughter and hostages that he blamed Daedalus, claiming Daedalus had said no one could get out of the labyrinth alive. The king wanted to roast Daedalus alive.

(An alternative story is that the king's wife had a perversion, and rather fancied a strong and powerful bull as a lover. She persuaded Daedalus to build her a wooden structure that looked like a cow, and used this subterfuge to arouse the bull, fitting herself into the 'cow' to achieve satisfaction. The Minotaur was the result of such a sexual union. If Minos had found that Daedalus was involved in such an affair, it is no wonder he was upset about Daedalus.)

Because of King Minos' control of the seas around Crete, there was no way Icarus and Daedalus could escape that way. But Daedalus, said to be the greatest sail-maker of his age, saw the link between wind and lift, and constructed wings for them to fly on. In a later version of the myth, thought to date from the fifteenth century, the wings were made of feathers and wax, a detail that does not appear in the original Greek myth. Father and son were said to have climbed Mount Ida (Idhi Oros) in the middle of Crete, just over 8,000ft high, and used it as a launching site to fly. They headed north, but Icarus flew too near the sun, the wax melted, and he fell into the sea. In the myth, his father made it to the island of Icaria, named it after his son, and appears in other myths later in Sicily.

Almost everyone accepts this as wishful thinking, an original story passed down by word of mouth and turned into legend, as oral history cannot work without legends and myths. One exception was a Yorkshire architect called Arthur Quarmby, who claimed it *could* have happened. He persuaded Yorkshire TV to make a film of the story, and I was invited out to Crete in 1990 with a YTV producer called Nick Gray, Arthur Quarmby himself, and Bruce Goldsmith, one of the world's best hang glider pilots. We wanted to see if it was possible for two men to foot launch off Crete and fly to another island. If it was, it would not be me doing it, as I was not skilful enough. The second chosen candidate was Robbie Whittall, then only 20 years old, but hang gliding champion of the world.

Quarmby's theory, which he developed from a glider pilot called Walter Neumark (one of the originators of paragliding), is that in certain weather conditions Crete has a 'standing wave'. This is a weather condition where the wind blows over a mountain and 'sets' into a particular shape. There is an up 'elevator', where the air climbs thousands of feet, followed by a down 'elevator', where it falls steeply, and it continues in a sort of vertical zig-zag downwind across the sky. Certain areas of the world, such as New Zealand, for example, or the Scottish Highlands, are famous for 'wave' flying. Alvin Russell's 'magic' flight on the Long Mynd was made in wave. All conventional gliding height-gain records, up to 50,000ft are made in wave. The phenomenon is powerful, smooth for the most part – I have only knowingly flown twice in wave, once in Scotland, the other time in Siberia when making the first microlight flight around the world in 1998 – but with strong turbulence at the edges. If Icarus did make his legendary flight, his fatal fall could have occurred because of this turbulence, rather the wax melting too close to the sun's heat, because of course the higher you go the colder it gets.

In certain conditions you can see wave. The rising air gets cooler, and carries moisture that turns into cloud at the top of the wave. As the air falls again, it warms and the cloud disappears. Wave cloud, called lenticular, looks like a fat white cigar lying horizontally across the peak. It is stationary, or moves back and forth as the wave itself changes frequency with the wind strength. Some people mistake wave cloud for UFOs.

Only advanced flyers know much about wave. They also say that the first wave, the primary wave, is virtually impossible to get into with a glider, and you have to join on a secondary wave, perhaps 10m downwind. By definition, Daedalus and Icarus were not advanced flyers if they stood on Mount Ida all those years ago, looking south at their launch site, over their shoulders to the north at where they wanted to go, occasionally looking up at the lenticular clouds, presuming that the wave started south of Mount

Ida itself. The two men had to go downwind to go north, so they needed a southerly wind, which Quarmby told us was the prevailing wind in spring and autumn on Crete.

To be successful, we would have to find a point from which to launch. Bruce and Robbie would have to be able to soar the mountains in ridge lift – like a ping-pong ball on top of air rising up the slope – and then catch the wave to climb thousands of feet, before turning north and diving through the down cycles to catch the next elevator up. They would plan to fly all the 80 or so miles to Icaria, or even just to the nearest island off Crete, Antikythera, 17 miles away.

As it happens, it is not impossible. With the right research, and the experience of local conditions that months of soaring the area would bring, one day conditions could be right and an attempt made. But the terrain is extremely inhospitable, and landings anywhere are likely to be ankle-breakers in one landing in three.

We concluded that it would be more possible to *thermal* off the island, to fly into and climb within a rising bubble of warm air, from a site near its north-western corner. This site is not far from the little airfield at Maleme where more than 6,500 German parachutists were killed in the 1941 invasion of Crete. We thought the two modern pilots could fly to the island of Antikythera with a normal cloud base of 8,000ft and a certain amount of nerve, by following a thermal in a southerly wind out over the sea. When the thermal dissipated, as thermals do over water, our pilots could make the island on a downwind glide. It would be safer on paragliders. We even found an ideal take-off site.

There was one moment on Crete that made us all thoughtful. We were halfway up the north side of Mount Ida in a little village called Anogia where all males – men, boys and babies – had been shot dead by the Germans in the last war after a British commando team led by the legendary Patrick Leigh Fermor kidnapped a German general and sheltered in the village. We found a priest, Papa Nikoulas Andreadakis, who had kept weather logs three times a day since 1952, information he used to telephone through to Athens for the forecasters there. The priest did not speak English, and we were struggling to communicate with him, trying to learn something about local weather. He found a book with photographs of different cloud formations, and we turned to the page with wave cloud to ask if he ever saw them. He thought for a few moments and spoke to the interpreter.

'Yes, I do see these clouds from time to time,' we were told. 'But only when the wind is blowing from the south!'

This startling information meant it *was* possible to have made the flight that the Greek myths said Icarus and Daedalus had done. With a south wind, the two heroes would have been able to launch and look for wave to lift them thousands of feet above the mountain. In such conditions, the wave would provide up elevators in which they could linger, and dive through the down elevators, and head north to Icaria.

But Bruce Goldsmith and Robbie Whittall never made the Daedalus flight. It would have entailed months out of their lives, and more to the point, I could not raise the sponsorship needed to make it work, despite intense television interest. Yet it is still possible, with the right pilots and organisation, to try. Arthur Quarmby falls into a long tradition of original, often eccentric and sometimes even mad thinkers (as we measure some forms of madness) who approach a situation differently to anyone else. If they are wrong, it is for the right reasons.

Icarus and Daedalus were not isolated myths. In English history, the first man to attempt flight is said to have been King Bladud, founder of the city of Bath and father of Shakespeare's King Lear. In 852 BC he tried to fly over Troja Nova – London – with artificial wings attached to his arms after weaving a few magic spells. They did not work, and he fell on to the temple of Apollo and was killed.

King Bladud is one of the first in the long line of so-called 'tower jumpers', those driven souls who defied gravity to achieve pure flight. They were thought insane, but interesting to look at. Crowds would gather to watch them fly. Modern American hang glider pilots call these types of spectators 'wuffos'. One wuffo was actually heard to say at a hang glider take-off site, 'Hey, honey, hurry back to the car and get my camera, a guy's gonna get killed.'

Another famous tower jumper was the English monk Oliver, also known as Eilmar, who leapt from the tower of Malmesbury Abbey in AD 1020 with 'wings' fastened to his hands and feet. It seems to be accepted that he did make some sort of a glide. He landed heavily, broke both legs and was crippled for life. He put his unsuccessful flight down to the lack of a tail.

In Scotland in 1507, an Italian immigrant called John Damien, inspired by the example of King Bladud, launched himself from the walls of Stirling Castle but fell to the ground. He was heading for Turkey, according to chronicles at the time, but instead broke several bones, including his thigh. He blamed his failure on the fact that when he made his wings he used feathers from a chicken, a bird that does not fly. Another excuse was the same as Eilmar's, that he did not have a tail. It was thought then that when birds landed, a tail was an important part of their undercarriage.

Another Italian chose France for his tower jump. In 1536, in Troyes an Italian clockmaker called Denis Bolori jumped from the cathedral tower, and flapped his way to his death on the pavements below.

Judging by the number and quality of attempts to fly in the last five hundred years, France is the country most likely to produce those willing to take the most chances, either by jumping out of towers or producing flying machines.

In 1678, a French locksmith named Besier jumped from a garret in a town called Sable. Historians are dubious it was flight, and think it was another 'parachute' jump. Besier survived the plummet, and news of his attempt set off the English inventor Robert Hooke, who concluded that man does not have the physical strength to power wings, which he thought required artificial propulsion.

In 1712, a French acrobat and actor called Charles Allard tried to fly from Terrasse de Saint-Germain to the Bois de Vésinet, with wings attached to his arms. He was killed by the fall.

Later that century, in 1772, France's Canon Pierre Desforges built a 'voiture volante' for which he claimed a flying speed of 60mph. Sadly, all that happened when he sat in his contraptions and flapped his wings was that he went nowhere. Two years earlier he had built a pair of wings for a flying experiment. That failed because the peasant to whom the wings were fixed refused to go through with the attempt. The French Revolution occurred nineteen years later, and from that peasant's point of view none too soon either …

My favourite French tower jumper is the Marquis de Bacqueville, who in 1742 tried to soar across the Seine river in Paris with paddles attached to his arms and legs. He announced he would fly from his house on the corner of Rue des Saints-Pères and the Quai Malaquais, across the river to the Tuileries Gardens. He tried, failed, fell into a washerwoman's barge, and broke his leg. You can walk to where his house was in modern Paris, look down at the river, and keenly imagine his feelings as he trembled at the edge of the window, wondering if he could really fly. We still have that sense of apprehension but most of us, thankfully, fail to end up in a washerwoman's barge, though some do break legs.

Tower jumpers were everywhere in history. In Italy, in 1499, Giovan Battista Danti, a mathematician, jumped from a tower in Perugia wearing some sort of apparatus. It included feathers, but one wing malfunctioned and he fell heavily on the roof of St Mary's Church and 'hurt his leg'. He was also said to have glided across Lake Trasimeno. The story, in C. Crispolti's *Perugia Augusta*, in 1648, seems to have been based on a real event.

19

In Spain, in AD 852, a Moorish savant called Armen Firman donned a huge cloak and leapt from a tower in Córdoba. He survived the plummet to the ground in a primitive parachute descent.

In Turkey in the eleventh century, at the hippodrome in Constantinople, now Istanbul, the so-called Saracen of Constantinople tried to demonstrate flight to the sultan, with a huge cloak stiffened with battens. He fell to his death.

In Portugal, Bartolomeu Lourenço de Gusmão (1686–1724) designed and built the 'Passarola', and in 1709 requested a patent for the flying machine from the King of Portugal. On 24 June 1709, he even demonstrated the machine … but it failed to fly. Later that year he launched a small craft of some kind from the Castelo Sao Jorge in Lisbon. Gusmão is said to be the first to demonstrate hot-air balloons. His Passarola is described by Charles Gibbs-Smith, from whom most of these stories come, as a very advanced design.

Tower jumpers were still trying, even in the nineteenth century. A Swiss called Jacob Degan, a watchmaker, carried out flying experiments in Vienna and on the Champ de Mars in Paris, in 1806–17. And in Germany, a tailor called Berblinger achieved legendary status by falling into the river at Ulm testing a machine similar to Degan's.

Yet history would have been so much different if the towering genius of the Renaissance, Leonardo da Vinci (1452–1519), had actually ordered his apprentice to build a machine in which he had every intention of achieving flight. Working in Florence, Leonardo came so close to devising the first flying machine, though it was not with the flying designs and flapping wings that appear in most mainstream media (and which were dismissed in a tabloid English newspaper as 'turkeys'). Five hundred years after Leonardo put pen to paper with his doodles, one of his designs actually achieved flight! It was built by an Englishman, Michael Pidcock, without the help of anyone in the British or Italian aviation establishment:

> My attachment to this machine was born one day in 1989 when my co-researcher Suzanne shoved a large book at me across her dining room table. 'There you are! There's the glider that you keep maintaining never existed!'
>
> Up until this moment I had been sceptical about Suzanne's claim to have seen a drawing by the great Leonardo da Vinci of a glider. At this time I was on a project for a BBC documentary, constructing models of the Artist's machines and supplying them with the magic ingredient – Electricity!

I had felt entitled to opine upon the scope of his ingenious machines: for 18 months I had been studying his flapping wing devices, known as 'Ornithopters' and I had never come upon a drawing of a hang glider. Yet among a great many machines were doodles of fledgling hang gliders! Doubly exciting, the drawing had all the appearance of airworthiness. Well, so it seemed to my eager and untutored eye! The thing flew right off the page! Carlo Pedretti, world's supremo da Vinci expert, had written 'A reconstruction of it would be far more meaningful than any other of Leonardo's flying machines – and it would certainly work'. It took me all of three seconds to decide to build it.

The reason I had never seen the drawing was that it had never been published. In 1966, two manuscripts were discovered in the National Library in Madrid where they had lain for 150 years. Among the closely filled pages was a design for a man-carrying kite and another, a striking precursor of the modern hang glider.

At the time, no one took any notice of it! Hang gliders would not make their debut for another 7 or 8 years. What an irony! Rediscovered after 470 years and still just a little bit ahead of its time.

The following weekend found me in London, where I met Ian Grayland, designer of Clubman hang gliders, and Nick Minnion, his business partner and test pilot, who were to become my early technical advisors.

More than once, Leonardo wrote in the margin of his aeronautical studies: 'Get an apprentice to build the model'. Well, now it seemed I was to be the apprentice. Armed with skills derived from years of wooden boat maintenance, I embarked alone upon the uncharted waters of Renaissance glider construction.

'Canes, wood, varnished silk and ropes', the Master had specified. Mindful of the English climate, I decided to pass on the varnished silk – good wing fabric though it had proved until the advent of polyesters. Apart from that, I would limit myself to materials and technology available at the time of its conception.

The text accompanying the drawing further states that the man is positioned with his feet at the base of the inverted mast and his chest at the cross bar; that the machine is to be flown from the top of a hill whence the wind will raise it and that the aviator will control it by pulling on guy wires.

From other designs we know that the curved undercarriage is a leaf spring, for soft landings.

It struck me as ironic that this was his only winged machine that did not closely follow the structure of a bird wing. For most of his life the Artist was working on his detailed study 'The Flight of Birds', and his machines were born of these observations. 'The Machine lacks nothing but the life of the Bird and this shall be supplied by Man,' he wrote earlier. And yet this design appears as a purely geometric shape. After some time I came to see it as a stylized form of the end two sections of a bat's wing. Being membrane covered rather than feathered, da Vinci had wisely adopted it for all his later wing forms. 'Let your Wing imitate nothing other than a Bat'.

As usual with da Vinci designs, no dimensions are given. Knowing the position of the pilot's head and the chest on the drawing and taking the height of a Renaissance man to be 5 foot 6 inches, gives the overall length of about 25 feet. This I calculated would give a sail area of approximately 250 square feet. I phoned Ian Grayland and asked him what sail area would suffice. 'Make it 250 [square feet] and you will be on the safe side.' Ecco!

The wing clearly looks elliptical, but what sort of ellipse? The kite drawn on the same folio is, he tells us, round. I assumed then that a meticulous draftsman would have sketched both machines from the same perspective viewpoint. Having no means of checking this with the Designer, I adopted that basic form and built a 1/10 scale model and took it down to the public garden where I live. The moment of truth! Breathless in anticipation, I climbed on to the compost bin and launched it. With a quarter of a pound of ballast, it flew 10 metres or more at a respectable angle of descent.

I now earmarked the next few weeks to constructing the full-sized machine. Having received the general blessing of Professor Pedretti on my interpretation of the sketch, I went early one Sunday morning to the local car park. With a length of twine and a couple of masonry nails hammered into the tarmac, I described in chalk an ellipse of approximate dimensions and scalloped off one end for the tail. I was instantly struck – as every time I look at it – by the beauty of its shape. I then traced it on to a polythene dust sheet and sent it to Brian Hayes, sailmaker in Stourbridge.

The next thing to address was the 7.5 metre spine. A telegraph pole was definitely out! A giant bamboo would have served admirably; it had been known in Europe since earliest times, but I felt sure that no 8-metre bamboo would have been readily found in nearby Venice in the 1490s.

Leonardo was the first engineer to carry out rigorous load-testing of beams. As far as I know, Box Beams were unknown to him, so I decided on a form well-used by him in the design of the portable bridges, the Truss Beam. This is the triangulated structure of a modern crane boom or roof span, in fact extensively employed by Roman military architects.

I made a few breaking strain tests on types of timber. Ramin was stronger for its weight than spruce, which had been my first choice. Building the Truss Beam turned out to be a nightmare on account of the impractical joints.

The bamboo wishbone leading edge was more successful. As far as I know, no one in these islands has mastered the art of heat-forming bamboo! Here I was on my own. The design required a fairly rigid wishbone, 35 feet long. I decided to heat-form the bamboo, each roughly half-inch diameter and then bunch and bind 7 of them together. One in the centre and six around the outside gave a nice circular section. I staggered the joints between the lengths regularly so that at no point on the circumference were two joints together.

Finally, the spars, the sail and the leading edge frame were complete and a few friends joined me and several bottles of wine on the roof for the occasion. It was a festive day, all the pieces fitted together, nobody fell off the roof and everyone agreed that it was indeed a splendid sight and did much credit to the Great Man!

At this time I consulted the Safety Officer of the BHGA who explained the load-testing procedure which normally requires that the airframe be capable of sustaining five times the pilot's weight. But rightly surmising that we wouldn't be doing aerobatics, he suggested that three times would suffice.

I had anticipated a mild ripple of excitement among the good burghers of Earl's Court at the sight of an 8-metre Renaissance glider suspended between two trees, but most were too polite to mention it. I realized that, to the layman, it was just any old hang glider that someone had been eccentric enough to build in wood.

The words 'stressed moment' took on a new meaning as my beloved glider groaned under the imposition of each new 10-kg sandbag! The bamboo cross-strut bent too readily; it clearly had to be reinforced. I added six more bamboo to stiffen it. By the time we reached 200 kg, the nose was brushing the ground. Bouncing it up and down convinced us that it would have well withstood the remaining 25 kgs we were aiming for.

I added a 15-foot high superstructure to the trailer of my racing dinghy which would support the wishbone in a vertical position. The main longitudinal spar protruded forward at an angle so it overhung the roof of the tow car. Then we loaded it and drove down to Nick Minnion's house in Sussex.

A week or so later, it came as a shock when Nick said, 'well, let's try her!' He attached a line to the front of the spar and the other end to a point towards the tail. His friend and I lifted the sides and, on command, we trotted forward. We had only gone ten paces when she was airborne! Up to that moment, it had been the Building Project. Now suddenly, it became the Flying Project! I almost drowned in the tide of satisfaction that flooded over me.

Weeks later we took it up to the head of a steep valley on Truleigh Hill and rigged the control frame, which Leonardo drew as an inverted mast. The wind was fresh and after bucking around for about 10 seconds, the machine plunged forward at an angle of 45 degrees and hit the ground quite hard. The bamboo under-frame bent into a U-shape momentarily but was not broken.

The test pilot's time did not come cheap and it became apparent that sponsorship would have to be sought before serious flying attempts could begin. My meagre savings had by this time evaporated. I sent out 30 proposals, well-documented, bound and with colour photographs, circularized the major PR companies. Everywhere the story was the same;

heavy on encouragement, light on cash! I still find it very hard to accept that there is no funding for a project like this. The Royal Aeronautical Society lost my file and then said 'No' anyway. The Science Museum aeronautical department laughed and said they wished they had the money to revamp their own gallery.

Months passed and by this time Nick Minnion had lost interest in the glider, the frame of which was mouldering in his garden. This turned out to be a blessing because I was recommended to Kelvin Wilson, known for his spectacular hang glider flight from the Angel Falls in Venezuela, who brought new life to the project and was more keen to talk about the flying than the money he would make out of it.

Through Kelvin, Michel Carnet, who runs 'Sky Systems', arranged for a local landowner to store the wing in his barn.

The narrow roads through the South Downs turned out to be riddled with low power lines and overhanging trees. Many times I had to leap out of Kelvin's car, squint at an overhead cable and make the difficult decision whether we could pass under. Kelvin was in a cold sweat and vowed he would sooner fly the Angel Falls blindfold than repeat this trip!

Summer of 1993 arrived and still not a whiff of sponsorship. On the previous outings we had been so under-manned I had not taken photos. I therefore decided to revitalize the now rather sad-looking spars and kite her again for the cameras.

I spent a pleasant few days in Truleigh sawing through dodgy joints and regluing them. Finally, the machine was ready and a date fixed with Kelvin and the guys at Sky Systems for the kiting, which was to happen in an adjacent field.

October 21 dawned, as forecast, grey and windy. A friend had kindly volunteered to record the event on his video gear. By mid-day the Bird was partly rigged and lying in the field. We then tried to fix the heavy bamboo cross-spar into its iron sockets. It wouldn't go! We exerted all our strength and still it overhung by 9 inches. We lopped off the surplus inches with a hack-saw. There was no way that a terylene sail could have shrunk, so the spar must have grown! Bamboo is incredibly virile stuff.

Kelvin arrived and, for the first time, inspected the machine assembled. He selected a small slope on the undulating stubble field and with Michel Carnet held the wing aloft in the wind, gauging its balance. Next they paid out the mooring lines and the Wing rose 20 feet into the air.

'Where do we hang on?' he said.

'Don't!' I shouted. 'It's not safe. It's been sitting in the barn for two years. I have to rebuild the main spar. Let's just kite her!'

The instructors at Sky Systems clearly had other ideas and the bit between their teeth. In the face of such mass expertise, who was I to argue?

A few seconds later Leonardo da Vinci's Hang Glider, after a gestation of exactly 500 years, lifted into the breeze, carrying with it the suspended body of Mike Millwood and, unless I am mistaken, the spirit of its creator.

It took me a while to take in the indisputable fact that it had made its first man-carrying hop! The experts said favourable things about the stability of the Wing. I am presently engaged upon rebuilding the 'spine' with more solid joints. I am aware that the control frame as sketched by Leonardo is awkward, to say the least, but we are looking forward to renewed flight tests.

My aim is that, if it proves as stable and manageable as we are hoping, we shall fly her on the hill outside Florence in Italy specially marked down by the Master for the inaugural flight of his first full-sized Machine.

'The Great Bird will make its first flight from the back of the Swan [referring to Mount Ceceri = Swan] filling the whole world with amazement and all the records with its fame and it will bring eternal glory to the nest where it was born.'

I too find it beyond belief that a project like this cannot attract any sponsorship at all, given the cretinous things PR agencies get excited about and pour their clients' money into. How could the Royal Aeronautical Society actually turn down such an opportunity? And surely Italians have enough pride in their history to test whether or not their own Leonardo da Vinci was more than 400 years ahead of the German Otto Lilienthal?

Back in history, manned flight was first achieved in balloons through the work of the Montgolfier brothers. The first two men to fly, in a Montgolfier balloon, were the Marquis d'Arlandes and Pilâtre de Rozier (1754–85), both Frenchmen. Pilâtre de Rozier was also the first man to die in a balloon, in an accident on 15 June 1785 – about four years before the French Revolution – trying to cross the English Channel. He fell at Wimereux, where the French erected a 'needle' – like Cleopatra's Needle in London – and is buried himself at nearby Wimille (north-east of Boulogne) in a large tomb. Every time I fly down the French coast in my trike microlight I lean over to try and find the needle marking where de Rozier fell; I have still to discover it.

But balloon flying, while exciting and sometimes dangerous, isn't floating through the air on wings, choosing where to go and getting there. That is the core of man's dream of flight, and throughout the nineteenth century, with all the hope and vision of the Victorian age, men laboured to realise that dream.

British pioneers include William Samuel Henson, who on 1 April 1843 published a picture of his Aerial Steam Carriage in *Mechanics' Magazine*. It was a monoplane, with fixed wings and a tail, driven by propellers, and way ahead of its time … but it was planned to be driven by a steam engine. Henson built a model with a colleague, John Stringfellow, but it did not fly. Henson married, and emigrated to the USA in 1848.

John Stringfellow (1799–1883) came from Chard in Somerset. With Henson, he designed a steam-powered monoplane in 1848. A model built to the design (wingspan 10ft, length 5ft 6in) achieved a flight of 130ft. Stringfellow abandoned his aviation work for twenty years, but the foundation of the Royal Aeronautical Society in 1866 rekindled interest. Stringfellow designed a beautiful steam-powered triplane model with a 28ft^2 wing area in 1868, the engine of which is now in the National Air and Space Museum in Washington, having been purchased by the American pioneer Samuel Langley.

In Scotland, in 1868, a Mr J.M. Kaufmann of Glasgow, designed and built a steam-driven 'flapper' that also had fixed wings. When power was actually applied to flap the wings, it fell to pieces, but it did feature in the Crystal Palace Exhibition.

After Leonardo, the next man to get close to actually achieving flight was a Yorkshire baronet, Sir George Cayley (1773–1857). French historians see him as the true father of modern aviation. His work can be seen in an historical line of development that goes through Stringfellow and Pénaud to Lilienthal and the Wright brothers. Cayley spent most of his life on his Brompton estate, north-east of York, laying down many of the rules of flight, and discovering the unique properties of curved wings. But much of his work was ignored at the time, and outside a small circle of real flyers he was almost unknown until fifty years ago.

Cayley was an old man when he got around to building some of the flying machines he designed. In 1852, then 79 years old, he built a boy-carrying glider, allegedly flown by a 10-year-old son of one of his servants, in a hop from the top to the bottom of a hill. Cayley's coachman, John Appleby, was persuaded to pilot a bigger machine, again from the top of a hill. He survived the experience, but promptly offered his resignation, saying 'Sir, I was engaged to drive coaches, not flying machines!'.

Yorkshire Television made a programme about Cayley, using original drawings to build again the type of machine John Appleby flew. In 1974 Derek Piggott, a famous sailplane pilot at the time, persuaded it into the air, towed by a car. Both machine and pilot landed safely.

France, as was to be expected, was a hotbed of experimentation, and led the way through the nineteenth century in daring and imagination. General Resnier de Goué (1729–1811) is one example. Born in Angoulême in 1801, at the age of 72 he glided on wings of his own design off the ramparts of Petit-Boulieu, 100ft above the ground and 225ft above the Charente river, and landed safely in the water. On a later flight he broke his leg, but the splendid fellow lived to be 82.

Another French general, Félix du Temple de la Croix (1823–90), patented an aircraft in 1857 that had flown as a model. He claimed that it took off from the ground on a site in Brest on the Atlantic coast under its own power. Of two models, one was powered by clockwork, the other by steam. Neither were built full-scale, so his life was never at risk.

The first powered flight in the world was made on 24 September 1852 by Frenchman Henri Giffard, but it was in a cigar-shaped balloon. He used a 3hp steam engine to travel 17 miles from the Paris hippodrome to Trappes.

The earliest known photograph of a heavier-than-air machine was one built by Jean Marie Le Bris, who experimented along the French coast at Brest between 1856 and 1868. He is alleged to have made a flight in his glider to a height of 300ft, and landed safely. A second flight broke his leg. Le Bris, formerly a sea captain, ran out of money, gave up flying experiments, became a special constable, like a sheriff's deputy, and was murdered by ruffians in 1872.

Another Frenchman, Louis-Pierre Mouillard (1834–97), designed and flew a glider in Algeria, but frightened himself silly with his one successful flight. His writings, especially *L'Empire de l'Air*, influenced a lot of people, including Octave Chanute and the Wright brothers.

The most tragic and brilliant of the pre-Lilienthal Frenchmen was Alphonse Pénaud (1850–80). He grew up in 1870 to be a handsome young man, son of an admiral but unable to join the French navy because of a disease of the hip. In his ten years of development he was said to have been more inventive and shown more achievement than any other man in a comparable field of endeavour. In April 1870, he invented the twisted rubber band method for propelling model aircraft, still in use today, which he flew in the Tuileries Gardens. His originality and designs dominated the 1870s. He won a prize for his theory of flight from the French Academy of Sciences, and was one of the first to recognise the importance of Sir George Cayley. In 1873 he designed a man-carrying powered aircraft that foreshadows the mainstream of design in the twentieth century, but lacked a sufficient power source. Pénaud was a vital link between Cayley and Lilienthal. After becoming depressed at lack of materials to build a full-scale model and criticism of some of his ideas, he shot himself. He was not yet 30 years old.

All these are pioneers of aviation, of mainstream flight as much as the new aviation. But the last joint ancestor we have is the greatest of them all, a German, Otto Lilienthal (1848–96). He was the first man truly to fly, to be seen to fly when he said he was going to, and to be photographed flying. His achievement broke the psychological barrier that, up to that time, had persuaded most of mankind that human flight in heavier-than-air craft was impossible.

Otto Lilienthal was born in Anklam in Pomerania, north-east of Berlin, in 1848. With his younger brother Gustav, he began experiments in aviation as a teenager. They built wings of birch and canvas and ran down hills, flapping them, but failed to fly. Their uncle predicted disaster for the pair, but their widowed mother encouraged them.

Both boys went on to higher education, Gustav to study architecture, Otto to attend technical academies in Potsdam and Berlin. Otto had his studies interrupted by the 1870 Franco-Prussian War, in which he served as a 22-year-old soldier. His fellow soldiers recalled that he talked of nothing except the dream of flight. Gustav lost interest in flying, but Otto persisted.

He began his career in engineering, and in 1880 opened his own factory in Berlin, making small steam engines and marine foghorns. In his spare time he studied bird flight, convinced that the process of learning to fly would be 'one step at a time'. This was in contrast to others who experimented with flight, like the Anglo-American Sir Hiram Maxim, inventor of the machine gun, who built giant full-blown flying machines and then devised powerful engines to try and get them into the air. Though he never succeeded, Maxim was a persistent critic of Lilienthal's approach.

Lilienthal re-examined Cayley's research done forty years earlier, and like Cayley, believed the 'arched or vaulted wing includes the secret of flight'. Cayley thought the vaulted arch should be induced by air pressure, while Lilienthal felt it could be built into the wing.[1] In 1889 Lilienthal published the classic *Birdflight as the Basis of Aviation*, which included tables of lift provided by various cambers.

In 1891, Lilienthal began experiments in his garden in Berlin with fabric-covered wings, leaping off a springboard and gliding to the ground. He jumped from as high as 8ft and flew across his garden safely. The following year he built his own conical hill in Berlin in a place called Gross Lichterfelde (the hill is still there), running down it with wings and achieving flights of 50m. One witness was the American Samuel Langley, experimenting at the time with steam-powered aircraft. Langley was publicly disparaging about Lilienthal's wings, calling them 'heavy and clumsy', though he conceded they performed handsomely in the air (Langley's own flying machine, called the 'Aerodrome', was useless).

Lilienthal believed that practising flight was much better than theorising about it like Langley. He explored the Rhinower Hills near Berlin in 1894, and every Sunday would go there to fly. Launching himself from hills 50m high (150ft) he achieved extraordinary flights up to 380m. His control method was weight shift, like a modern hang glider pilot, but he placed himself much higher in the aircraft, his head through the top of the wing and his feet below, and was therefore less effective. He shifted his weight as much as he was able to, back and forward for pitch, and from side to side to roll. But just because of his position inside the wing, it had less control than behind the triangle control bar that the Australian John Dickenson bequeathed to hang glider pilots seventy years later.

Yet Lilienthal could fly! In all, he conducted 2,000 flights, and achieved worldwide fame. Sometimes, inevitably, he had accidents, but he constructed a device like a rebound bow or a warding-off stick (he called it a *prellbugel*), which absorbed the energy of heavy landings and saved his life at least once. He did not fit a *prellbugel* on 9 August 1896, when flying one of his standard machines in the Rhinower Hills. A gust of wind tipped one wing up, he stalled, and fell about 60ft to the ground. Lilienthal died the following day of a broken spine. His last words, in an age when everyone wanted to know them, were alleged to have been 'sacrifices must be made'.

---

1. I remember an exactly similar argument on hang gliding hills in 1977 between Len Gabriels of Skyhook Wings, who put pre-shaped batten into his sails, and Steve Hunt of Hiway, who used flexible battens and tried to sew the camber shape into the wing.

Without Lilienthal, the history of flight would have started later and been, in consequence, completely different. The Wright brothers began their experiments in flight following the news of his death. Had he not died, Orville and Wilbur might not have even started. Blériot might not have been first to fly across the English Channel. The aeroplane might not have contributed to the First World War, nor Alcock and Brown flown the Atlantic, and nor so much else. Lilienthal is central to the history of flight, and the central link between mainstream flight and the new aviation.

A contemporary of Lilienthal was a Kent-born Englishman, Percy Pilcher, who was taught to fly by the German pioneer. Pilcher was educated at Glasgow University, where he became a lecturer in naval architecture before taking up flying (and is wrongly labelled a Scot). He built three different types of aircraft. The 'Hawk' was virtually a hang glider, unpowered, in which he flew nearly 300 yards. The other two, the 'Beetle' and the 'Gull', were modified wings built to take a small petrol engine that he was experimenting with to achieve powered flight. He was on the verge of adding a propeller and a 4hp petrol engine when on 30 September 1899, at the age of 32, he staged a gliding exhibition at Stanford Hall in Leicestershire, the estate of Lord Braye. The machines were left out in damp weather, and though sodden and heavy, Pilcher decided to fly. The waterlogged Hawk climbed to 30ft, and then a soggy bamboo rod in the tail gave way. He fell to the ground, dying two days later without regaining consciousness.

The Australians had a pioneer, Lawrence Hargrave (1850–1915), who lifted himself into the air by four box kites near Sydney in 1894. The kites were towed by a train. In America, Octave Chanute, born in France in 1832, went into aviation at the age of 59 in 1891, and built a number of gliders, biplanes and triplanes, even one with four swinging wings. Chanute was the author of a seminal book, some of whose drawings are reproduced here, called *Progress in Flying Machines* (1894). Chanute was an adviser to the Wright brothers, encouraging and supporting them, and his ideas were vibrant enough that, seventy years later, they had a key role to play in how hang gliding started.

Then came the Wright brothers in the opening years of the twentieth century. They broke through the barriers of flight and were taking to the air for flights of more than an hour while Europeans could stay in the air only for seconds. The Brazilian, Alberto Santos-Dumont, made the first heavier-than-air flight in Europe, first for 2ft over 7 yards, then for 10ft over 65 yards, finally winning a prize on 23 October 1906 for a flight of 240 yards in 20.2 seconds, reaching the magnificent height of 20ft. Wilbur

Wright went to France in 1908, facing widespread scepticism from the vociferous local French flying community, which he silenced by a series of brilliant flights that measured in miles where Santos-Dumont had flown in yards.

mainstream aviation has been well chronicled, and I do not want to follow others down the same path. But similar patterns have been formed in the new aviation that began, neatly, seventy-five years after Lilienthal's death, so it is necessary to touch briefly on some mainstream events.

Before the First World War, the French made almost all the running, while the Americans faded. Partially, this was because the French, in their 900-year rivalry with England, conceded the sea to the Royal Navy, but claimed the air as their own. They had such a head of steam on, liberated by seeing Wilbur Wright fly, that they virtually threw rule books out the window and tried everything. In the USA, by contrast, the Wrights went around threatening anybody who built a flying machine with alleged patent infringement, as if flying itself was something that could be patented! As a result, there cannot be one American in a million who could name the first aviator to fly coast-to-coast in the United States (Calbraith Perry Rodgers, in 1911, flew for fifty days east to west on a Wright machine called the *Vin Fiz* – wrecked so often one could have built four new machines with the spare parts he used). The *Vin Fiz* is now displayed in the Smithsonian Institution in Washington DC. The first man to fly the other way, Bob Fowler, took 113 days from Los Angeles to Jacksonville; you could walk it faster. Despite the fact that almost every journey coast-to-coast in the USA is now by air, these pioneers were soon forgotten. It is hard to find common knowledge today of any pilot in American history between the Wrights in 1903, Jimmy Doolittle in 1922 and Charles Lindbergh in 1927; perhaps Eddie Rickenbacker, the First World War ace, and General Billy Mitchell after that war, because he got into a lot of trouble.

In France the list of aviation heroes is long and revered; Louis Blériot became a legend when he was the first man to fly a heavier than air craft across the English Channel. Hubert Latham was one of my heroes, beaten by Blériot across the Channel, but first to install an ashtray and smoke cigarettes in the air. He was killed in 1912 by a charging buffalo he was facing down in Africa, but was dying anyway of cancer ... a stylist! Frenchman Roland Garros was the first man to fly non-stop across the Mediterranean, with eight hours' fuel, landing in Tunis after seven hours and fifty-five minutes. Louis Paulhan came to England in 1910 and snatched the £10,000 prize for the first flight from London to Manchester, beating English hero Claude Grahame-White. Jorge Chávez, yet another Frenchman, was the first man to cross the Alps, killed on landing when his aircraft collapsed just 30ft from the ground.

Looking at a list of the first hundred people killed in aviation after 1903, it is significant to see where they came from. They include passengers as well as pilots, and like hang gliding in its very early days, it was often machine failure that caused the deaths. Eight of those first hundred killed were British, nine Italian, fifteen American and sixteen were German. But the French had obviously thrown themselves heart and soul into flight, for thirty-five of them died. This covers a period between September 1908 and November 1911.

Before the First World War, almost all the records in the world were held by Frenchmen. They were everywhere, racing hither and yon, fighting off eagles, capturing the rich prizes on offer, landing in every city in Europe and many in Africa and elsewhere. Other nations caught up between 1914 and 1918, but the French have retained to this day an elan and commitment to aviation like no other nation.

The First World War changed things, producing faster and safer machines, and the men to fly them. In 1919 the first international passenger service was established, on a British initiative, between Paris and London, servicing the Versailles Peace Conference. John Alcock and Arthur Whitten Brown first flew the Atlantic non-stop in 1919, the same year Ross Smith flew to Australia – all three men were knighted for their achievements. In 1922 Jimmy Doolittle made the first coast-to-coast flight across the USA in under twenty-four hours: Jacksonville, Florida, to San Diego, California in twenty-two hours and thirty-five minutes. Records tumbled in great excitement as in 1923 John Macready and Oakley George Kelly crossed the US coast-to-coast without stopping. In 1927, Charles Lindbergh flew non-stop from New York to Paris. A year later, the Australian Charles Kingsford Smith made the first crossing of the Pacific from the US to Australia, while solo flyer Bert Hinkler – 'Hustlin' Hinkler' – flew from England to Australia in sixteen days, then the longest solo flight in history. His flying helmet caught the imagination of designers and was turned into the cloche, that evocative fashion of the 1920s. You could hardly pick up a newspaper without someone having completed a record flight, and it attracted those people excited by risk … and glory. What else should a young man aim for?

The heroic age of aviation continued into the 1930s with names like Amy Johnson, Amelia Earhart, Alan Cobham, Jim Mollison, Wiley Post, Jean Batten, Parmentier, Moll and Campbell Black, but they trickled off as the Second World War loomed. Aircraft got bigger, faster, much more expensive, as they must, but it was no longer really flying anymore and it became the primary means of transport, and of course, a branch of the military. The wild men of aviation began to be cleaned up and swept aside in the early 1930s with the prudent introduction of health and safety, belt and braces, nothing left to chance, all the old adventure values out the window.

The real end of the heroic age of mainstream aviation probably came with Howard Hughes' flight around the world in July 1938 in a specially built Lockheed. It had all the latest technology, and Hughes completed the circumnavigation in three days, nineteen hours and eight minutes, New York to New York. Afterwards, he conceded that almost any pilot could repeat the journey, 14,791 miles through the Northern Hemisphere following Wiley Post's route.

'All you need is the right aircraft,' he said.

But you also needed dozens of people to back up each pilot, and hundreds to allow him to take off, fly and land. Flying ceased to be an individual matter and became a team effort. You did not now need an Antoine de Saint-Exupéry, the poet of flying, or a V.M. Yeates, author of *Winged Victory*, or a Cecil Lewis, who wrote the wonderful *Sagittarius Rising*, co-founded the BBC, won a Hollywood Oscar and was said to have had 500 lovers. After learning how to actually fly, new flyers needed an intimate knowledge of all the new regulations. A pilot could as easily be flying a bus. Because the trend in the mainstream had to be bigger, higher, faster, further, those inside such aircraft had to be protected. Who could stick their head out to smell the air and experience the clouds if they were whizzing by at 300mph? Flying became less an experience and more just an efficient way of getting from one place to another.

Cockpits were enclosed, dashboards packed with instruments, pilots forgot the seat of their pants and relied totally on instruments. They were insulated, as were passengers, from the air itself through which they passed. What happened in the weather was only incidental, because they soon flew above it and looked down at the earth from inside a silver tube, breathing other people's air, and often emerging hours later in another country. The pilot, nowadays, might as well not be there at all except as a reserve, because computers can do the flying for them.

For a short while after the Second World War there was still room for heroes, for the 'right stuff' of Chuck Yeager, John Cunningham, Neville Duke, Eric Brown, Bill Bridgeman, Jacqueline Cochran and Peter Twiss. But these test pilots were at the apex of a huge triangle of people who made vital contributions to their flights, but did not themselves fly. More and more, the most interesting of flying, discovering what happens at the edges, was being done by proxy. Look through the chronicles of aviation; individuals appear less and less, and shiny fast aircraft more and more.

Even in small aviation, few people flew open cockpit anymore, they became fully enclosed, radios were introduced, there were strict flying patterns, clubs to join, behaviour to be regulated. You do not buy maps that show you the way a river flows, or where a motorway crosses it, or which identify a town or village. Maps take you from one radio beacon to another and give you a bearing to your airfield; you can even use a satellite Global Positioning System (GPS) and hardly look out the window at all.

Looking at modern airliners it is hard to describe the experience in them as being graced with the word 'flying'. One goes through the air from one place to another, but it is not *flying*. This is an aesthetic judgement, that by the end of the 1960s the soul had gone out of flying. We were, unconsciously, betraying the sacrifice made by all those people who wanted to achieve flight. Flying clubs seemed to be full of people in blazers who were far more heroic around a table full of drinks than actually in the air. They may have been heroes as young men, but they were no longer young, and anyway, their values had changed.

If the pioneers came back and saw that what they had been reaching for, the stars they dreamed of, had turned into a Jumbo Jet or the average club flyer, would they think it was worth the sacrifice?

It is significant that, even in his 70s, Chuck Yeager, hero and defining figure of Tom Wolfe's *The Right Stuff* and the first man to fly through the sound barrier, took up hang gliding. He saw it for what it was, the 'flyingest flying there is'.

There is a passage in a story by F. Scott Fitzgerald, in a theatre in Paris just before 1930. An expatriate himself, Fitzgerald looks around the audience and sees it packed with American and other tourists. Where once it was the wealthy and discriminating who came to Paris, people of taste who created the atmosphere in the 'City of Light' within which great painting and literature can flourish, now it was anyone at all, *hoi polloi*. A large, woman in front of him sweated and fanned herself, and as the curtains opened she said, 'it's luverly, just luverly'. At that moment, Fitzgerald thought, the Jazz Age died.

This is not snobbery. Virtually unseen by anyone outside it, hang gliding has opened up a whole new ethic in aviation, aesthetically quite different, indeed reacting in revulsion against many values of the old aviation. This accounts for the extraordinary reaction from the public to those fourteen young men who jumped off sand dunes in southern California over the weekend of 23 May 1971, significantly the 123rd birthday of Otto Lilienthal. They knew where in aviation history they had to go back to if they were to start again, even if they did not know at the time they *were* starting again. They were, indeed, aware of the deep loss of the real experience of flight, and wanted to discover again what it was.

Those of us who joined them were not about to make the same mistakes about where to take the new aviation, now we had a second chance to begin once more from where Otto Lilienthal left off.

Chapter 3

Roots of Hang Gliding to the First Lilienthal Meet

Most of us, contemplating flight, buy a wing from an expert. But after the Wright brothers showed the way into the mainstream, and aviation developed throughout the twentieth century at breakneck speed, there remained people who did not accept wings, tailplanes and engines pulling aircraft through the sky as the *only* way forward in aviation.

In southern California in the early 1960s, a group like this was linked together by a magazine produced on a Roneo machine, first called *Low, Slow and Out of Control*, later just *Low and Slow*. They bounced ideas off each other, built fantastic contraptions, bruised themselves trying to launch themselves into the air by foot, and always went back to the drawing board.

Among the ideas they discussed were those of Francis Rogallo, a NASA space scientist. Rogallo, born in 1912, became interested in flight at the age of 7 at the start of the Jazz Age, but made no really original contribution until 1945. He had been an aeronautical researcher since 1936 and throughout the Second World War, after which he chose to devote his spare time, working with his wife Gertrude, to design what he called a 'simple, practical, inexpensive and reasonably safe flying machine'.

His idea was to construct 'a flying machine with no rigid element or element designed to produce rigidity; a completely new concept, never seen before, with no model in science'. With Gertrude, Francis set up a wind tunnel in their kitchen and conducted experiments. Attempts to interest his employers NACA (a predecessor of NASA) at the time came to nothing. In 1948, the couple filed a patent for the 'Rogallo Wing', pointed at one end, looking like a cloth version of a paper dart. It was entirely flexible, nothing rigid at all, and suspension lines did as much to give it shape as the cut of the sail. It achieved a certain popularity when developed as a kite for children, but no commercial future was seen for it.

The story might have ended there, among tens of thousands of patents taken out by inventors that went nowhere, except that in 1957 the Russians put a satellite into space. Eisenhower's America, smug in the belief that no other country equalled it in science – or anything else – was galvanised into action, and billions of dollars were poured into the space race. Looking for ways to bring satellite and space capsules back to earth, NASA spent an estimated $50 million exploring variations on a Rogallo wing, adapting Francis' original totally flexible principles, and began designing semi-rigid variants, stabilising the leading edges with compressed air beams, or even with aluminium tubes.

US government establishments, having completed the basic studies of a development, often hand them on to private companies to see where they can take the idea. Contracts to do so are lucrative. Two companies, Ryan and North American Aviation, were asked to develop the Rogallo wing, and produced flexwings of different shapes and sizes. They built flexible re-entry gliders; helicopter-towed flexwings; radio-controlled, self-steering cargo delivery gliders; even rocket-powered escape Rogallo modules.

Photographs appeared from time to time of the weird aircraft under development, with highly sophisticated aircraft bodies suspended under rough-looking, delta-shaped sails. But in 1962 the development of flexwing aircraft slowed dramatically. NASA made the decision to bring back capsules from space flight using conventional parachutes, and the flow of money was diverted elsewhere. More photographs were released publicly, which became the inspiration for at least two holy lunatics. Two separate lines of research continued, one in the United States, the other in Australia, that led to the official birth of hang gliding on Lilienthal's 123rd birthday.

The American was a student called Richard Miller, an enthusiast of the 1960s Age of Aquarius, with strong ideas on individual freedom, personal motorless flight, and even 'transcendental aerodynamics'. From 1964 onwards, Miller began constructing 'bamboo butterflies', Rogallo wings made from bamboo and polythene, held together with Sellotape, budgeted to become wings for $10 in materials. Miller hung from a box-like structure under the wing, two parallel bamboo struts buried in his armpits, much like Lilienthal. And like the great German original, Miller threw his legs and lower body around to steer the contraption. He flew off sand dunes in southern California; one early rule of thumb was, 'don't fly higher than you are prepared to fall'.

There is a classic series of photographs taken of Miller hanging off one of his machines just after take-off, with three friends behind him, all with broad smiles on their faces, two with sunglasses. Miller has sunglasses, too. A curious dated quality haunts the photograph, as if they were not from the 1960s but at least fifteen years earlier. Miller looks like a 'beat' poet, someone that Jack Kerouac would have written about, an aerial Dean Moriarty.

There exists wonderful movie footage of young men flying bamboo butterflies in the late 1960s, long-legging it down the sand dunes with friends trying to hold the wings level. They sometimes achieved a few short, manic, brilliant seconds of flight. Often, flight wasn't achieved so much as a twanging, tumbling crash, but the butterflies were easily repaired, or replaced, and experiments continued. Yet rigging was cumbersome, and the box-like structure under the sail had not really changed from Lilienthal's time.

The key American development in the new aviation happened in 1971, two years after mainstream aviation had taken man to the moon. The development was triggered by a letter from Miller to a school teacher called Jack Lambie. The letter read, 'The 123rd anniversary of Otto Lilienthal's birth will be on May 23, 1971. What can we do to celebrate?' Lambie had been conducting classroom projects for his California high-school students, leading them to build a replica of the biplane gliders developed by Octave Chanute before the end of the nineteenth century. Lambie called it a 'Hang Loose':

> I had been screwing around with hang gliders for years. I built my first one in the '50s, and then in '65 and '66. There was Richard Miller, Bruce Carmichael, Paul MacCready, all the gang, building these bamboo butterflies. But we didn't know how to fly them. We were doing it with arm balancing. We would run along, get the nose up, and just about the time it started to fly, the drag would go up. We didn't have hang bars. Or we would run along, I would start to lift, and then, ohhhhhh we'd drop. In fact, one time we were out flying in the dunes and MacCready ran and jumped off the hill with his arms out and went further than we were going in the hang gliders ...
>
> Then I built a Hang Loose. I built it with a 28 foot span, real light so the kids in the playground could fly it at very slow speeds. The next day I went out and flew it, and it really flew! I was astounded! And this was to prove that hang gliders do not work!
>
> So Miller, Carmichael and the gang would all take turns, and this thing flew time after time, floated down the hill. Don

Dwiggins took photographs of it. I gave Don a story I had written for *Soaring* magazine and he re-wrote it kind of happier and more exciting and put it in *Sports Plane* magazine. It got on the cover. And then some people said 'we want plans', so my brother Mark and I drew up some plans in one evening, and charged $3 for them.

We thought we'd sell maybe 40 of them and so I had 100 printed. The article came out in *Sports Plane* and it came out in *Private Pilot*, and Doug Lamont just went out of his gourd and said, 'we've just got to put this in *Soaring*'. It was the first article on hang gliding in *Soaring* Magazine. I had literally shopping bags full of mail. Just about all the old timers in hang gliding are on my mailing list. I've got letters from Dave Kilbourne, oh, just about everybody built a Hang Loose at one time or another because you could build one for $25. They'd never admit to it now but they all built Hang Looses. Yeah, I could go through my list and you'd find all the old timers on it.

We sold over 4,000 plans. I just couldn't believe it. All those letters coming in, and the beautiful 8-page letters from airline pilots! I saved them all. Some of them start out, 'Yeah, I flew fighters, I did this …' a whole history, 'but this is the way we want to fly'. So we had really unlocked a desire in man to get out and fly himself. Airline pilots, Air Force pilots, 14 year old kids, everybody! Beautiful letters. They all start the same way. They tell their life histories, their dreams of flying, what a wonderful thing this is, could we send them the plans, here's 3 bucks.

So Richard Miller wrote to me and told me about Lilienthal's birthday and said, why don't we have a meet? There had been six of us who fooled around with hang gliders and we said, 'OK, we'll do it'. This was supposed to be a secret meet. We didn't publicize it. Mark and I went out and found a hill and just decided to do it. If they throw us off the land they throw us off. Fourteen gliders showed up. There were 12 Hang Looses, one monoplane, and Taras Kiceniuk in his Bamboo Butterfly which they had learned to fly, with the arm rests, beautifully. He looked like Nureyev doing a ballet in that thing.

Something in that meeting touched the soul of America. The American public had seen hang gliders before, because of the public battle in the US between two Australian pioneers, Bill Moyes and Bill Bennett. But it may have been the whole idea of Americans launching an aircraft by foot. *Reader's Digest* called it 'the flyingest flying there is' in its account, and Lambie could be forgiven for thinking that his Hang Loose, which had dominated the pictures and the event, was really going to take off. It did not work out like that. It was Taras Kiceniuk's bamboo butterfly – a Rogallo wing – that swept the stage.

One of the fourteen pilots at that meet was Bill Liscomb, then 21 years old, the son of Bettina Gray, the former actress who married into the Bancroft family that owned the Dow Jones Index and the *Wall Street Journal*, later acquired by Rupert Murdoch. Two husbands later, Bettina became wealthy when her first husband died, because she had borne him a daughter, also called Bettina. Her brilliant photographs captured so vividly the innocence and grit of the early days of the new aviation. Bill Liscomb wrote later:

> My goal in life, at the age of 21, was to first get all my aircraft repair certificates, and then acquire pilot ratings. I was attending San Bernadino Valley College, and in my first semester studied repair and maintenance of aircraft structures, among other subjects. One day a fellow student showed me a newsletter that changed my life. It was called Low and Slow and was about hang gliders. I was vaguely aware of hang gliders, having seen them in some aviation history books. They were ancient, frail machines, abandoned with the advent of the powered aircraft. This newsletter touted the upcoming Otto Lilienthal hang gliding meet in Newport, and supplied the address for the 'Hang Loose' plans.
>
> I lived in Riverside, California, and had several friends that attended UCR. We were into riding ten-speed bikes en masse at great speed in the darkness of night. My Hang Loose plans came, and work on the airframe progressed slowly until a carpenter friend came on a visit and helped provide the energy to finish the flying machine. I built the craft in my sister's garage. My cycling friends would slip by to check on my progress. At first they would marvel at this modern antique, then retreat into small groups in the corner and snicker and giggle among themselves. Some support. With the help of my brother-in-law the decision was made to adorn the polythene covering the craft with the air signs of the Zodiac – Libra, Aquarius and Gemini – with a can of spray paint.

One night it was completed. My cycling friends assembled to admire the finished product, and after some speculation and serious thought, we decided to take the glider to a field a couple of blocks away for taxi trials. It was quite a sight to see this throw-back carried tail-high across an overpass to the field. The field was bisected by a rarely used road, complete with sidewalks and curbs. Six or eight of us picked up the glider and trotted along in the damp evening air, expecting the magic of flight to carry me away. No such luck. We simply backed up further and ran harder. On the third try, we could not stop before encountering the slight drop, the sidewalk, curb and street. I was aware of tumbling bodies around me, and I must have flown 15 or 20 feet before grinding to a halt on the asphalt. The flight resembled a trajectory more than it involved the usual forces associated with taking to the air. The glider escaped injury, and our minor abrasions were tended to back in the garage.

The only problem left was getting the fragile machine to Newport. The roof of a car or an open trailer would probably destroy it. My brother-in-law saved the day by renting a large truck for me.

At 7am on the morning of May 23, 1971, I woke up under the grey overcast sky common to Southern California in spring, also known as the June Gloom. Dick and I assembled the glider as more pilots arrived. At the pilot's meeting the owner of the property introduced himself, and told us the land was reserved for use as a cemetery, casually adding that the mortuary was just over the hill in case any of its special services might be needed. Hang gliding was lunatic fringe before it even got off the ground. It seems so strange that in fulfilling one of man's oldest dreams, to fly like a bird, he is judged to be less than competent by his peers. This was something I never quite understood or got used to. These people of quick verbal jabs had not dreamed of airplanes during their childhood, content to walk along never looking up, both in spirit and in body.

By late morning, the overcast burnt off and the wind began to freshen. I had visions of soaring for hours over the gentle grassy slope. My friends and I carried the craft up the hill and gave it one last check. With helpers on the wings and tail, I was ready. We started the take-off run. The glider began to tug me skywards by my armpits, and just as my feet lost traction the main spar failed. My first flight was a very short entry in my logbook.

The glider was only slightly damaged. I had not brought any tools or materials to repair it with [me]. I mean, after all, it would soar for hours on its first flight. We did manage to round up a 2 by 4 and some wire. We used a hammer and a screwdriver to split the 2 by 4 into 1 by 2 (approximately) spar splints. We nailed these to both sides of the breaks and wrapped the splice with wire. Field repairs, circa 1880.

We had lunch and gave it another try. I climbed into the 'cockpit' and this time the glider held my weight. It was slightly out of trim in pitch which, coupled with my light weight, caused it to pitch up sharply to an alarming altitude of maybe ten feet. It was not the flight of an hour I had dreamed of, but I had flown. We adjusted the surfaces of the glider as best we could and tried again. I concentrated on keeping my weight as far forward as possible and ran down the hill. The glider pitched up sharply again, but not quite as bad as the first time. More adjustments with the same result for flight number three.

A meeting of the minds determined that the centre of gravity was too far aft and we needed a pilot who weighed more than 135lb. Dick weighed 165[Ib] and was the next choice. As the old saying goes, the bigger they are, the harder they fall. Dick also pitched up, not as sharply, his flight resembling the trajectory of an artillery shell. His impact knocked off the helmet he was wearing. More weight. My brother in law weighed 180lb, and we figured that he would either hit the ground really hard or the glider would actually fly properly. On his third flight he made it to the bottom of the hill! His landing was also an acrobatic manoeuvre previously unknown to man. As his rear touched the ground (gear up landing) he let go of the glider. He did a half roll and the glider did a half loop.

The day was over in what seemed to be a few minutes. My friends and I wore out the airframe of that first glider in one afternoon, and left it in a garbage can at the end of the day. The plastic covering had been stretched, torn and taped, the airframe repaired by so many splints that it probably gained 10lbs. My armpits were bruised, my buttocks punctured by wild thistles and my legs were tired. But what a day! It changed my life. The next day my picture was in the LA Times.

A five-minute video of that tremendously important meeting can be seen on You Tube (http://www.youtube.com/watch?v=t-XC0dxerYs&feature =youtu.be). It's a compilation of all the film – no video or any sound – of the flights made there. I am glad they left the crash sequence in at the end, all those California boys with lean bodies and long hair and only one motorcycle helmet between them.

More meetings were organised, more aircraft turned up, but very soon it was apparent that the Hang Looses and rigid machines were being swamped by Rogallo wings. The Rogallos had a much worse performance than the rigids, but they caught on, and the new versions started to appear with the triangle control bar underneath that made all the difference to rigging and control. It was not, though, an American invention. It came out of Australia, and a man still virtually unknown even within the sport called John Dickenson. The story was pieced together for the first time in its entirety by an Englishman called Mark Woodhams:

In 1963 John Dickenson was working in electronics, not aviation, and had just moved to Grafton, New South Wales, Australia, with his wife Amy. As a child John was obsessed with things that fly. But as he grew up, circumstances forced him to train for a more down-to-earth profession. However, the urge to fly cannot be lightly put aside, and it was on a Woolgoolga beach that John was spotted flying a modified Benson gyro-plane by officials of the Grafton Water-ski Club. The annual Jacaranda Festival was approaching and John, by now a club member, was drafted in to build and fly a water-ski kite as part of the show. If he could build and fly a gyro-plane, a ski kite should give him no trouble.

The Club expected John to make a conventional flat-kite, the sort that does not really fly but goes upwards in drag reaction to the tow boat speed. This idea was abandoned when John discovered that every previous kite flyer at the Jacaranda Festival had been injured, and that was what everybody turned up for! It was at this time that NASA released the Gemini photograph, the space capsule suspended under a Rogallo wing. This seemed to be much more suited to the aquatic environment. John saw it in a magazine and was inspired.

44

It is precisely at this point that history was made. Armed with only the photograph, with no dimensions and no back-up information, John started to make models based on the flexwing principle. And they flew – really well! By May 1963 he had a half-size model in which he could be towed. The full-size version was developed and the maiden flight was in September 1963. The *Daily Examiner* of October, 1963, records the event for posterity. The aircraft had a weight-shift single hang point and the 'A' frame that is common to all modern Rogallo hang gliders. All the major innovations that lead directly to hang gliding as we know it today were developed in the space of about 6 months! On the 11th October, 1963 John filed for the patent and Provisional Protection was awarded for the application, numbered 36189/63.

The first hang gliders had wooden leading edges, aluminium cross-booms, steel A-frames and the sails were made from blue plastic sheeting. Total cost, $24. By 1964 all flight and construction problems had been sorted. John's Ski Wing, for that is what it was called, was now made entirely out of aluminium, except for the mild steel A-frame. The sails were partly battened, and made of nylon, and the rigging was wire cable. John had designed the nose plate so that the leading edges swung into the keel, and the cross-boom pivoted, fore and aft, for quick knock-down and car-top transport. And most importantly, although launch was still being towed up behind a boat, the landings were often made off the tow-line in true free flight.

It is interesting to note that work on personal rogallos in the United States was still a year or so off, and when it did start it would go the bamboo, plastic and parallel bars route.

In 1964, a Brisbane newspaper published a picture of John's creation and a man called Robin Bishop saw it and wrote to his friend Francis Rogallo, explaining that an Australian had privately developed the rogallo principle into a perfectly viable man-carrying aircraft for so little money it was laughable. Understandably interested, Rogallo wrote to John Dickenson in September, 1964, requesting information. On November 24, 1964, the entire plans and general specification of the Ski Wing were sent to him at [the] Langley Research Centre in Virginia. In just about every detail the craft described in the drawings is identical to what became known throughout the world as the 'Standard Rogallo' and latterly the 'Bog Rog'. We had to wait for another ten years before this type of hang glider started to become obsolete.

In Francis Rogallo's reply to John dated January 29, 1965, he says and I quote 'I hope to make some copies of your drawings and perhaps have some individual or groups build a glider like yours locally. Your design looks better than other ski kites I have seen and I wish you great success with it.' This is praise indeed from the master.

By 1964 the publicity surrounding the Ski Wing was beginning to create a demand and John started making and selling the glider to water-ski enthusiasts. Rod Fuller now drove the boats, John did the demo flights and people like Ray Leighton bought the early examples. However, for one reason or another the business of marketing the hang glider as a tow-launched craft was making slow progress.

They were flying a lot of exhibitions and everyone was very enthusiastic, but converting interest into sales was an uphill struggle. John thinks it was the daredevil publicity that made people wary. After all that work, they had a complete system to sell and John was not making any money out of it. He was beginning to wonder if it was all worthwhile.

In 1966 a move to Sydney and a meeting with Mike Burns seemed to open up new commercial possibilities. Mike was a graduate aeronautical engineer who had independently developed a Rogallo-type tow glider called the Ski Plane. His company, Aerostructures, now started to build the Ski Wing whilst John demonstrated it and taught people to fly. About this time John set an Australian 2-hour endurance record and people like Bill Moyes, Bill Bennett, and 'Gelignite Jack' Murray began to sit up and take notice.

In March 1967 Moyes and Bennett signed up for trial flights. John duly taught them both to fly and Bill Moyes bought a kite from Aerostructures. Shortly afterwards, the company went bust owing John all the commission from the wings that had been sold.

Bill Moyes and John Dickenson became good friends. John willingly donated the design and constructional information of the Ski Wing to Moyes, and in the years between 1967 and 1969 a great deal of collaborative work was carried out in the search for higher performance. It seems that Bill was a fearless flyer and his chase for records and hang gliding publicity created an enormous press following. Bill Bennett was similarly motivated and altitude records see-sawed between the two barnstormers. In 1969–70 Bennett moved to the US with some gliders based on John Dickenson's designs and set up a manufacturing business in California. Moyes was already set up in Australia and beginning to make it pay.

It is ironic that at a time when hang gliding started to fire the public's imagination world-wide, John Dickenson should begin to retreat from involvement with its future. Pressures at work, the financial implications of the move to Sydney and trying to salvage a Diploma in Management at the Tech; all contributed to his withdrawal. By late 1969 John had stopped flying and building, and by 1973 the collaboration with Bill Moyes was over, though they are still good friends.

It is undoubtedly true that many people from many countries made very real contributions to the development of the hang glider. The phenomenon of parallel development has clearly operated to a great extent. Richard Miller in the US was blissfully unaware of the work of John Dickenson in Grafton, as was Mike Burns in Sydney. It appears that Tom Purcell Jr flew a Rogallo tow vehicle in 1961, and Jim Natland and Barry Palmer were also pioneers in the mid-sixties.

Despite the efforts of all these visionary engineers, the name of John Dickenson must stand alone as the man who created the first completely developed flexible wing hang glider, with all the features we now take for granted. He did it in 1963, way ahead of anything that was going on in the United States. He did it in a small town in Australia away from the so-called centres of learning. He even had a provisional patent for it. The whole process was completed in a ridiculously short time at hardly any cost. Ironically, he never made any money out of his invention.

Despite all this, his contribution is not generally recognised, not even in Australia. Surely John Dickenson's rightful place in history is alongside Dr Francis Rogallo?

Development in hang gliding is often unselfconscious. Magazines cover events monthly, and in the early days, changes were so momentous that it was almost impossible to draw breath and discover where we had come from. I had heard Bill Moyes talk about John Dickenson long before Mark Woodhams' discovery, but Dickenson's significance escaped me at the time. Dickenson's vital invention was the triangular control bar, the so-called A-frame, which Leonardo da Vinci might have got around to if he had authorised his apprentice to build his hang glider in 1493 and actually tried to fly it. The A-frame is a much more logical device for adding strength to the flimsy wing than the 'mast' that da Vinci envisaged.

Years later, Mark Woodhams added to our insight into the development of the basic hang glider by adding the name Rod Fuller, as Dickenson's partner:

> Fuller, then 26, was the first person to actually fly the flexible wing hang glider designed and created by Dickenson in September 1963. It was the photograph of Rod flying along the Clarence River, towed by a water ski boat, in the Grafton 'Daily Examiner' that ultimately led to the free flying revolution. This glider design, with its triangular 'A' frame, swing seat weight shift control and simple folding structure was copied worldwide. Rod's involvement with towed flight was because of his water skiing expertise. At the time of these flights in 1963 he was Northern Rivers District Water Ski Champion.
>
> Rod's first flight came close to disaster when the prototype glider was unexpectedly towed to the top of the line in a stiff breeze. It was only the quick thinking of Rod and expert boat driver Pat Crowe that allowed the craft to be steered away from an approaching bridge and landed safely back on the river. It is interesting to speculate what might have happened to the development of hang gliding if this first flight had ended less happily.
>
> What is not generally known is that the flying partnership of Rod and John Dickenson perfected the principle of flight control of the revolutionary new wing, and it was for this work that Rod was later awarded the FAI Hang Gliding Diploma. Weight shift control of gliders up to this point had not provided very satisfactory results, as Otto Lilienthal had found to his cost. However, the flexible wing and its ability to change shape according to the plan form load placed upon it, ushered in a mode of control that had long been avoided.

We all take it for granted now, but in the early days the pilot swinging from a single hang point for control was a completely untested technique. The length of the hang straps, the relationship of the hang point to the centre of pressure, the position fore and aft of the A frame and the height of the A frame itself, were all variables whose interplay had to be tested to determine effective flight control. Rod and John between them established the principles by which control authority could be maintained safely in a flexible wing vehicle.

John Dickenson talks about their early partnership developing the weight shift flying techniques between 1963 and 1965:

'Both Rod and I became addicted to flying the wing. I was well aware of the history of Otto Lilienthal and his unfortunate demise. I believed it necessary to develop both the wing and the flying techniques to a very reliable extent before the wing could ever be flown over land. Being able to continue this task over water provided a huge advantage, as we could crash into the water with only a tiny risk compared with mistakes or accidents made over land. During this period from September 1963 to December 1965, when I moved from Grafton back to Sydney, I was in constant consultation with Rod Fuller and so I can say that the development of the flying techniques, of the pendulum weight shift control system was perfected by Rod Fuller and me. I think you are aware that bitten by the flying bug, Rod Fuller went on to become well known as a sailplane pilot, becoming an instructor, qualified to repair sail planes, and authorized to issue certificates of air worthiness following repair.'

All of the hang gliding test flying activity happened far away from the usual centres of gliding design and development, in the quiet waters of the Clarence River in New South Wales, Australia. Rod's modest and unassuming character meant that his true importance to the history of hang gliding was not recognized until quite recently.

But Dickenson's insight could also have been lost to the wider world had it not been for those two formidable Australians, Bill Moyes and Bill Bennett, and the fierce competition they had with each other to profit from hang gliding. It is hard to say which of the two is more important, but Moyes has sometimes been called the father of hang gliding.

Moyes, born in 1932, started flying after barefoot water-skiing got too boring for him. He was towed to 8,600ft in a hang glider behind an aeroplane, scattering battens and nearly killing himself. He has flown from the Grand Canyon, taken off from the top of Mount Kilimanjaro in Africa, been seriously injured five times and there are very few bones in his body that he has not broken. At the age of 52 he had a mad ambition to drop out of a balloon in a hang glider, land at the top of Mount Everest, and plant the Australian flag. Bill Moyes is very Australian. He started flying in kites in 1966, when he was 34:

I had been water-skiing since the early '50s. My partner and I were looking for something new to do. We were bare-footing and had done everything we could do on the water. My partner used to drive a taxi for 'Gelignite Jack' Murray, who had a kite, a ski-plane, a Rogallo wing with a pair of floats and controlled with a joystick. It was pretty primitive so he suggested I try a new wing that had been built by John Dickenson, the guy we call Dr Cyclops.

The Rogallo wing that we have today is John Dickenson's. When NASA decided they didn't want to use the Rogallo wing they allowed Francis Rogallo to publish his notes. John Dickenson got hold of those notes in 1962. He designed the trapeze bar and the weight-shift system that was the basis of what we have today.

In 1966 John was flying his wing to heights of 20 or 30 feet, towing behind a boat on skis. He never did anything too wild. He wanted to produce the wing to sell and was trying to interest people in it, taking it around the ski clubs and the kite flying clubs that flew the conventional pentagonal kites.

Those pentagonal kites consisted of sheets drawn tight on a frame and flown at a high angle of attack in a constant stall. They are dreadful things. The driver has to be completely alert all the time. They don't fly, they just drag. I had never flown one of those when I met John Dickenson. At that stage he hadn't sold one of his ski wings because he hadn't found anyone to test-fly the thing for him properly.

The first time I tried it, it was a comedy. It happened on the Hawkesbury River. Because it was somebody else's boat they had first crack at it. The first guy went out and the kite climbed away pretty quick. The driver of the boat has to co-ordinate with the kite all the time and has to slow down if the kite climbs too quick. The first guy crashed. The rear restraining wire took his ear off so they carted him off to hospital.

The second guy went out, climbed rapidly, panicked and pulled the bar right in. When he hit the water he broke his leg. So they took him off to hospital too. The third guy wasn't three feet off the water when he let go of the control bar. He too was gashed by the wires. By the time the fifth had gone to hospital there was no one left to drive the boat.

Eventually we found a driver who would only do what I told him to. I told him to go at 30 mph and off we went. I flew the kite for 8 miles, turned around and came back. I let go at about 150 feet and glided down. I knew exactly what the thing was going to do and it did it.

Within six weeks of that flight, Bill Moyes had set a world altitude record, towed up to 1,045ft at Tuggerah Lake, and he began chasing this and other records. In 1967 he flew at the Sydney Showground during a boat show and subsequently got hired to do the job regularly. He started to travel the world giving demonstrations of tow-kiting. He met Bill Bennett when Bennett was the official witness at the Tuggerah Lake record attempt. Bennett was in the aircraft that flew alongside Moyes to verify the height gain of more than 1,000ft. In contrast to Dickenson (who says he taught both men to fly), Moyes states he taught Bennett, and they flew together for about a year before Bennett went to America in 1969. The two men became fierce rivals, and more than twenty-five years later, remain so. You can still hear Moyes roar, 'I always beat you, Bennett, my son always beat your son, and my grandson will always beat your grandson!'

The peculiar flavour of Bill Moyes's strong personality can be caught in his account of a tour of Europe, where he spent six weeks in plaster:

That was in Denmark where I was flying in the World Water Ski Championships. The officials had said I couldn't use the boat for practice because I was distracting the men laying out the slalom course. But I wanted to finish trimming the kite. The wind was pretty strong so I had six of the team run down a hill with a rope towing me into the air. The first flight was quite good. I wanted one more flight to finish the adjustments. We went back up. By this time a crowd of about 2,000 people had gathered in the landing area. When the crew came running

> down the hill again with the rope they ran into this mass of
> people and couldn't go any further. I was still over the trees
> and came down through them. I smashed my wrist, elbow,
> face, teeth, [and] a few other things.

Nice line, that, isn't it? ...'a few other things'. Bill Moyes claims the first
soaring flight on a Rogallo in May 1968, flying tethered at La Perouse. He
had been towed into the air, but after some minutes noticed the rope was
slack.

'Aren't you holding the bloody rope?' he roared.

The man shook it about to show there was no load on it, so Bill let the
rope go and flew about for thirty-two minutes.

Bennett went to the US, where there was a much bigger potential market
than Australia, and he and Moyes slugged it out in front of the television
cameras and news photographers. Bennett towed over the Statue of Liberty
wearing a suit that made him look like the Rhinestone Cowboy. Moyes
jumped into the Grand Canyon. They were both towed higher and higher
until Moyes got an aeroplane to tow him up to 8,600ft:

> In those days Bennett and I used to upstage each other. He'd
> do something and then I would top it. He'd do something else
> and then I would top it and then he would attempt to top that.
> It went on for years and years. I had established the tow record
> for 2,870 feet in 1968. In 1971 Bill topped it with 2,900 feet.
> So I thought I might as well make a proper job of it. I hooked
> on the back of a plane and took it to 8,600 feet. There were
> quite a few problems as you can imagine. I was lucky to meet
> a tow pilot in America called Chuck Doyle. He was a pioneer
> of the barnstorming days and he was familiar with towing
> because he towed banners. He was a Northwest Airlines pilot
> and had his own fleet of planes. He brought his fleet of planes
> along and we first tried it out behind a Stearman. I thought it
> would have plenty of horsepower.
>
> I underestimated the horsepower that a plane can put out.
> Anyhow, that thing nearly tore me to pieces. It flew along at
> 60mph with the sail fully luffed. It tore all the rubbers out
> and battens flew out like a shower of spears. I was lucky
> to get down alive. I just lost a bit of skin, which we did
> in those days. We bled almost every time we flew! After
> half a dozen unsuccessful flights we decided we weren't

using the right equipment. We switched to a Super Cub with modified tips and a lower speed. We managed to get it down to 45 mph and since I also used a smaller kite it went quite successfully.

I started behind the plane using a pair of skis with no fins. I kicked the skis off when we got airborne and away we went. The plane took off and we didn't get much over 45 mph until about 5,000 feet, and he had to pull the flaps up as the engine was overheating. The speed went up to 60 mph and I had a sail-luffing problem again, but not as badly as before, and we managed to creep up to 8,600 feet.

Was it a straightforward flight? Well, actually it was a crazy day in Autumn in Wisconsin in America in 1971. Temperature was about zero on the ground and minus 23 at altitude with wind chill on top. The wind was blowing about 50 mph at 2,000 feet and only about 20 mph on the ground. So when we reached the 2,000 foot level I thought there was something wrong with the plane because it was going backwards. We flew backwards for five miles until we climbed out of the strong wind layer. Then we went forwards again. But I was about 10 miles upwind of the airport when I released and I kept the glider headed away from the airport and flew backwards all the way down to it. The wind was so strong.

That was the end of that type of competition between Moyes and Bennett, though they remained rivals in other areas. They both became major manufacturers of hang gliders. Moyes set up Moyes Gliders in Sydney, Australia. Bennett founded Delta Wing Kites in Van Nuys, California. It was Bennett who made the Phoenix 6B that Alvin Russell took the agency for in England in 1976, and that carted me to second place in the 1976 British National Championships.

Moyes believes it was his flight into the Grand Canyon on a wing made with aluminium and dacron in 1970 that finally put paid to the bamboo butterflies in the US. The first Lilienthal meet had only one Rogallo, and that had no triangle control bar, but as the new aviation started to grow, it was Rogallos that dominated, because they had Dickenson's control bars and were car-toppable. You could fold them up, stick them on a roof rack, and drive away. The meeting after Lilienthal's 123rd birthday was named after another American pioneer, Montgomery, where there were just two Hang Looses, but a great many Rogallos. Lambie was amazed:

Little did we realise that Rogallo, the flexible wing, was going to be the winner. We just didn't know. Volmer Jensen and Paul MacCready came out and looked at us crashing and bashing and said, 'Aw, it's just like jumping on a bicycle with no steering and pushing off and going down a hill. It's interesting but it has no future.' Then Volmer went out and built that good one with the controls, the VJ-23.

Volmer Jensen, in his 70s and a holy lunatic if ever there was one, designed, built and flew a rigid-wing hang glider called the VJ-23. It was one of dozens of rigid hang gliders whose designers, consciously or not, tried to lead hang gliding back into the mainstream three-axis control aviation developed by the Wright brothers, except they were foot launched. But hang gliding wouldn't go there. Jensen's VJ-23 did have a big influence on the British-built CFM Shadow, one of the most sophisticated of modern microlight powered aircraft, but that, too, is a cul-de-sac in microlighting (although Eve Jackson became the first person to fly a microlight from England to Australia in a CFM Shadow in 1986–87, and I made a similar flight, but at speed, and also in a CFM Shadow, from London to Sydney for the Australian bicentenary on 26 January 1988). CFM stood for Cook's Flying Machine.

MacCready, of course, as we will discover, went on to build the Gossamer Condor and revolutionise man-powered flight, mainly because of his hang gliding roots.

Before the end of 1971, the first soaring flight had been made in the US on a Rogallo wing. At the Lilienthal Meet earlier that year, the longest flight had been 196ft, and the longest time in the air, eleven seconds. But so fast had progress been that on 6 September, not even four months later, Dave Kilbourne soared a Bennett-designed 16ft Rogallo on Mission Ridge near Fremont for twenty-five minutes!

Can you imagine the grit that Kilbourne must have had, to rig on top of a hill a 'flying machine' that previously had only flown down? He had this theory that it was possible to turn into a lift band that glider pilots said was there on other hills, but glider pilots didn't fly Mission Ridge. Kilbourne proposed to steer his wing to stay in that lift band and go up. It was only a theory, though, with no other proof than to try it himself. The risk was that he would hit the hill and kill himself. There was no water around for a soft landing. As he stood on that ridge, the wind beginning to fill his sail, his feelings must have been very like those tower jumpers in aviation's past. But he succeeded where they failed. I met him once, years later, flying at the coastal site of Torrey Pines, near San Diego, California, as if he was any other flyer. No one pointed him out to me, and it was only by accident I discovered that he was, indeed, *the* Dave Kilbourne, first man to soar a hang glider in America. He seemed to have no awareness of how important that flight had been. It was probably modesty.

With the exception of Bill Moyes and his Australian travelling circus, most of us outside the United States watched the magical new aviation as if with noses pressed heavily to a plate glass window. We read whatever we could about the heroes of our sport. There was the great Bob Wills, whose role in the Smithsonian film *To Fly!?* made my hair rise when I saw it. At the end of the sequence trumpeting the triumph of mainstream aviation, the film shows a Jumbo taking off in all its mighty noise and size and power, and cuts suddenly to a distant helicopter shot of Hawaiian cliffs and a lone hang glider pilot circling … and silence. That film's editor had an early insight into the significance of hang gliding in man's urge to fly. Bob Wills, in his short career, exemplified all that was best in American flying.

There were other legendary American names … Chris Wills (Bob's brother), Rich Grigsby, Taras Kiceniuk, Chris Price, Tom Peghiny, Dave Cronk, Dick Eipper, Dean Tanji, Roy Haggard, Keith Nichols ….

When Johnny Carr, the great English pilot who four years later was just pipped into second place at the 1979 World Hang Gliding Championships, saw Tom Peghiny in 1975, he couldn't speak to him. Johnny just watched Peghiny (who was quite unaware of the effect he was having) saunter absently by. Johnny whispered to another English pilot, 'That's Tom Peghiny.' The idea of actually talking to Peghiny was quite beyond him. By the beginning of 1975, that was our view in Europe on American hang gliding. They flew off mountain peaks, built aircraft and made flights to which we could only aspire, and won competitions with names like the US Masters of Hang Gliding and the United States Open. They knew things about flying that were beyond us. They were demi-gods, at the peak of achievement. And we were looking up the long, high mountain wondering how we could possibly get there, too. They were the superstars. We were merely fans.

Chapter 4

Early British Years

It took more than a year for hang gliding to cross the Atlantic and arrive in Britain. The first Englishman credited with flying a Rogallo hang glider was a student of engineering, Geoff McBroom. He studied at Cardiff University, and with a number of colleagues, including the future balloon manufacturer Don Cameron, and he built and flew a primitive Rogallo wing. There was a certain amount of wuffo press attention ('wuffo you're doing that?'), nothing like as romantic as the Americans, and around the country people began to take interest. In Shropshire, my friend Alvin Russell read about McBroom, and visited him in Bristol where he was setting up McBroom Wings, bought one of his hang gliders and became an agent to sell them.

In Oldham, another British pioneer was Len Gabriels, an engineer and aeromodeller:

> I suppose it is the dream of every aeromodeller to fly, especially in something he made himself. Some time in 1972 I saw an artist's impression of a man-carrying rogallo wing in my son's Look and Learn comic. It provided the inspiration for a model that I built. The first couple of wings were based on sketchy information from the comic. I read about Geoff McBroom's experiments in Bristol in November 1972, and I wrote to the 'Self-Soaring Association' of California but got no reply. So I started experimenting myself with models.
>
> My models gradually led to a full-size wing. It didn't work very well. I am sure now that we were trying to fly it on slopes that were too shallow. We didn't appreciate the poor glide angle, consequently we didn't get off the ground. We should have picked steeper slopes.
>
> Our first real glider was the Skyhook Mark 3. This flew really well. I advertised plans in April 1973 Aeromodeller Magazine. I didn't know of any other people flying hang

gliders in this country at the beginning. By April, 1973 I was aware of Ken Messenger, and before that I knew of McBroom but he was in hospital because his glider crashed. Anyway, within a couple of months I was selling 12 sets of plans a day for the Mark 3. The idea was that people could build the machine themselves from materials that were easy to obtain. I've still got a book of names of people who ordered my plans. My wife Hilda kept it. We thought perhaps we had better get organised after the enquiries came flooding in. The names in that book make interesting reading. Most of the people who subsequently set up as manufacturers had plans from me.

Quite soon people began nagging me for kits. With two friends – they are no longer in the sport – I started to make glider kits. The Haynes Brothers began manufacturing gliders around this time, down near south London. Geoff McBroom and Ken Messenger were two other manufacturers I remember. At that time we were the only company in the north of England. It was as if hang gliders were the answer to everyone's dream. People who had wanted to fly for years became interested all at once.

Hang gliding attracted strong-minded individuals. One who admitted openly he was only attracted because of the danger was Nick Regan in Sussex. Later famous for his refusal to wear a crash helmet, and the robustness of his replies to pressure from Johnny-come-latelies to conform, Regan became interested in the summer of 1972, and began building his own wings in October. They were essentially a John Dickenson creation, designed by Nick with simple drawings, and took four weeks to complete. Their first flights were in early November 1972, from Farnham Park, South Harting Down, and then Hankley Common; they lasted about fifteen seconds. The wing, weighing 35lb, demonstrated reasonable control and they were almost beginning to get the hang of flare-out landings by Christmas.

In south London in 1973, John, Robin and Terry Haynes saw pictures of a man flying a Rogallo. Using the photograph as a model, they built their own wing, and went up to Box Hill to fly it. Terry was the first to succeed in getting airborne but when he landed at the bottom of the hill he broke his arm.

The man who did more to popularise hang gliding in Britain than anyone else, our equivalent to Bill Moyes and Bill Bennett, was Ken Messenger, a successful businessman from growing tomatoes in Marlborough, in Wiltshire. He had spent his twenties on competition motorcycling and Formula Ford racing, and then water-skiing:

It was through skiing that I got into hang gliding, via tow-kiting. Bill Bennett was in England for a couple of days, and I was watching him demonstrate towed Rogallo water-ski take-offs, followed by free glides. I was so fascinated I followed him to Dunstable Downs where he gave a demonstration free glide from the top. This was just one flight because of very adverse winds, and the short time at Bill's disposal. He was only airborne for 10 seconds. But it was enough for me! I ordered a glider from him on the spot, asked him to ring California that same evening to get it put on to a plane. It arrived a couple of days later, but by then Bill had left the country. There I was, left to work everything out on my own from the 10 seconds I had seen of Bill in the air, and the few minutes' conversation I had managed to get with him.

I took things very slowly and cautiously, running into the wind, being picked up by it and then lowered gently down again. It was months before I felt safe enough to glide from any worthwhile height. I chose Milk Hill. When the big moment came it was well worth all the preparation. A full minute of belonging completely to the sky, swinging my legs left and right, forward and back as instinctively as if I had been doing it all my life, watching the horizon yaw to and fro, rise and fall obediently at each command, while rich green Wiltshire hill pasture slid by 400 feet below. Ten seconds setting up approach and landing as slow and gentle as a gull. And this was still only the very beginning.

My confidence had had a good old build-up and I felt all the thrill of the early pioneers. I could see many possibilities beckoning. These included setting up in business as Birdman Sports, importing and manufacturing Bennett Gliders and trying to spread the good news in the UK by combining private pleasure flying with public demonstrations. In those days it was all downhill flying. It had not occurred to anybody that a Rogallo would be capable of soaring. So the obvious move was to keep getting higher up to take off; why not a great deal higher up? The top of Snowdon, for example? It had the advantage of easy access via a railway. At the same time it has always stood as a symbol for adventure and endeavour in the public mind, and would make an excellent focal point for publicity for the infant sport of which the public were still totally ignorant. Birdman Sports (myself and Dave Raymond, who later went on to do the Roger Daltry flying sequences in the 1975 Ken Russell film 'Tommy') decided to get the backing of the media and go ahead, which we did on September 12, 1973.

The weather was perfect, warm, clear, practically no wind. What little there was came from the south-east allowing take-off from the extreme summit, a narrow platform with just enough room to get airborne, ending in a spectacular 2,000 foot sheer precipice. The mountain was crowded with tourists and climbers, and the trains kept bringing more and more of them to the top without taking any back, because none were going to budge until they had seen what happened to the crazy fellow unpacking the butterfly wings. All the media were there.

We got the glider assembled with tension growing all the time, none of the spectators having seen a hang glider before, or a man, for that matter, who was planning to run flat-out with one over the edge of a 2,000 foot precipice. There were quite a few worried faces around, and I was told afterwards that a group of people were on their knees, praying.

The tension built up further as I went round doing the last routine safety check of the machine, more thoroughly than ever before. I had never trusted my life so completely to a set of wing nuts and bolts. Then I lifted up and held the A-frame, and let the sails inflate gently above me the way I had found always worked on the Marlborough Downs. I hoped it would work up here, and started my run.

I have been very much higher since then on hang gliders, flying from balloons and in the Alps, but I have never experienced a bigger thrill than during this descent. There I was, gliding through the air with nothing between me and the wild Welsh mountain scenery thousands of feet below, with a feeling of exhilaration and awe. At the same time there was just the right amount of anxiety in the situation to keep my adrenalin flowing. I tried to calculate a safe speed, well clear of stalling, when the ground was so far below that it gave the impression I wasn't moving despite the familiar sound of a

20 mph wind in my ears. The glider's nose started to behave in a sudden unexpected way as I approached a funnel formed by the mountain's arms. I was puzzled, and as an obstinate lift force grew stronger, I tried to counteract with further and further forward weight shift, until the wind sounded more like 30 to 35 mph than my customary 20[mph]. Finally, I approached a large wood, and had to make up my mind whether or not I would have enough height to clear it. I played for safety there just as I had over the speed, and went for a series of S-turns to lose height and land short, in perfect comfort.

Then it was a case of champagne at our hotel and waiting for the media to do their job. They were very quick off the mark. The full flight was on the six o'clock news that evening and proved as big an eye-opener for the British public as we had hoped. I gather this was the first full national coverage of a hang glider in action in Britain.

It used to be said in San Francisco in the late 1960s that if you rubbed two hippies together, you would get a business. The same seemed to apply to hang glider pilots. Messenger's exploits helped the sport to grow, and during that winter the number of pilots in the UK grew to 500, and by the following winter it was 2,500. Messenger founded Birdman Sports, while Len Gabriels threw away a marvellous opportunity to call his company Gabriel's Wings, and chose instead to name it Skyhook. Nick Regan seemed to be the only early flyer not to set out to make wings for other people.

From just running off a hill and landing at the bottom, the ambition of the pioneers turned to try to stay in the air. If gliders could be slung off a hill, and soar, why couldn't hang gliders? The first man in England to take off, go up, and soar is said to have been John James (aka Haynes) in the middle of 1973, a full two years after the Dave Kilbourne flight in California. In the autumn of that year, Gabriels went for a record:

Pendle Hill, near Clitheroe in Lancs, is the place where on Sunday afternoon, November 11, 1973, I soared for 25 minutes and 46 seconds for (I believe) a British sailwing record. The details of that flight will probably be of interest to others who are hoping to do something similar (who isn't?) and would like to know what it takes.

The main ingredients obviously are a suitable hill, a good glider, the right weather conditions and a willing band of helpers, plus the luck to get it together at the same time on whichever day of the week you usually fly.

This Sunday, everything was right. We arrived at 1 o'clock and whilst debating where on the hill to go we suddenly saw another flyer, Mick Hurst of Keighley, airborne off the north-west face, so we decided we would go to the same spot. We settled on an area which was about 50 feet lower than the top of the hill, as I have learned to expect turbulence behind the edge of a steep hill, usually in the form of a 'rotor' in the air.

Anyway, the wing was assembled, wind checked (15–20mph), and off I went. I turned to the right and flew close along the ridge for about 400 yards and then slowly outwards, and finally left to come back towards my take-off point, which I passed and went on towards the end of the ridge. When I turned to go back again, I found to my dismay that I was now well below the take-off point. Despite efforts to regain the lost height by keeping as close to the hill as I dared, I was unable to do so and finished up at the bottom after a flight of about 4½ minutes.

Forty-five minutes later and we were back at the top, ready for another go. After some slight alteration to the rigging to provide just a little bit more lift at the rear, I went off again. This time, as before, I flew to the right for a few hundred yards and gained height, again turning slowly at the end so as to avoid flying inefficiently. On the way back I was again some height over the take-off point, but this time decided not to go beyond this point but to turn around as I grew level with the crowd (about 30).

After several passes back and forth like this I knew that if I wanted to, I could stay up for as long as the wind blew. However, I began to find out that it was a lot colder just hanging there than when climbing the hill.

Also I found that the rigging still wasn't quite right so that I had to pull on the control-bar to counteract a small nose-up tendency. Not a lot, but like dripping water wears away stone, after about 15 minutes my arms began to ache a little and the thought nagged at me, what would happen if my fingers lost their grip and I let go? At times I would let my arms go to full stretch trying to feel a stall coming on, but it never happened.

I found that the kite would fly very slowly like this, much more quietly and with the rear of the sail filled out tightly. It also climbed a little more easily.

About mid-flight I wanted to know how long I had been airborne, and flew about 50 feet over the crowd and shouted, 'how long?'. The skid lid (always wear one) prevented me from hearing their replies so eventually they were holding up their fingers to indicate about 15 minutes (at least I think they were telling me the time!).

After a further few minutes, my fingers were really painful with the cold and the pleasure had gone out of the flight, so I started to think about landing. I flew very low over the crowd and they scattered in all directions as I shouted that I intended to land. I was promptly told to try and land as near the car as possible. As they set off walking along the hill, I passed a few more minutes by going backwards and forwards along the ridge. I wanted to be sure they could see the landing when it came in order to clock me off properly.

Eventually I judged that my time-keepers were in position so I turned off the end of the ridge, flew over a gully about 400 feet deep to turn into wind on the other side, and finally landed as light as a feather about 200 yards from the cars.

A few minutes later the crowd arrived off the hill, by which time I had thawed out and began to regret that I had not stayed up a bit longer. Still, there always is another day. Finally the time was checked, witnesses' names and addresses taken, and off we went homeward, everybody very happy.

By the summer of 1974, many of the pilots who later achieved fame in international competitions had taken up hang gliding. These included Johnny Carr, Brian Wood, Bob Calvert, Robert Bailey, Graham Hobson, Keith Cockroft, Graham Slater and, John and Jeremy Fack. Each manufacturer seemed to operate only within his own 'turf'. Waspair and the Haynes brothers had the wealthy and populous south-east, but were challenged directly by a new company called Hiway, run by John Ievers and a pugnacious Australian called Steve Hunt. Ken Messenger's Birdman had the south-west of England. Geoff McBroom had Wales and the Midlands. Len Gabriel's Skyhook had the north. Two associations were formed, the British Kite Soaring Association (BKSA), which Ken ran, and the National Hang Gliding Association (NHGA), run by a man who called himself John

James, but whose real name was John Haynes, brother of the two directors of Waspair. This is not an unusual start to a united national organisation, but there were bitter feelings about Haynes pretending to be independent when he was connected to a major manufacturer. If you turned up in Birdman country flying a Wasp machine you were not very welcome, and vice versa. They were like baronies across Britain, and cultures and flying styles grew up around particular manufacturers. In the south-east, for example, pilots were often robust, more working class, even aggressive, but not threatening. Birdman flyers saw themselves as a better class of flyers than others, more genteel. Very British.

Two championships were run in that year, on Steyning Bowl near Brighton and from Cam Long Down near Stroud in Gloucester. All early competition was either 'how far can you go?' or 'how long can you stay in the air and hit a spot?' Hundreds of people saw these events, either in person or on television, and wanted to learn. There was no defined method of teaching. Len Gabriels describes how he did it:

> I used to supply flying instructions with each machine, and taught loads of people to fly. After talking for half an hour about what they had to do, I used to take them to the top of a steep hill, not too high, and get them to hold the glider and talk them through the movements. I would set them up, holding the keel to show them what angle the thing should fly at and slowly run them off the hill. I told them, 'hold the bar here' and off they went. They would fly down 100 feet or so to start with. Two hours of this and the average guy would be flying fine. Nobody ever hurt themselves learning this way, either. The glider was so stable it would just fly in a straight line. If it was stalled it would just mush.

The big site everyone in the south aspired to go to was Rhossili on the Gower Peninsula in South Wales. It was a hack up to the top, carrying a hang glider, but two thirds of the way up you could launch from the so-called 'pimple'. Once on top of the ridge you could fly so long as the wind was anything from west to north, using the ridge in a westerly and the cliffs in a northerly. If you went from top to bottom that was still 600ft, higher than almost anywhere else we could find in Britain at the time.

Brian Wood was a former motorcycle racer who learned to fly that year. He was simply a natural pilot. Brian was told what to do, 'pull for speed and dive, push to climb or slow and eventually stall, lean left to go left, lean right to go right', clipped in and flew (that is still how hang gliders are controlled, fifty years later). On Wood's third weekend flying he stayed in the air for thirty-five minutes, beating Len Gabriels' Pendle Hill record. He entered the championships at Steyning, and won, and did the same at Cam Long Down. A week after that he went to Rhossili to see if he could beat the duration record of more than ten hours established in Hawaii by an American pilot (for some years duration flying was all the rage):

After a long and very wet journey which started in London at 3.30am on Friday, we eventually arrived in Rhossili. I understood that we were to fly off a large hill that came right off the beach, but as we drove down through the village to the car park that overlooks the beach, my eyes nearly popped out of my head. A kite soared over the Worms Head Hotel, turned and ridge-soared down to the end of the cliffs. Yes! They were cliff soaring!

I had been told that it wasn't a very good idea to try and soar from cliffs, but here was a guy soaring up and down these cliffs. Say no more, half an hour later I was up there myself. The conditions were perfect. That night I said to Robin Haynes that if the winds were good in the morning I was going for a long one (flight, that is). After a sleepless night I ate a sickly breakfast that Eric Short had cooked, loads of baked beans – the flyer's breakfast 'to give you plenty of lift!'

We soon arrived at the site and I took off just after half past ten on the north-facing ridge and flew up and down. Sometimes I went around the cliff facing north-westerly to get the best of both, and keeping out of the way of the other flyers. The only thing that worried me was that I was about half a mile away from the car park, and also those cliffs were far too steep to land on.

If I got sink I was in trouble because the sea came right to the bottom of the cliffs. Well, after five hours everything was OK and I was still warm, but then some black rain clouds came in and it poured. The wind and rain got stronger and I could hardly see the others so I flew back to the Hotel. The rain stopped but the winds got stronger and stronger. I did not know that it was blowing about 40 mph. I guessed the winds were bad because I was the only one in the air, and I was also flying at about 60 feet, both in front of the cliffs and above the beach. Yes – soaring a flat beach!

The winds soon returned to normal and I was now frozen and wet, but I thought I would plug on. All the others appeared from the pub indicating that they had food and drink ... the swines! Ten minutes later Eric 'Ossie' Short was flying towards me with a king post bag on a long line with food in it. But the line was too short and we were getting too close for comfort, so I flew off down the ridge so the others could carry on flying. Twenty minutes later Tony Beresford followed me along with the same bag on a longer line. This time I stayed as still as I could and Tony flew over me and the bag came straight into my hand. He let go of the rope and I tied the bag to my control bar. Inside I found a Cornish pastie that looked like it had been run over by a steam-roller (Eric Short had dropped it back to the others from about 60 feet). When I opened the can of shandy which I found inside, it blew up in my face (that was also dropped in the bag). In the end I flew for 8 hours and 26 minutes. Boy, was I glad to get down and into the Hotel for a drink and a hot bath. So we are only one step behind the Americans now and with a bit of luck I hope by next summer we will be the Duration World Record Holders. Look out Yanks, here we come.

Over the period of Brian Wood's flight that day, two flyers were blown back into cliff rotor (when air curls over a cliff it rotates, creating often fatal conditions), landed on telephone lines and were taken away to hospital by ambulance. A third also had an accident but refused medical treatment, although he had considerable difficulty walking due to an injured back. One of the three was a man called Brian Gaskin, another holy lunatic who walked away from hang gliding a few months later, then threw himself into what later became known as paragliding.

Wood's flight was my way into hang gliding. I interviewed him the following Sunday at BBC Radio London's studios, then in Hanover Square. When he walked through the door, stocky, bronzed, his face and hair wind-blown with a wound across his nose where he had cracked it against the control bar at the end of his long flight, I thought, 'that's who I want to be'. In return for making a half-hour radio programme about hang gliding, he threw me off the 500ft Devil's Dyke near Brighton. I still remember the one minute I spent in the air, dangling like a sack of potatoes with arms, as among the most thrilling moments of my life. A pilot waiting in the landing field shouted 'push!' when I was 10ft off the ground. I pushed, stood on my feet, shouted with exhilaration, packed up, rushed up the hill, rigged again, flew, fell in from 10ft, de-rigged, slung the glider on my back and walked up the face of the steep hill (because no car was around), and was trying to rig again when someone pointed out that it was now too dark to fly. I bought a glider that day, and when it was delivered, went to Rhossili with Brian Wood and Eric Short and all these super-heroes. They threw me off the top until, on my tenth flight, I learned to soar. I think, even without Brian's flight, I would have been attracted into hang gliding. My then wife Fiona became pregnant with our son James the same month I flew off Rhossili. She is adamant there is no connection.

That winter of 1974, the two warring associations came together and became one, under the guidance of two men, BKSA secretary Dick Bickel – who was towed across the English Channel by boat in a hang glider the following year – and a former RAF wartime Spitfire pilot, Bob Mackay, NHGA secretary. One of the guiding forces was a classical representative of mainstream aviation, Ann Welch, who had produced a number of books on gliding. Though she did not fly hang gliders she became, and remained decades later, president of the new association, the BHGA. Chris Corston became the BHGA secretary. A new magazine was produced called *Wings!* Its first editor was Nick Regan, who treated the sport like a small, exclusive club.

Looking at the first issues of *Wings!*, decades later, it was very clubby. Everyone seemed to know each other. Accounts of flights were carried all the time and first names were used because no one needed to know their surnames. The magazines are whimsical, full of humour, with a lot of Bob Mackay's poetry:

> Oh I must go up to the ridge again,
> To the lonely ridge and the sky
> And all I ask is a soaring kite
> With a bar to steer her by.
> Then a strong wind and a steep slope
> With the white clouds flying.
> For, as we all know,
> Unless it's so,
> There's no bloody use me trying!

'As we all knew' then, Bob weighed over 18 stone, 260lb, and he needed a strong wind to stay up. There were always sly digs about his weight and his Spitfire stories, but at bottom, Bob was a flyer like the rest of us. He seemed to defy the advancing years, not just with the courage to fly those primitive kites – I cannot believe, when I look at them, that I actually strapped myself in and jumped off hills in them – but his big personality and wit made him a seminal character as the BHGA grew. At this time he wrote the excellent 'North North West':

> There's a green wide soaring mountain
> To the north of Katmandu,
> At the foot, a little cross upon a mound,
> Where a sad-eyed dusky maiden
> Tends the grave of 'Mad Carew'
> On the spot where his hang glider hit the ground!
>
> Back in eighteen eighty-two
> Was the year that Carew flew
> It was somewhat a spectacular event!
> He would not have been the lad wot
> Had the first 'shot' if he had not
> Slung his hammock from the ridge pole of his tent.
>
> It was during the Monsoon
> That a squall inopportune,
> Blew so hard that our young hero's tent was rent!
> To the earth it was well guyed, so …
> It should not have come untied, no …
> It should not have, but it did,
> And up he went!
>
> From his hammock, arms stretched wide
> Carew grabbed the tent each side;
> It was fastened to the ridge-pole at each end.
> Thus our pilot, young and callow,
> Did create the first Rogallo,
> It could climb and it could turn but not descend!
>
> After conquering his fear,
> Hanging there it was quite clear

One or two modifications must be done.
What he needed to control it
Was to pull down on the pole bit,
Thus he started to design a new 'Mark One'.

Soon the master of his craft
He would pull wires fore and aft,
His Mark One design was basically sound.
But no matter where the wires went,
First and foremost his requirement
Was to get his PROTOTYPE back on the ground!

O'er the mountain Carew flew,
To the north of Katmandu,
Then there followed a phenomenal descent,
Where the Afghans when they found him,
Bits of kite strewn all around him,
Hailed him 'King sent from Allah!' in magic tent!

So although we can't be sure
Was there Mark Two, Three or Four,
Story tellers wondrous tales bring from afar.
Full of weird and magic tips
That sound strange on Afghan lips.
Such as 'reflex trailing edge' and 'soaring bar'.

In the bar at Katmandu
Though she'd had a drink or two
T'was the Major's wife that sang the sad lament,
How the Mad Captain Carew
Was the only man she knew,
Who could do it, in a hammock, in a tent!

There was an exuberance about the actual experience of flying in 1975 that has nothing to do with the fact that we were all younger back then. Our flying was so different from anything else, from mainstream aviation and from parachuting, that each time we lifted our feet off the ground was an event, be the duration ever so short. Sitting at 200ft with the wind rushing around you, just a rope and a plank for a seat, no parachute, no instruments, the glider sounding like a motorbike it flapped so much … Tony Fuell's account of 'A Spring Day' captured it perfectly:

> 'But headlong joy is ever on the wing' – John Milton 'The Passion'
>
> There wasn't much joy around in Regent Street that Friday night. A lengthy telephone hassle had left me drained and sick of the city. I was waiting for my wife Diane to pick me up and we were going to her parents at Eastbourne. With luck, I might get some flying in. Suddenly, in the gloom of the office-building foyer where I was sheltering, a flash of white suit, white shirt, white teeth – Gary Glitter! The pair of us waited in the steadily-darkening room and watched the rain falling down outside. We exchanged brief, meaningless stranger's smiles, he looking at me doubtless wondering when I would start asking silly questions. Then the rain eased. A long green Rolls Royce drew up to a stop outside, and GG ran across to it to be driven away to wherever rock idols spend their weekends.
>
> Shortly afterwards Diane turned up, kite on top, two cats and a baby inside, set to go. Through the Friday traffic, that old weekend feeling building up inside the car. Truckin' music on the stereo, cruising down to the South to see what the future might bring.
>
> First it brought bad news: 'The Dyke's off.'
>
> 'WHAT?!'
>
> 'It's off, allright. AND Firle!'
>
> 'Oh Jeez …!!'
>
> Yes, hang gliding in the South-East of England is not having an easy time of it at present. Nevertheless, Saturday, early morning looks fine. The bunting on the tail of the kite is blowing about as I look out of the window. High puffy clouds chase across the sky from a Northerly direction. Quick whip through the check-list of possible sites says it's gotta be Secret Spot No 4 (didn't think I was gonna tell you where, didya?) A brief telephone call to make sure, then into the car and off.
>
> Driving along, the sun comes out. I drive up the narrow twisting road to the top of the hill. The wind is making the grass blow about. Quick check with the ventimeter, 18–20mph, pretty steady. Tony Beresford is there getting his kite out too, and together we set off down the rutted track along the Downs.

Lord, what a beautiful day! The sun is shining like it's just been switched on, the wind is warm, hawks fly above soaring on the wind. Make room, fellas, I'll be there soon ...

At the site I rig up and clip in. Tony gets the nose, I stick my head through the A-frame and nod to let go. I run a few steps, ease the bar out an inch, and I'm off. Six inches, a foot, three feet, five feet, I pull the bar back slightly and move out over the bowl. The air is smooth and the lift is incredible. The sun is hot on my back and I can see the kite's shadow moving slowly down the hill below me. It is time to gain height, so I let the bar go out again and the shadow stops moving as I begin to rise. And rise ... and rise ...

Good grief, will it never stop! At about 250 feet above the ridge I can see the Downs for miles in either direction. I can see the Devil's Dyke and for once I don't mind not being able to fly there. It hasn't been necessary to turn the kite to get this lift, it's just been there for the taking. A quick glance at my watch, 11 o'clock on a fine Spring morning. Surely nobody has a right to feel this good?

Time to go places. A gentle turn and off along the ridge. With this much height I don't have to worry about the hill contour below, and I fly around areas I've never even seen before. The kite is talking to me, the wind is blowing in the wires, the booms flexing, and the sail chattering quietly. Well, old thing, you're really doing me proud today.

At this height you really are conscious of the fragility of the whole machine. I do hope the designer Miles Handley did his sums right! Those two straps look awfully thin! But such worries soon pass away as I fly up and down. A few cars stop on the bottom road to watch me. A late rabbit runs over the paddock below. More cars arrive with kites on and soon I see minuscule figures toiling up the hill. I give them a hoot and they wave back.

A few more passes up and down and then I'm back over the bowl. It's not quite so smooth now and I'm having to work to keep things going. Down below they said that later the wind had changed and was gusting up to 26 [mph] or so, and much of the lift had gone. Half an hour coming up and the turbulence was jumping me around a lot. My arms were tiring, and so I thought I'd give it a rest.

Gerry Breen, thanks a lot! Your patent top-landing method works a treat. As I still had lots of height I was able to go back quite a way, turn and set 'er down, if not like a feather then less like a lead brick than my usual attempt. In the meantime, everyone else was sitting on the hill waiting for the wind and chatting. Later on we had some more flights. Saturday night we had a roast pork dinner and beer.

Sunday was the same. Lovely day, a bit gusty, lots of turbulence at Secret Site No 4. Lots of people flew, though, and the spectators loved it. Nobody got hurt, there's no accident report. All the kites behaved themselves and so did the flyers. Driving home I thought, I'd really like to let everyone know how stoked I was, and a little of what it's like to fly like a bird. As I started with a quotation, I'll end with one:

'The clouds and the wind are free, passing over all countries, belonging to all men. Let no man take to the skies with malice in his heart or hatred of his fellow men. On earth there are frontiers, in the sky there are none. Let those who have the good fortune to become airborne remember that the blood of all men is of one colour' – Edmund Cooper, 'The Cloud Walker'.

The site where Tony flew, Ditchling Beacon, is no longer secret. We all liked to fly in smooth lift back then, thus the popularity of Rhossili, and flying in the early morning and late evening. Most of us flew seated, and only the very best flyers flew prone. The 'turbulence' that Tony wrote about was thermal activity, the earth heating up and bubbles of warm air rising to form clouds. One day quite soon we would learn to ride those bubbles, once we understood that they were the only way we could break away from the hill, but in the beginning thermals – turbulence – made us nervous and eye our rigging and wonder if it would come apart at 300ft.

The seminal event of 1975 for every hang gliding nation except the US and Australia was the first FAI World Hang Gliding Championships held in March in Kössen, Austria. Britain sent an official team – Brian Wood, Ken Messenger, Gerry Breen, Bob Calvert, Dick Bickel, Malcolm Hawksworth, Robin Payne; some of those names still resonate. Other Britons flew unofficially. The competition, essentially derived from parachuting, was solely judged on time in the air and a spot landing. It did not matter if you stood up. One pilot flew across the target, stabbed the bullseye with his feet and landed somewhere else, and scored highly. The winner was

Dave Cronk, from the US, with another American, the legendary Roy Haggard third.

The stars of the event were the Americans; young, confident, they were to us like eagles. Bob Wills in particular seemed like Superman. He was going off not long afterwards to double for James Coburn's hang gliding sequences in the movie *Sky Riders*. What was happening in Britain was happening all over Europe. We all looked at the Americans, or heard about them later, as if they were fabulous creatures from another planet. Roy Haggard, a genuine genius of hang glider design who came back to haunt us five years later, turned up with a new kite called the Dragonfly that actually looked like a wing instead of a steerable parachute. And it flew like one. If you bought a glider in Europe a week before Kössen, it was three years out of date a week after Kössen. That event was when the Americans let the genie out of the bottle. They showed us what was possible. We resolved to learn it as well as they could. Why not? Britain did poorly in the championships. Best position was Tony Beresford in thirteenth place. The mountain flyers, Swiss, Austrian, French and Germans, did much better than us. Brian Wood was lucky to come home at all:

> Safety is a thing that everybody who flies a hang glider thinks of [at] sometime or another, or all the time. For me safety means not just the kite but the hill, conditions, etc, so when we set off for the World Championships we were all thinking about the 2,000 feet mountain from which we were to take off.
>
> The Championships themselves were run very badly in some ways because the organisers had reckoned on about 50 entries from all over the world, but instead they received 50 from England alone and about 330 from other countries. Well, after a lot of arguing and quarrelling between the officials and flyers, the meeting eventually took place. As expected, the Americans won most of the top places.
>
> On one of the free flying days Eric Short and myself were doing some filming for World Wide TV as they had seen us doing our formation flying stunts and thought it would be good for their film. Whilst on top of the mountain rigging my glider as always, I checked it for faults. I found one! The fault was that the nylon end-caps on my Wasp CB (CB is Curved Boom) which hold the sail on the tube had been knocked off on the chair-lift (another row we had with the organisers as this happened continuously and I had already fitted three new

72

end-caps and now had no more left). This cap alone did not hold the sail to the end of the tube; the sail itself was sewn in a sealed pocket, but the end had a tear about one inch long on a two-inch diameter tube.

The film crew were waiting below for us and I thought it would be all right, because a sail can never come forward up a tube while you are flying. What a mistake! Eric and I took off and did a tight 360 turn left, then a right 360 together, but because the 360 turns were so tight my inside wing momentarily stopped flying … and that's when the sail went up the leading edge to the cross-tube.

The feeling I had first was a bad stall on the 360 turn but as the nose dropped and the kite started plunging down, it began spinning like a top. The G-force threw me all over the place and I knew I was a goner. The reason I thought I'd had it was that we'd seen luffing dives on film and were told that the pilot weight-shift would make no difference. The main thing that saved me was the altitude, 1,500 feet at the time it happened. Because of the long wait to hit the deck my bottle went, and I thought I'd have a go, so I climbed out on the cables as far as my prone harness would let me. Gradually the kite's 360 turns started to slow down and then … crack! the sail went back up the leading edge and I knew if I could keep flying it straight it should be OK. I headed for the pine trees but over the trees the sail went back to the cross-tube and the kite started plunging and spiralling again. This time I was about 500 feet off the ground which was coming up fast. The kite came down in a small clearing and at the point of impact I pushed the control bar as far as I could and landed in 4 feet of deep snow nearly on my feet. I just lay on the snow, my heart almost pounding out of my ribs.

The only damage to the kite was that the right hand leading edge had bent one foot out of line because it had touched down first.

After this I would recommend that you always check that your glider's sail fixings are safe. The simple way to double the safety, which is already used by some manufacturers, is to put a small self-tapping screw with a washer at each end of the sail into the leading edges, so that if the end cap or plug goes, there is the screw to hold the sail. This job will only take minutes. Take it from me, it's well worth doing.

Nobody had died yet in England, but the number of would-be flyers pouring into the sport meant that, sooner or later, life-threatening accidents were more likely to happen. Many of the sites where hang gliding is now established were being pioneered, and on the most popular there began to be crowding. Rhossili had its brief years of glory – one only goes there now to train or check the performance of a hang glider; because it's not a thermal site it is not really serious – and development was quickening. Only a month after the Kössen World Championships those who had known the early days were already lamenting the change from the cosy club to a national organisation, summarised in a Bob 'Spitfire' Mackay poem, 'The Way Ahead'.

> There's far too many of us now,
> And more to come each week.
> So when 'that twit' comes asking you
> Think before you speak.
>
> 'Is hang gliding dangerous?'
> 'Very!' you reply.
> 'Can I try it locally?'
> 'If you're keen to die!'
>
> 'Are there many accidents?'
> 'Every kite gets bent!'
> 'Where do most of them occur?'
> 'The end of the descent!'
>
> 'Does it cost a lot to do?'
> 'Not if it's done right.'
> 'How much if you do it wrong?'
> 'Two hundred quid a flight!'
>
> 'Do you do it near here?'
> 'Yes …' you slyly say
> 'We have a very good site only
> Eighty miles away!'

Chapter 5

Learning How to Fly Cross-Country

The six years from 1975 to 1981 saw a complete revolution in hang gliding, in Britain as in the US. In the beginning, there was much spirited debate about the Selsey Birdman competition (now the Bognor Birdman) in which contestants try to fly 50m with only a 5m platform to run along, just under 8m high. Within two years an American had flown more than a hundred miles. Within four years, this distance had been flown in England. Yet Selsey was one of our roots and does not deserve the scorn it attracted from pilots worried about the Mickey Mouse image it gives the sport. Selsey has its share of the holy lunacy of our founding fathers.

Thousands of people were attracted to the southern coastal town of Selsey for one day a year to watch contestants try and win £10,000 by flying 50m. The 'flyers' are not allowed to use helpers to boost their flight, and all end up in the sea, most of them dressed as chickens or cod-aircraft, quite happy to be ridiculous. But a small, dedicated band, including a former lieutenant commander in the Royal Navy, Mike Collis, author of *Pilot's Creed*, and a microlight manufacturer, David Cook, really set out to win. The organisers stage the event for charity, and have been alarmed at the seriousness of some of the Selsey attempts. One year the chairman of the Selsey Birdman took the cheque out of his pocket and looked at it sadly when Cook made what appeared to be a winning flight. But Cook's attempt was judged to have been unfairly boosted by people pushing him off the platform, and ending in the sea themselves, so Selsey was still there to be won. Collis nurtured hopes for years of winning with a foot-powered hang glider, peddling a propeller on its nose, and called 'Tweetie'.

Yet a year before the debate around the worth of Selsey, which focused on an aspect of the new aviation that was truly a dead end, as pilots get no lift enabling them to fly off, there was already a real and valid discussion about how to actually fly, to leave the ridge like a bird and disappear. A young pilot who went on to beat many of the best in the world, Graham Hobson, began to think about turbulence. He had come across turbulence in flight, as we all had. But instead of pulling the bar in, as Ken Messenger did on Snowdon, or landing, as Tony Fuell did on Ditchling, he began to explore the very nature of the turbulence. Hobson's sense of wonder at what he was discovering, a long time after it was formalised in mainstream sailplaning, comes through in an article he wrote at the time:

I am writing with the news of two hang gliding deaths and one serious injury still weighing heavily on my mind. It makes me ask myself if I am in the right game, especially when I received the news at the end of a day's thermal soaring to altitudes of probably 1,000 feet. The answer to this question you will probably glean from the following account.

Before I continue I would like to say I don't know exactly what a thermal is, and the lift which I am referring to as a thermal is that which one can get whilst soaring in the usual ridge pressure band beneath a passing cloud. Suddenly, the control bar pulls strongly and the ground drops away rapidly. Often this lift is spasmodic and accompanied by a considerable amount of turbulence, but if the pilot can 'hold on' (and I admit it can be quite frightening) and work his way out from the ridge then some fantastic altitude can be gained, enabling dynamic manoeuvres such as 360s and 'figure of eights' to be safely undertaken. Eventually, however, the lift peters out and, losing height, it is again necessary to fly back into ridge lift.

With this spell of hot weather we have been having, my friend Bob Calvert and I have had more than our fair share of this type of flying. On one notable day, we were soaring a small 150 foot local ridge in a 22 mph wind with clouds forming on the other side of the valley 3 miles away which, when they arrived, often hefted us up to about 1,000 feet. After realizing what was happening we patiently buzzed up and down the ridge waiting for the next cloud to come so we could, hopefully, catch its thermal. It must have been amusing (and surprising on such a small ridge) to see first one kite and then the other pop up to become just a small triangle in the sky, and then when it came down again, the other.

Probably the most exhilarating moment came, however, when we both hit the same thermal and ended way up there in the blue sky, side by side, with 100 feet between wingtips and at some mutual understanding, suddenly pulled into two simultaneous tight turns, myself cranking off rapidly to the left, and Bob to the right. It must have looked good from below! Incidentally, all this occurred during one flight in which Bob set a new Pennine HGC soaring record of 2½ hours (which has already been broken). At this point I would also like to mention Phil Robinson and his girlfriend Linda, and Paul Adams, who were aloft with us, not forgetting our unfortunate friend William Jones who broke his arm hang gliding.

These experiences have made me wonder about further possibilities in hang gliding. Until now my most enjoyable flying has been soaring on the many ridges we have around here. Although the experience (as you would know) is incredible, I sometimes feel a little bit imprisoned by the fact that I must stay in a relatively narrow air space in order to maintain lift, and watch the same piece of ground sliding slowly beneath my feet. I must admit I have been looking for a free-er form of flying, and now perhaps I've found it! Certainly after my recent thermalling experiences I have felt that more freedom is possible by gaining height in a thermal and then flying cross-country. I was very excited by an article in the American magazine, 'Ground Skimmer' by Chris Price who was thermalling in the Arizona desert and flying from ridge to ridge and thermal to thermal.

Of course I realize that in our country such flights would be carried out on a much smaller scale. But after seeing one friend gain probably 1,600 feet of height and having myself shared the air with a conventional glider at Hay Bluff at an altitude which my friend (who was on the ground) and I reckoned to be in excess of 2,000 feet (and that's no exaggeration, I swear), I am fascinated with the idea of using this height to eat up the miles.

Probably there are people who would say that thermal flying is too dangerous because thermals are unpredictable and turbulent and as such, flying them should be discouraged, particularly now that the public eye is on us more than ever. My only answer to this is, ironically, another question: why do you fly hang gliders? Think about it and see if you can blame some of us for adventuring. You might think it's a little weak, but it's all the answer I need.

This insightful account, full of innocence, was written in July 1975, in a magazine that also carried articles on how to make a 360 degree turn without hitting the hill, as I had done on my first attempt. The magazine included an account of Dick Bickel being towed across the English Channel flying a tow kite behind a motorboat; no advance at all on Bill Moyes ten years earlier.

This is not meant to be a how to account of hang gliding, but it is necessary to explain a little about the air we fly in. Like all gliding aircraft, hang gliders will always descend through the air at a speed called sink rate. In early Rogallos, the sink rate was often higher than 500ft a minute. As hang gliders developed, sink rates dropped close to 200ft/min. If gliding aircraft are always going down, how do they go up? Simply by finding air that goes up quicker than the wing goes down. Such air is called 'lift'.

There are at least three standard forms of lift. The first, which Graham Hobson called 'ridge lift', is when the wind meets a hill and rises over it, creating a band of air that can sustain wings. Birds, gliders, hang gliders and paragliders can take off into this lift band, and go up. In prehistoric times, pterodactyls were thought to have used ridge lift to fly up and down looking for prey below. It is much like a ping-pong ball riding on a jet of water. So long as the air goes up faster than the aircraft descends, the aircraft will stay up. But the aircraft has to remain within the lift band.

The second form of lift is the so-called thermal that Hobson discovered, as it were, by deduction. Thermals are caused by the sun heating the earth, and the earth heating the air above at different rates; a brown field will heat up quicker than a green field. The air above the brown field also heats up quicker, and when the temperature difference between the brown field's air and the surrounding air is great enough, the bubble of warmer air breaks off and starts to rise. The rate it rises depends on the change in temperature with height (called the 'lapse rate'). This bubble is doughnut-shaped, with a column in the middle rising quickly – the core of the lift – and a turbulent outer layer called 'sink'. When the bubble rises high enough, the moisture it carries turns into cloud (a cloud doesn't have a thermal, it is where a thermal ends up).

If one heat source is constantly pumping out thermals then a line of clouds forms downwind, fed regularly by the heat source. This is called a cloud street. I cannot resist telling you that the best lift is found on the sunny side of the street.

The third form of lift is called 'wave', described in more detail in the Icarus and Daedalus story. But we did not know very much about wave in 1976, until there was another letter to *Wings!* magazine, this time from another northern pilot called Paul Maritos, with information from the same Graham Hobson who had asked what a thermal was:

Monday afternoon, 5th April, 1976, saw the Birdman Competition drawing to a pleasant conclusion with the presentation of the trophies and a succession of farewells. One by one each flyer had a last soar along the ridge and then leisurely de-rigged and departed in the breeze and sun of an afternoon more like August than April.

Eventually only two kites were left, my Vynair and Graham Hobson's Skyhook. By 4 o'clock we had had our fill, Graham had landed, arms aching from the turbulence and complaining of hunger. He reckoned that was his lot for the day. I borrowed his helmet and decided to have my last session too. We carried my glider to the edge and, apprehensively, I decided to fly, uncertain that I would penetrate a wind now blowing 30 mph on a relatively small ridge.

My first reaction on take-off was incredible relief as the sail went fairly quiet and I went slowly but steadily up and out. There was some rough air about from thermals, but it wasn't too bad. Gradually I found myself getting into the habit of waiting for a thermal to take me up to about 500 feet, do a 360 or two and wait for the next one, just like waiting for a bus!

Anyway, Graham saw all this going on and I knew he'd be up there sooner or later, with or without his helmet! (I had lost mine the day before). About this time the lift was becoming smoother and I was going higher. When Graham took off, all I could see of him was a tiny kite scooting back and forth along the ridge, and I thought how mad he would be if he didn't gain any height. Next time I looked he had gone, and then I saw him in line with the sun and above me!

It really was incredible. For nearly an hour we could go anywhere within an area of about a half mile square at a height of 1,000 to 1,500 foot, gently searching out the edges of the lift. The smoothness was out of this world. Talking about it afterwards we both found that we'd had time to 'tweak' the rigging wire – feeling the tension, or lack of it – and to fly hands-off.

It was quite an experience and a search through the conventional gliding books in the library put things into perspective. We had happened to be in the air when conditions had just been right for, we think, a combination of ridge lift and wave lift at that particular place.

'Wave lift' describes a situation where the air flow, having risen over a hill or ridge and fallen in the lee of it, continues to repeat this pattern, up and down, as it travels along for some distance downwind, so forming waves of rising and falling air. This is quite likely after a day of steady winds. Perhaps what happened to us was that for one hour the 'upsweep' of a wave from one of the hills upwind of us had coincided with the normal ridge lift. We'd gone high, for us, but to put things into perspective a conventional glider in the same place might have gained 10,000 feet and not just 1,000 feet. Roll on the day when kites can do that.

Any form of rising air, for whatever reason, is lift. At the end of a hot day, when the air cools, heat traps like thick forests begin to release their warm air. Flying over the heavily wooded areas of Tennessee on Lookout Mountain, for example, this form of early evening lift is called 'magic lift'. The sun can disappear, the moon appears, and all the time the magic lift – smooth, gentle, stronger than a hang glider's sink rate – keeps you up for hours.

We knew about ridge lift in 1975, but all the other forms of lift were ahead of us. Paul Maritos' account of wave in Wales was published at the same time as Alvin Russell's account on the Long Mynd, when he 'sat on' a glider. There was a certain amount of teaching from pilots of more conventional gliders (they were, at that time, not much interested in speaking to us, we were the plebs of flying), but most of our knowledge came from what we ourselves learned, and talked about to each other. One pilot would start climbing in a thermal on a ridge, others would see him high and rush over to get into the same thermal. A column would form, beginning circling in different directions, with hang gliders riding up the rising air. There was a lot of strained shouting between pilots, worried about colliding, until we broadly agreed that the first one into the thermal decided the direction a good-mannered pilot should circle. When the thermal, sometimes called a blob, topped out ('blobbed out'), pilots looked over the back of the ridge and wondered whether to go for it and find a thermal downwind, to leave the security of the ridge lift and go into open country.

There was only one genuine hang gliding cross-country in England in 1976, that is, leaving ridge lift and going into open country. That cross-country flight, known as an XC, was made in July by the great Bob Calvert. But he wrote about it on such a scrappy piece of paper in such an illegible fashion that the editor of *Wings!* at the time – Tony Fuell, of secret site No. 4 – didn't even read it, and threw it away! It is one of Tony's lasting regrets, to miss publishing the account of our first XC out of ridge lift. Calvert flew a Hiway Cloud base, a wing not very much better than the American kites at Kössen fifteen months earlier. He thermalled up from Pendle Hill and out of ridge lift in extremely turbulent conditions, flew cross-wind over Clitheroe, and turned left at Waddington to land after 7 miles, having been in the air twenty-five minutes.

But that intrepid pair, Graham Hobson and Paul Maritos, were still in pioneering mood, and soon appeared in print again, with a piece about flying a mile high over Snowdon. This was still in the period, 1976, when we tended to fly without instruments, without an altimeter to tell us how high we were, or a vario that measured the rate of climb or sink.

We also had no parachutes.

The discovery of the techniques of flight was done in an innocent way, relying on intuition rather than formal training. Compare this account of Hobson and Maritos' flight with that written by Ken Messenger three long years earlier off the same mountain:

> Ever since Bob Calvert let his curiosity get the better of him and investigated a 'Cu-Nim', as he put it, and ended up flying seven miles upwind, half the time hanging on for dear life, there has been a fever spreading through the Pennine crowd to search out big lift conditions with a high XC potential. It was whilst engaged in this search that Paul Maritos and I discovered the superb lift generated from the south-east face of Snowdon, the highest mountain in Wales.
>
> The tale begins four days earlier when a few of us flew off Snowdon in still air. The day was very hot and very blue and we were hoping for good thermals. Having gained considerable thermalling experience on our local 150 foot hills, we were wondering if we would be able to make use of this knowledge to soar on the west face for a little while at least. Bob Calvert was second off and turning left along the face he maintained height in the lift produced by heat rising from the hot rock face alone. He then flew out looking for thermals and started to descend. It was clear that soaring was not possible, but from what I saw I was convinced that had

there been any wind at all blowing on that face, then we could have stayed up.

It was with this thought repeating itself time and again in my mind that we returned, Paul Maritos, his girlfriend Sue, Phil Robinson and I to Snowdon, armed with a forecast for a light easterly and clear blue skies. We were hoping to get up on the railway but were refused as our gliders were interfering with the large holiday crowds who were also using it. So we had to walk and this we did in two hours steady plodding up the railway track. After about 90 minutes we arrived at a point on the top of the Llanberis Pass and were able to enjoy the breath-taking view down to the bottom a couple of thousand feet almost vertically below.

I have always found it interesting comparing the types of flying that we do with that done in other countries, and have heard many times that the greatest difference is that Continental flying is only ever done in light winds, never exceeding 15 mph due to extreme turbulence in the mountains, whereas we fly in much higher winds. As none of us were experienced mountain flyers, knowing only soaring on relatively small ridges, we had no alternative but to pay particular attention to what we had heard about this. So you can imagine our consternation when we looked down into this valley, at the 26 mph wind that rushed up over the edge and tugged so annoyingly at our kites!

The weather man had assured us that the wind would die off to nothing in the afternoon as a westerly sea breeze came in, so we continued our weary way and made the summit in another 30 minutes.

On top we discovered only 2 or 3 mph coming up the south-east coombe, and I must admit I was disappointed, thinking that a steady 8 mph would have been ideal. We decided to take off from a point about 30 feet below the top, on the apex of the shoulder separating the west and south-east coombes. What a launch point! To our right the SE coombe fell sharply away into a gigantic bowl, the forward wall of which was the peak of Snowdon itself. To our left lay a vivid blue lake nestled in the depth of the east coombe like a puddle at the bottom of some monstrous dried-up well.

Paul was the first to rig and get off, helped on the wires by Phil, whilst I cleared a way through the unbelieving spectators. I felt there was a strong possibility of soaring but what happened surpassed my wildest imaginings. Paul took a couple of steps into the 2 or 3 mph wind and was airborne. Turning right he flew along the face and went up, and up, and up. Within a minute he was 360ing in the blueness 500 feet above the top.

I was next to rig, hoping Paul wasn't just in a lucky thermal. I waited 10 minutes and Paul was now about 1,000 feet above the top and the wind had not varied, convincing me that it was truly soarable. I couldn't wait any longer. I clipped in and took the leap and immediately experienced the same abundant lift.

(Paul Maritos takes up the story)

Like Graham I had gone to Snowdon hoping for something to happen, only to have my hopes fade when there turned out to be virtually no wind on the summit. With only occasionally 4 or 5 mph of wind it looked like a flight down. The only bright feature was that apparently there were thermals coming through, from the way the wind felt and shifted. Influenced by this I decided that whatever lift or lack of it there was, I would at some point soon after takeoff fly back towards the mountain whilst I still had some height just in case there was something there.

We picked out a suitable landing area and rendezvous and eventually managed to persuade most of the spectators to move out of range. I remember especially urging those on my right to move, as I wanted to turn soon after takeoff. With a short run and a height-loss of perhaps 10 feet I was away and hugging the hill. I lost no more height on the first pass and soon beat back.

There was clearly good lift and it was obvious I'd gone straight off into a thermal. With virtually no wind and drift it was sensible to go straight into flat circling and within a very few circuits I was above the summit.

There was turbulence but the lift was correspondingly powerful.

At first I was apprehensive about passing behind the summit and the two shoulders which bounded my take-off area, but little by little I got the feel of things and found that my kite speed seemed unnaturally high relative to the ground. This was presumably because it was all lift and no wind.

Looking down on the summit I could no longer distinguish people but saw that Graham had moved his kite to the take-off point I had used and was preparing to launch.

Graham Hobson: Before long I was also looking down on the summit 500 feet below. I had discovered that the easiest way to stay in the lift was to 360 continuously rather than beat to and fro across the face. This was only sense as the 'face' was really only a point, the summit of Snowdon, and because there was so little wind there was no drift back over the top. In fact one was free to fly a couple of hundred yards back and have no problems in 'penetrating' back to the face.

As with all thermic lift, the turbulence was severe at times and it wasn't long before my arms were aching, but I knew that, as always, I would feel better in a little while when I had 'sussed' out the situation and was able to relax. I was more concerned about locating Paul's whereabouts as I was also pretty high now and he couldn't be much higher. I peered up into the sky for some time in a vain attempt to find him, and then he slowly appeared from behind my left wing a good 300 feet higher. We were both working the same thermal and slowly slipping downwind.

About 300 yards behind take-off and maybe 1,000 feet above the summit I decided that I hadn't been in the air long enough to warrant flying off on a cross-country attempt, and that I ought not to waste an opportunity to really learn something about true thermalling. Not so with Paul! He was by now a good 500 feet above me and probably an incredible 1,500 feet above the summit and I knew that he would be clearing off. Flying back to takeoff I had to take my eyes from him and concentrate on my own flying, but on reaching the summit I turned and again searched the heavens for Paul. I will never forget the fantastic sight that met my gaze. Paul had not followed the thermal completely downwind but had turned NW heading for Llanberis and flown over Llanberis Pass. Imagine the peaks of Snowdonia all around and the top of the pass stretching away from Snowdon, green and hazy, then start looking up … and up in the blue, two or three thousand feet and suddenly spying, small and unreal, a blue shape that you know to be a hang glider and a pilot!

Simple arithmetic will tell you that at this point, Paul was 4,500 feet above the bottom of the Pass. Intrigued, I followed his progress as he flew towards Llanberis, at the same time concentrating on my own flying. Each time I flew the 'downwind' leg of a 360 I would search the sky for him and each time he was more difficult to find. Now he would be circling over the slag heaps of the Elidir Fach mountain, now just a blue flash on the horizon as he turned over a distant town, and then he was gone. Unable to see him any longer I shouted down that he had flown over Llanberis and would land about 7 miles away. This estimate was based on the fact that at the last sighting Paul was below me and above Llanberis and I assumed he would glide for at least another 3 miles. However I was quite wrong as he decided to lose height over Llanberis and land.

Paul Maritos: Gradually becoming accustomed to the scale of things, and being consistently 1,000 feet above the summit, I noticed how my style of flying and thinking were adapting. The turbulence could have been very disconcerting and tiring, but with so much height I could let the kite rise and fall or drop a wing and then correct itself, knowing that there was enough height to pull out of anything. Or so I hoped!

As time passed it was apparent that there was a succession of thermals and in one I reached a height which I judged was the highest I could hope for. The whole Snowdon massif looked like a one-inch tourist map, the crowd on the top giving the appearance of a colourful fungus which had taken root at the very tip of the mountain, their faces upturned. Many must have stared in disbelief. It was then I decided to fly off.

Having nothing with which to gauge my rise and descent rate, and knowing that I couldn't detect constant lift, only changes in it, I decided that the chances of a true thermalling cross-country flight were slim and so I headed cross-wind for Llanberis.

Flying down the pass with the summit still below and behind me and the ground 4,500 feet away was a quite unforgettable experience. I arrived over the quarries at Llanberis with 2,000 feet of height and circled, gradually losing height. Finally I crossed the lake to the town, circled and landed on the shore, much to the surprise of the bathers who at first thought the kite was a toy!

The whole flight had lasted 40 minutes and I had flown 4 miles as the crow flies and now I know why the Americans with their various launch points and super-kites are pulling off 20 mile flights!

[Graham Hobson] – Now I had Snowdon to myself and was beginning to get concerned at the lack of Phil Robinson's presence in the air. I could see his glider laid flat and Phil working on it, the wings kept coming in and out and still he didn't take off.

Meanwhile, up in the air my flight was developing a recognizable pattern. I discovered that I could spend about 10 minutes very high above the summit and then, however hard I tried, I couldn't check a slow spiralling descent back to the level of the summit. I then had to scrape around at this level before again encountering strong lift and slowly working my way up, high above the world. Each time I found it harder not to lose the lift and fly down in the periods of reduced lift. There is no doubt that these periods of good lift were big slow-moving thermals, the like of which I had never encountered before.

The turbulence was severe and one was never quite sure whether it was wholly due to the thermal or just some of that mountain turbulence that we had heard so much about. You could be turning at minimum sink and going up in an apparently smooth one when the nose would suddenly shoot up as if it had been given a punishing uppercut and you would have to fight your way over the bar in a vain attempt to prevent the inevitable stall. Or the tail and wing would dramatically rise and you'd hang your weight out for all your sore arms were worth, and still nothing would happen except that the kite would continue to go up in this crazy position. Then there was the time when you'd made a wrong turn and flown into sink; here you didn't try any corrective measures (what use would they be when the harness straps were slack because you were falling so fast?). All you could do was hang on and wait until the kite pulled out of the dive and the sail stopped banging, and then set about recovering all that lost height.

As a rule, however, this massive turbulence was rare and one could readily learn to accept it as inevitable without much concern. What was far more disconcerting were the

ALVIN RUSSELL —
A REMEMBRANCE (page 4)

COVER PHOTO:

Chris Johnson races a wave on the prototype Hiway Scorpion at Rhossili.

CONTENTS

Edited by Tony Fuell.
Published by the British Hang Gliding Association, Monksilver, Taunton, Somerset.

N.B. The views expressed by our correspondents are not necessarily those of the Council of the BHGA, its officers or members, nor of the Editor.

"WINGS!" EDITORIAL

Articles advertising, cartoons, photographs — to Tony Fuell, 74, Eldred Avenue, Brighton, Sussex.

EDDY-SHEDDING

by Tony Fuell

Are we getting a fair deal from our Manufacturers? Nobody in the UK is making a lot of money out of manufacturing hang gliders. The 'industry' is still based largely on small companies. Most of them exist on a financial knife-edge, and it has to be recognised that in the intensely competitive world of hang gliding, a manufacturer is under pressure to cut corners wherever possible.

The pressure for change must come from us, the buying public — even if it means dearer machinery. Everyone who buys a hang glider puts his life in the hands of both the man who designed it, and the man who built it. A new glider these days will cost well over £300. When you're paying over this sort of money, you are entitled to expect both proper design and development work, and good workmanship on your particular kite.

Unfortunately, it seems that some manufacturers don't believe this. I work in the pharmaceutical industry, where quality control is the single most important factor in the manufacturing process. One person in three who works in the drug industry is connected in some way with quality assurance. Few hang glider manufacturers seem to have heard of quality control, much less apply it to the aircraft they build. Amazingly, several quite major UK manufacturers, and some American ones we've heard about, don't even have specifications or engineering drawings for the gliders they build. They rely entirely on jigs, and 'rule of thumb'! What happens to you in a year or two when you want a replacement keel for your Bumskreetch Special Mark I when Joe Bloggs has been making Mark III's for a year and can't remember exactly where the Mark I's holes go?

Here are some questions you should ask anybody who's trying to sell you a glider:

1. How many prototypes were built before he arrived at this design? (Is he using you as a guinea pig to try out his new idea?)
2. Is the glider registered with BHGA for insurance? (I wouldn't trust my life to anything that wasn't!)
3. Is it possible to rig the glider incorrectly, or put the harness on wrong? (If it CAN happen, it WILL happen, says Murphy). Does the manufacturer provide a rigging diagram, or an instruction book? (You should get both!)
4. Will the glider be assembled AND FLOWN by the manufacturer before you get it?
5. Is the manufacturer a member of BHGMF?

Anyone who manufacturers gliders has a big responsibility. He MUST ensure that every glider he sells to the public is safe. Each and every one. Not only the design, not only the prototypes, but each individual glider. His workshop systems must ensure this. He should keep proper records of every glider he builds. Basically it boils down to: DON'T ever buy a glider from a man you don't trust. DO try and look beyond the sales talk, and advertisements, and the performance achieved by a 'professional' pilot, and get the glider that's right for you. FLY BEFORE YOU BUY!

3

Alvin Russell – only known photograph.

13 THE MYTH OF DAEDALUS AND ICARUS
From an Italian woodcut of 1493.

12 BLADUD, MYTHICAL
KING OF BRITAIN

Above: Legend of Icarus and Daedalus, Crete, 1500 BC.

Left: King Bladud, father of Shakespeare's King Lear, London tower jumper.

15 LEONARDO DA
VINCI'S DESIGN FOR
A PARACHUTE
c. 1500.

Above left: Leonardo
da Vinci.

Above right: Da
Vinci's design for a
parachute.

Right: Da Vinci's
design for a hang
glider.

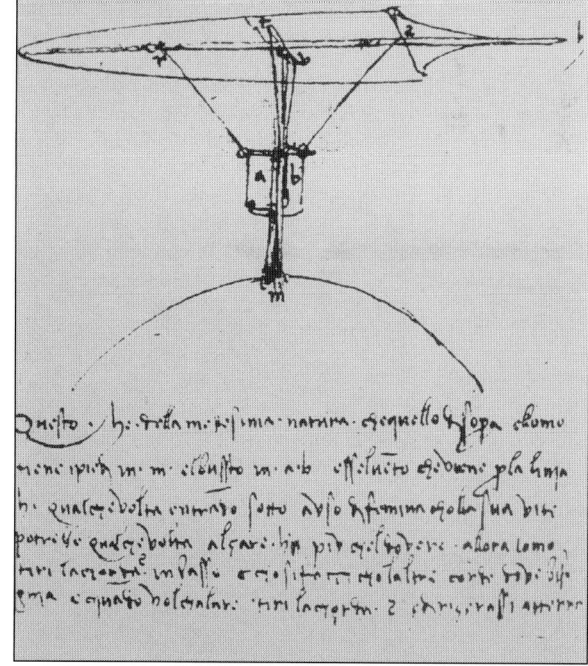

Above: Da Vinci's hang glider design built and flown in the twentieth century.

Below: First flying wing powered by rubber bands.

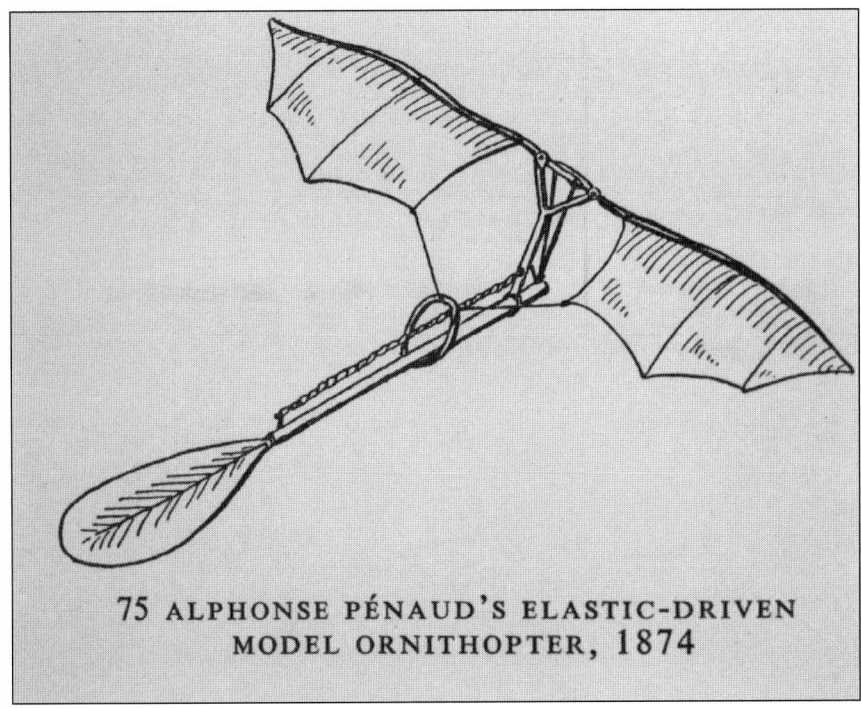

75 ALPHONSE PÉNAUD'S ELASTIC-DRIVEN
MODEL ORNITHOPTER, 1874

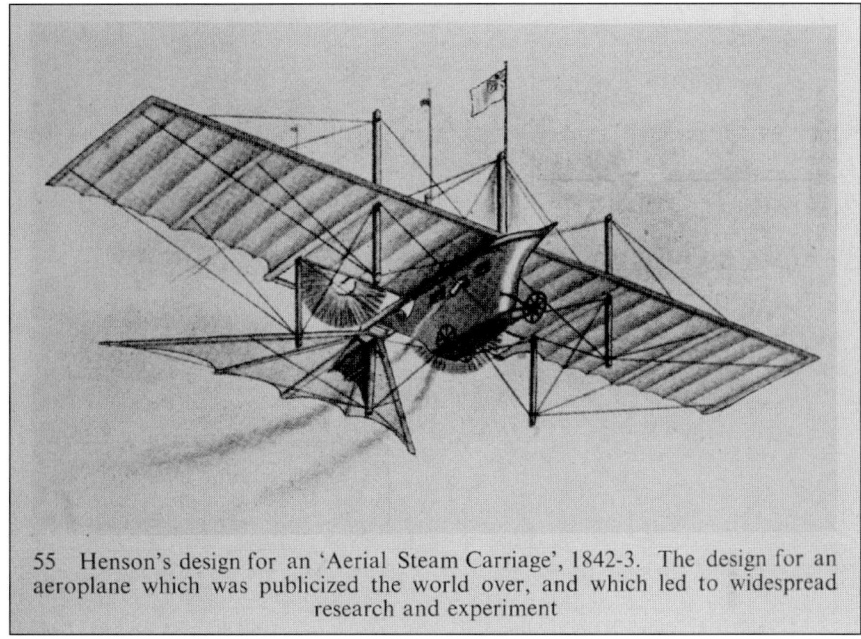

55 Henson's design for an 'Aerial Steam Carriage', 1842-3. The design for an aeroplane which was publicized the world over, and which led to widespread research and experiment

Above: Best nineteenth century design for a steam-powered aeroplane.

Below: Octave Chanute's early hang glider which was pre-Lilienthal.

92 CHANUTE GLIDER 1896-7

The Sun, Thurs-
Morch, 27, 2

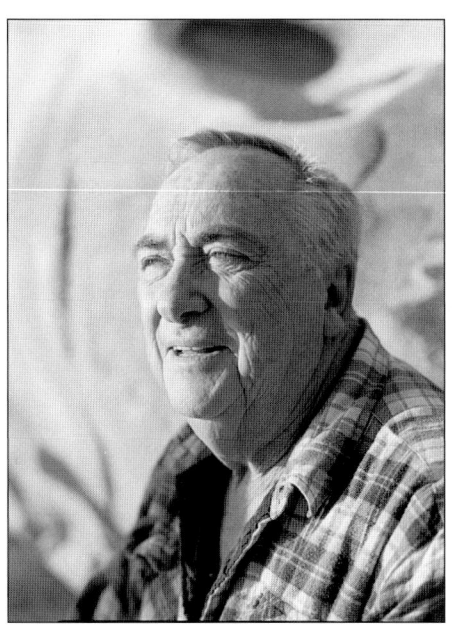

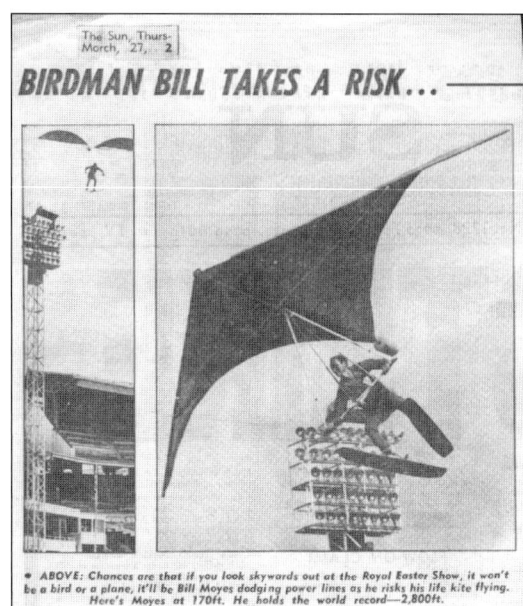

BIRDMAN BILL TAKES A RISK...

• ABOVE: Chances are that if you look skywards out at the Royal Easter Show, it won't be a bird or a plane, it'll be Bill Moyes dodging power lines as he risks his life kite flying. Here's Moyes at 170ft. He holds the world record—2,800ft.

Above left: Australian Bill Moyes – 'Father of Hang Gliding'.

Above right: Bill Moyes' active youth.

Below: Two US legends: Bob and Chris Wills.

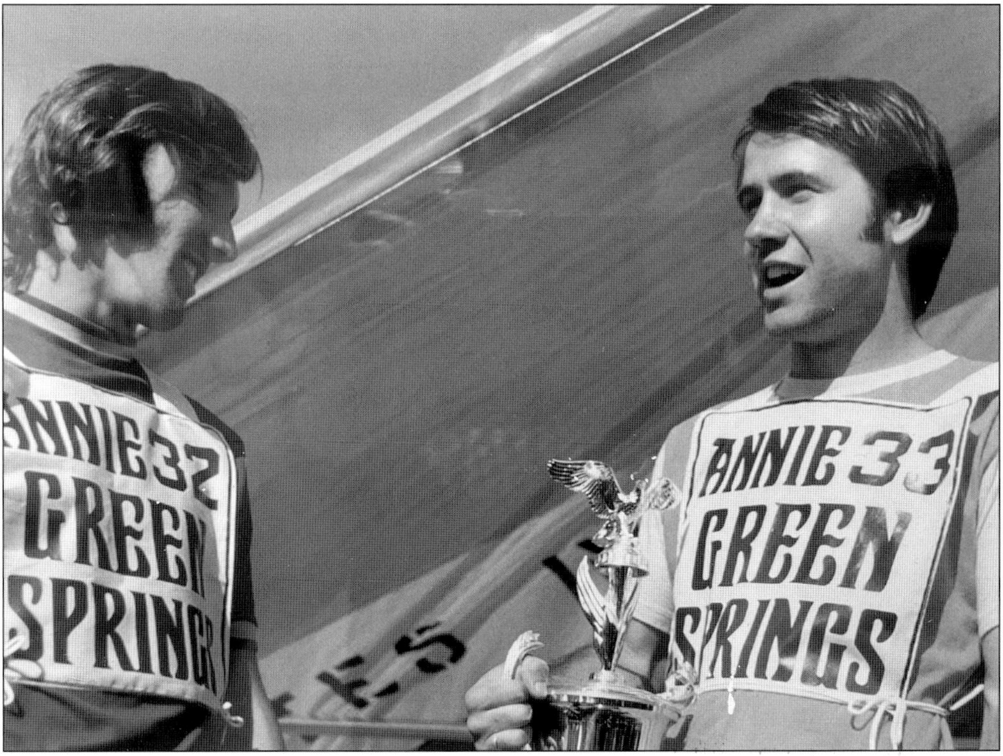

Above: Chris Wills under $10 bamboo butterfly.

Right: Bob Wills plus three people on a hang glider.

Above: Bob Wills nails spot landing.

Below: First British League, 1977. Left to right, back row: Peter Day, Chris Coleman, Graham Slater (hidden), John Hudson, John Fack, Mick Maher, Julian Thomas, Lester Cruise, Ashley Doubtfire, Mick Evans, Norman Millhouse, Mike Atkinson, Roger Black, Paul Baker (half-hidden), Dave Lyne, Dale Clothier, Frank Tarjanyi, Roger Middleton, Chris Johnson, Roger Wates, Ken Messenger, Dave Weedon, Graham Leeson, Mark Southall, Dave Worth, Miles Handley, Jeremy Fack. Front row: Tony Fuell, Tony Beresford, Bob England, Johnny Carr, Brian Wood (champion), Bob Calvert, Rob Bailey, Graham Hobson and Brian Milton.

Above: Chris Wills soars Torrey Pines.

Below: Before a competition take-off.

Above: Bob Calvert going for the target.

Below: British American Cup team, 1978. Left to right: Brian Milton (coach), Graham Slater, Mick Maher, Graham Hobson, Bob Calvert, Mick Evans, Robert Bailey, John Fack and Keith Reynolds.

Right: American Cup
take-off, 1980.

Below: Tethered training.

Above: Hung up – no injuries.

Left: Mick Maher hits a power line.

Joseph Guggenmos (Germany), Rich Grigsby (US) and Keith Nichols (US).

Author taking off; Kite now at bottom of the English Channel.

Rich Pfeiffer US, should have been 1985 world champion.

John Pendry (GB), was the 1985 world champion.

Above: British
American Cup team in
Tennessee, 1980.

Right: Keith Cockroft
performing a 90 degree
wingover in Rhône Valley,
France.

Above: Early powered trike.

Below: Keith Nichols (US) with oxygen on a XC.

knocks being received when scraping about at summit level in between thermals. At these times I was flying pure ridge lift, and the bubbles of heat that broke away from the hot rock face. I dared not get any nearer to the face than 60 feet for fear of being turned irresistibly into it. In fact there were times when I sweated as I have never sweated before, but then another thermal would come through and I could go up and be able to relax.

Phil still hadn't taken off and was clearly having difficulties rigging his glider. By now I was a little weary and was just waiting for him to take off before flying down.

It was at this point that a good thermal came through and I managed to work up in it to the highest point that I had attained all day. I decided to follow it back behind the West face and if things got really good I would follow it for as far as I could with no thought to the consequences for those who would have to go and find me. At about half a mile behind the summit I reached my crisis point; what should I do? Should I go on, hoping to stay with the thermal, remembering that I had no vario and God only knows where Paul had landed? Or should I turn back and be sure of my location being known by the others? I judged that I had lost height since leaving the mountain and that a true thermalling cross-country flight would have to wait until I got my new Skyhook kite and a vario. So I bade my thermal farewell and turned back into wind, 2,700 feet above the ground, 800 feet above the mountain, and with half a mile to penetrate back to the summit.

This was one of the most worrying periods of the whole flight because suddenly there seemed to be a great deal of wind and there I was stuck out in the middle of nowhere in the lee of a great big mountain! I kept thinking about that 26 mph on top of Llanberis Pass. Was I slowly penetrating into one of the most horrific rotors that God ever sent? I tried to reassure myself that the wind was only 2 or 3 mph when I took off and that the reason why the ground wasn't moving was because I was so high, but still the doubts persisted. I could not stop myself from pulling on all the speed I had available. The situation felt crazy because I was flying flat out and yet according to all my points of reference I was completely stationary, devoid of all motion in any direction.

As time passed, however, I became aware that I had in fact moved forward, as a lake that I had been over had slid imperceptibly behind. I neared the west face again and realised that I had lost a lot of height and would pass very close over the top (if at all?) before the mountain dropped away again on the east side. The turbulence was increasing but there was nothing too bad, then almost before I realised it my troubles were over as the kite sailed over the top on to the east side with almost 100 feet to spare. One never seemed to get used to the scale of mountain flying, and yet again I gasped at the view which slowly unfurled before me as I passed over the edge that had obscured my line of sight, and the east face once more shrank from me at a dizzy rate.

There was no sign of any wind so I concluded that my fears must have been imagined due to the novelty of my situation. Breathing a sigh of relief I turned and followed the face around to the right and soared over a shoulder of rock back into the SE coombe.

On arriving I sensed that there had been a change of conditions. The wind was stronger and across the face, coming from the left, resulting in very poor lift. Phil still hadn't taken off but was at last fully rigged and ready to go. From my vantage point about 150 feet above I could see the sails flapping to maybe 8 to 10 mph. Suddenly he was airborne and judging from the way his kite was yawing about the sky, going through some pretty rough air. I couldn't help grinning when I saw him fly straight out and make no attempt at soaring. A second later that grin was wiped off my face as the same turbulence reached me. I too just as readily forgot about soaring and decided that in this sort of air I didn't want to hang about close to the face any longer, so I pulled speed and followed Phil. Again there was felt to be a strong 'flat' wind blowing in my face and we both only just made it out of the coombe to land in a field at the bottom of the valley close to the road and only two miles from the summit.

On touch down I checked my watch and discovered I had been airborne an hour and ten minutes. I unclipped and walked over to meet Phil. It turned out that he had been unable to get his nose catch on (to connect the bottom rigging), and as a result of constantly shifting winds on the top, often filling the sails from behind and threatening to blow his glider away, it had taken him over an hour to adjust the rigging so that the catch would fit. As soon as this was done and he was ready to go the wind suddenly changed, making it so turbulent as to be unsoarable.

To my amazement both Sue and Paul arrived in the van. I had been expecting to have to go and find Paul but in actual fact he had only flown to Llanberis and had cadged a lift back to the car from there (there were no mobile phones then).

Looking up, I beheld the peak once again and tried to imagine two tiny delta-shaped objects turning to and fro high above that proud head. I promised myself silently that I would return.

We had talked about thermal soaring in still air and had heard about other people in other countries doing it but now we had gone out and done it ourselves. We know just what will be possible in the near future. We drove home to Manchester that evening in a jubilant mood.

These flights by Hobson and Maritos off Snowdon were probably the last important hang glider flights in Britain before genuine cross-countries began. They were also among the last flights like that made without parachutes and early flying aids like varios and two-way radios. Their account was published in November 1976; Alvin Russell was killed the following month, and Bill Bennett began selling his first parachute in Britain the following August (though I know I had one on when I fell into the sea trying to fly across the English Channel in July 1977. I remember drying it out after soaking it our bath to wash the seawater out of it. Looking through *Wings!*, parachutes don't seem to have truly caught on until March 1978!). The first *Wings!* advert for an electronic vario, essential for XC thermalling, was in February 1977.

We had begun to hear about big cross-country flights being undertaken in America. Very few of us subscribed to the key US magazine, *Hang Gliding*, successor of *Low and Slow*, first called *Ground-Skimmer* and a second private magazine celled *Glider Rider*. Because news from America was passed by word of mouth, the oral tradition took over; flights were embellished with each telling, and the legendary status of US pilots was heightened. We knew we were on a relatively small island, while they had 3,000 miles to play in, but all their flights seemed to be of a different order. We would do 7 miles, they would do 20; we would do 20, they would do

50; we reached 50, they would do 100. All the lessons they learned about XC flying and wrote about would pass on to us, but it was like they were on another planet. Cloud base for them was 10,500ft in Arizona; we were lucky when ours was 4,500ft. We had to fly in much worse conditions than the Americans. For a long while we thought their longer flights meant that they were much better flyers than we were.

In 1977, cross-country flights in hang gliders began to happen all across the world. Before the end of the year, in the United States (where else?) a flight was made of more than 100 miles. Bill Moyes and his circus of top Australian flyers had been travelling the world every year, with Bill like some mythical human bumble bee, pollinating development in each country he visited. We had moved through two generations of hang glider design since Kössen 1975 under the influence of the Americans, and we leapt into the fourth generation with the Moyes visit to England (there was virtually no contact at all between England and Scotland in hang gliding at the time) for the British Open with his new 'Stinger' kite, later called a Maxi, in August 1976. This was the first hang glider with a keel pocket and a flat, fully battened sail that didn't chatter (the noise made by a sail flapping like a motorbike engine, as all the early kites did), and it created turmoil among the British manufacturers. It was Ken Messenger's attempt to produce his own keel-pocket machine, the Moonraker, that Alvin Russell was still testing when he was killed. The performance of kites was increasing, and with it, along with at least a vario, the capability to climb high in a thermal and leave the ridge. The year 1977 was when we began to do it regularly.

The first British claim for an XC was in April when Messenger's test pilot, Mark Southall, ironically on a Moonraker, made an 11-mile flight from Hay Bluff to Pandy, a ridge north of Abergavenny in Wales. But this was really just a ridge run, philosophically no different than any other ridge run except that Mark had to jump back from one ridge to another, a gap of a mile. After Mark's flight, Gerry Breen, another early flying star, flew 15 miles from Tredegar. But they were superseded by a superb distance record that stood, despite many assaults, for most of that summer.

Nigel Milnes was a quiet pilot flying with the Avon Club based around Bristol in the west of England. He did not fly competitions, so he was little-known outside his area. His club had been a strongpoint for McBroom and Birdman machines, but this feudalism was breaking down. Nigel owned a third-generation machine built by Bill Bennett in the US, a Phoenix 6B, the same type that had taken me to second place in the Nationals twelve months earlier. Twelve months was a very long time in hang gliding in those days, and the Phoenix, though a superb kite to fly, was already old technology. The former Spitfire pilot Bob Wishart wrote an account of Nigel's flight:

Sunday, May 15, 1977, saw the Great Thermal Maker get down to some serious practice to the intense delight (and fright) of all things which fly. Of those 'things which fly', Nigel Milnes of the Avon Club journeyed with his Phoenix 6B to Swineyard Hill at Castlemorton Common in the Malverns, and after stepping off the hill at 2 pm, flew off to establish new British XC and altitude records of 22 miles and 6,000 feet respectively, a thermal flyer's dream come true. It reads like this:

Fifteen minutes after take-off, a thermal rocketed Nigel straight out and up to 1,300 feet above take-off with the vario 'off the clock' (1,000 feet a minute up was the vario limit, climbing the height of the London Telecom Tower in 30 seconds). From 1,300 feet he started circling in the core of the thermal and drifted back, wishing the hill goodbye as the vario showed a steady 500/800 up – 500 ft/min to 800 ft/min up.

Soon Sedbury appeared 3,400 feet below and Nigel decided to seek a new thermal, pulled on speed and headed west (downwind) but ran only a short way before finding more strong lift. This thermal hauled him to cloud base at 4,800 feet and though he could see straight down clearly, the horizon was obscured by the surrounding haze.

After 'stepping off' the thermal, he flew fast downwind and encountered his third thermal with 3,000 feet on his altimeter and was soon back at cloud base. He repeated this again just for the hell of it and then perceived a large town ahead, perhaps Hereford, HQ of the SAS, though with no compass on board he could not be sure.

By the time the town perimeter arrived below the altimeter said 2,500 feet and the vario showed a woeful 500 ft/min down. Suddenly he was into a gigantic smooth thermal which sent the long-suffering vario off the clock again and wound the altimeter up to 4,500 feet in less than two minutes of dizzy circling.

At this stage Nigel decided he was on a one-way trip to heaven and tried to get off this giant before coming face to face with St Peter. An enormous cloud loomed above and although he had the bar down to his knees – in full dive position – there was just no way he could avoid being sucked into it.

For 15 minutes he was tossed around in rough pea soup, the wing tips barely visible and the vario alternating between zero and 500 up, but there was nothing going down! Put yourself in Nigel's place for a minute and let your imagination roam – total disorientation, zero visibility, being chucked about the sky, squinting in disbelief as the altimeter passes 6,000 feet AGL … had enough?

Eventually, to his vast relief and surprise, he flew into a vertical 'tube' of clear air, literally a funnel through the cloud, in which the air mass was sinking at a steady 500 ft/min and from the base of which he could see part of a town (still, he hoped, Hereford!). Coring this 'anti-thermal' he fell out of the cloud at 4,400 feet, disorientated and most anxious to leave the vicinity quickly. The only problem was which way to go, no smoke being visible below to act as a wind guide (curse these smokeless fuels!)

Soon he remembered crossing a sewage works when approaching the town and after identifying that feature again, put it behind him and pulled on speed while the altimeter rapidly unwound until the figure 2,500 jogged him into seeking another thermal. There was little about. Plenty of zero sink but that was tame …!

Being by now extremely tired both mentally and physically, he decided to get away from the town and pulled speed until after 5 or 6 miles a disused airfield appeared 1,900 feet below. He amused himself by completing a circuit around it in a vain search for lift, so at 1,000 feet – which now seemed dreadfully low – he decided to seek an uncropped field and set up a landing. Having selected such a field and given it a serial vetting for those dreadful power lines and cables, often so obscure from above, he set up his approach only to perceive to his horror what appeared to be two bulls in the intended field when it was too late to abort and select another. 'Oh hell, what a way to go …' but it transpired that the 'bulls' were a pair of sleepy donkeys.

Touchdown occurred at 3.30pm. Nigel enjoyed the farmer's hospitality until his recovery crew arrived at 6pm. From the air he had clearly observed the Hay Bluff-Pandy ridge system.

Had he found continuing lift and not been suffering from 'putty arms', who knows where he could have landed? One fact is now obvious to us all – there are vast amounts of lift around for those with the skill and bottle to make use of it.

Flying styles differed, depending in which area of Britain you flew. Northern pilots, like Hobson, Calvert and Maritos, had converted totally to big XC flying, and had the sites and terrain to achieve their ambitions. Nigel Milnes flight in the West Country was also over good XC country, and other pilots were making smaller but decent XCs in the area. Down in the Southern Club, where many of the top competition pilots lived and flew, the best sites were on the north side of the South Downs, like Devil's Dyke. They were only a few miles from the sea, so they could not go straight over the back and downwind over Brighton, because there is an awful lot of water between Brighton and France. There were more southern flyers in the National League than from any other club, and they were competitive with one another, all the time. Every day, everyone tried to go top of the stack, higher than anyone else, and if one pilot went XC, he was followed by others who used him as a 'wind dummy' to see where the sink was.

The best account of the type of early XC flying in the south came from the inimitable Johnny Carr, the pilot with the loudest laugh in hang gliding. Johnny, an aerial Peter Pan, has been a champion ever since he began hang gliding in 1974, and more than thirty years later, was still at the top, selected to fly in the rigid-wing class at the 1995 World Hang Gliding Championships in Àger, Spain. Johnny always flew new-technology machines, including a radical design at the time called a Gryphon from the British inventor Miles Handley:

Wednesday Morning, June 1 – I finished work early and thought 'I really ought to go flying'. I could see small cumulus clouds puffing up from everywhere, so my brother-in-law and I jumped into the Volks and set off to Ditchling Beacon on the South Downs.

The trouble was I was a little wound-up because I had only just finished testing the new kite with Miles Handley at Steyning and, although the Gryphon flew perfectly there, Ditching is a different story. I have been going through a bad patch in my flying recently as we all do sometimes and, when I arrived on top of Ditchling, I nearly changed my mind about flying. I asked the lads what the conditions were like and was told 'EVIL' and that nearly finished the matter.

However, watching Jeff Lowrey climb to 1,000 feet smoothly (and the wind did drop to 18 mph at times) I decided to rig up. I had just finished rigging when there was a lull in the wind speed so I thought 'This is it' and asked Ian Grayland to see me off. When I was up, all was fine. The thermals were strong and after 5 minutes I latched into a thermal that took me over West Meston. I estimate 2,000 feet when it started to fade away – I looked back and Jeff was behind the ridge so I went down wind to keep him company. We were thermal flying half way to Brighton. Jeff then got another big up, and headed off towards the Devil's Dyke.

Naturally I couldn't hack that, so I went after him. He was by this time 200 feet higher than I was, so I was doing the best I could to catch him up. As I was still about 1,500 feet high I was not too worried. By now I could see the Devil's Dyke, Brighton Golf Course and Hotel, and directly below me was a main road – I could only just make it out and, as it was the only road I could see I assumed it must have been the A23 London–Brighton road. I knew now that nothing could stop me reaching the Dyke and I thought, 'Well, Mike the Dentist, I have got my own back on you good and proper!' (it was the first time the Ditchling to Dyke flight had been achieved).

As I came over the back of the Dyke Hotel I was losing height quite rapidly and I could see Tom Knight's kite on the hill. I could hear Jeff shouting at him and we were both getting sore throats screaming to him from above.

I could see Paddy coming on to the face of the Dyke and thought (rightly) he had followed the ridge contour from Ditchling – cheeky!

Jeff was still 200 feet above me as I headed for Truleigh, and had already arrived when I got there. I was at ridge level then and thought I would go down because the wind was NE and that is not very good for Truleigh, but I settled for it as it was my first cross-country flight. I could not see Jeff anywhere now and figured he must have landed somewhere downwind of Truleigh.

By now my arms were aching where I had been fighting like mad to stay up at Truleigh. Small thermals helped but sink seemed to put me back at ridge level after a few seconds. I waited until another bubble came along and climbed to 100 feet above Truleigh and pulled on speed and tried to make it back on to the Dyke (by now my arms were dropping off!) when a massive bubble came and I climbed to 1,000 feet approximately. I thought 'This is it – downwind, now or never!'

I decided to head for Mill Hill. 'It will be a gas to say I have flown all the sites in the Southern Club without landing first.' Then came the sink. Oh no! Will I make the car park at Mill Hill? Yes, No, Yes, Yes, It's there and I still have 150 feet or so left. I had worked out several landing fields en route but managed to go over them all. Now I thought 'The river – I could land this side. No, I reckon I could get over the other side. Yes, I'm over it. Fifty feet left and all that is separating me from Shoreham Airport is the A27.'

I remember thinking 'I have got to make it. No one could come this close and not fulfil a 2-year ambition.' I pulled on a little more speed and said, 'Yes! I am over.' I turned into wind with about 15 feet to spare by the big windsock off the Sussex Pad. I just could not believe what I had just done so I rang Steve Hunt at the Hiway factory and he went potty! Everyone went barmy at the factory. Steve said that Jeff had landed further over, 2 or 3 miles down the A27 at a boating lake in Worthing (bloody amazing). Paddy went down at Truleigh and flew off the end to land at Steyning.

Many thanks to Graham Slater and staff who came to pick up Jeff and me and not forgetting Steve Hunt who coughed up his promised bottle of Scotch and, of course, that peachy new weapon of Miles Handley's that I was able to do it on.

No one writes quite like Johnny Carr. The airport controller also offered a bottle of Scotch to Johnny, as promised. Johnny offered to pay a landing fee (Johnny has such style!). It was sportingly refused.

The first hang gliding master of XC flying in England was Bob Calvert, an aeronautical engineer from Blackburn, Lancashire (that is the town the Beatles sang about in 'A Day in the Life' – 'Four thousand holes in Blackburn, Lancashire', 'now they know how many holes it takes to fill the Albert Hall'). Calvert wrote generously about his flying techniques, and shared them with the rest of us. In July 1977, at one of the League competitions that began that year, everyone was sent over the back to do an open XC, including myself, also a competitor, who had ordered it. It was the first time open-XC had been done in competitions, and put the best pilots in the country up against one another to find out who was really good and what everyone really wanted to do. For many, including me, it was our first time over the back into open country, and we were stoned with adrenalin that night. The day was won by Bob Calvert, who flew twice as far as the next best pilot. When he later described how he had done it, the new editor of *Wings!,* Dave Worth, had been forewarned by Tony Fuell not to throw away the grubby notepaper Calvert always wrote on.

It was an open distance competition, in what were seen as perfect thermalling conditions, and unlike most pilots, Calvert had worked out a sophisticated technique, timing the thermals coming through, and only leaving when his vario showed 600 ft/min up (6-up). Even then, if the thermal weakened, he penetrated back to the ridge, though he grew alarmed when other competitors stuck with a thermal which he had rejected, and went over the back and started climbing away. He reported later that he took the next thermal, even though it was only 4-up, and it strengthened to 8-up, and he found it easy to gain height. He had been in the air four and a half hours at this time, it was 4pm, and we all expected thermal activity to decrease after 6pm as evening came on.

Calvert climbed to within 500ft of cloud base, constantly centring, and faced a choice as the thermal decayed, between going cross-wind to find a cloud he could see in the distance – where a thermal ends – or going downwind. Flying at min sink/max glide, he found another thermal that took him up 1,000ft and then ran into moderate sink, descending to just 500ft over the ground before his vario flat-lined. He then drifted down the valley, hoping the village of Kerry would pop off a thermal. It did, he found it and looked back to see Johnny Carr sink out, before looking downwind to see gliders maintaining on the Long Mynd. If he could get there, he reasoned, he could gain real height and win the task. He struggled for ten minutes, just conserving height, before he ran into sink, scraped over a large forest and landed on a small field with power lines and a slope with trees all round. His flight was more than 16 miles, the most done until then in a League competition.

The contrast between Calvert's meticulous winning flight, knowing exactly what he was doing, and the query written partially on his behalf by Graham Hobson – 'I have to say I don't exactly know what a thermal is' – just fifteen months earlier is an indication of how much had been learned about real flying. Calvert could fly anything, mainstream powered aircraft and gliders as well as hang gliders, so he was able to transfer his knowledge from one form of flying to the other. But the skills needed in sailplane gliding had to be adapted. Sailplane gliding is much less physical than hang gliding. You could not fly as fast in a hang glider, but you could climb faster, and take more risks with landing areas and losing the lift. Calvert made the switch and wrote about the changes in our own language. The transfer to the rest of us was easier, simply because he was one of us. We felt that his words were relevant.

I include these accounts of flying because there is a freshness to them, a genuine wondrous discovery of flight that has been missing from mainstream aviation for decades. You can read accounts like that in the early issues of *Flight* magazine, and drifting through issues published before the First World War is a joy, with the same free-wheeling spirit of the first years of hang gliding. But *Flight* is now devoted to hi-tech aviation and the advertising that attracts, and it is no longer a chronicle of the soul of flying.

Calvert did not take the British XC record that year. It was his major rival from Yorkshire, a large man called Robert Bailey, who taught hang gliding professionally, and who added 2 miles to Milnes' 22-mile record before the end of 1977. That record lasted all though 1978, despite numerous attempts to beat it. Then Nigel Milnes took the record back in April 1979, when he flew 34 miles with Jerome Fack and Bob England, again in Wales. Bailey felt the loss deeply and soon got his own back. His account of the first 50-mile XC hang glider flight in Britain that he made a month later to regain the record is one of the classics of its kind. There are passages that read like Hemingway's 'Big Two-Hearted River':

Saturday, 12th May, 1979, dawned bright and clear blue. The forecast sounded good; SW moderate with good lapse rate. I decided to head for Littondale, Arncliffe in the Yorkshire Dales, a three-mile ridge, 300 feet at takeoff, rising to 1,000 feet best.

On arrival, Dave Harrison was there and we rigged on the lower slopes as the wind was gusting and strong. We had a chat and decided conditions were favourable for an attempt at a Goal Distance flight to Richmond cricket ground. We also discussed the possibility of a cross-country flight together, which would help our chances of catching thermals. The morning was spent being thrashed in some really badly torn gusty thermals so I decided it wasn't good enough to set off and had a break for lunch.

In the afternoon the thermals cleaned up and I hooked into the cleanest, biggest thermal of the day – the whole valley seemed to be lifting. I shouted to Dave to come over as I centred to a steady 600–800ft/min up. He shot across but must have hit the tail-end of the bubble and could not get away. A few minutes later saw me at 4,000 feet ASL (Above Sea Level), and climbing steadily towards cloud base. The hilltop is at 1,500 feet above sea level.

I worked the first thermal for 15 minutes and reached cloud base over Great Whernside at 5,800 feet ASL. On reaching cloud base I noticed my drift while circling was very slow (8 circles – 200 yards) and as it was late in the day, 4 o'clock, I decided if I was to make distance I would have to push on quickly and not hang around in weak lift.

I glided straight back over Whernside and noticed another hang glider rigging. The view was fantastic and it was countryside I knew very well, having camped in Coverdale many times when I was a young man.

I was over Scarhouse reservoir now and could see the wind at ground level, still strong and gusty as the water was well whipped-up leaving white caps. How I wished there was some strong wind at this height to carry me faster across the countryside! Down to 4,000 feet and starting to look less at the view and more towards the clouds for my next lift back up to cloud base. Still straight downwind and the vario wanders from 4-down to a steady 2-up. Steady circles, 200–300 yards diameter, 4-up and tighten, then back to 5,000 feet (It was not as easy as that but I have got 45 miles more to write about!).

West Scrafton Moor coming up next. I don't need to look at the map tucked into my pocket as I know this countryside so well having planned this route back in snowy January. It looks massive and I think, 'If I hit heavy sink over the moor I will have a long walk out to the nearest road!' Again my concentration wanders and I am gliding to the south of Carlton and I'm busy looking at the river, the spots I've fished and tickled trout. Middleham is in the distance and looks miles away. 'Will I make Richmond?' crosses my mind.

Down to 3,000 feet and starting to concentrate more on reaching the next cloud, which looks far away. The clouds are small cumulus 2,000 feet thick, closely grouped in places with big blue gaps – and I am in a blue gap – sinking like hang gliders do – fast!

West Witton is below and looks really close. I can see the farmers in the fields, people on the river banks and my thermal-spotting sunglasses are not working too good! Down to 2,000 feet, I have blown it, no hills now. It's all flat out front and clouds are miles above and I need a lift back up. Good-looking area to the north so I fly cross-wind pulling just enough speed for maximum glide. Sure enough – it's there, 2/4-up which I work for ten minutes to gain 3,000 feet. This is no good as I'm getting nowhere so I head north to a brighter looking area. Noughts and 1-up all the way but I take no notice as I've been messing around in this bubbly trash far too long now. I hit a 4-up and tighten which gives me 500 feet. I'm just feeling confident and enjoying the view again when it leaves me. I open up – search – nothing, just noughts, so I head on down-wind. The clouds look really good 10 miles away. If I can only get back up. I guess this is the Dales sink hole, and I'm struggling.

Another mile in 0s and 2-downs and I'm down to 1,000 feet, real low but feeling confident that just a bit further on I'm going to hit something really good – which is going to get me back up on top to where the view is best!

I work another small thermal which gets me back to 2,000 feet and then dies. I open up the circle and find another active core, 4-up, smooth and big. It's my lucky day (thinks) 2,500 feet and it's gone. Maybe it isn't. It's really smooth round here and it feels like it's decaying – nothing active and pumping as it was over the Dales.

Onward, down-wind, then I see there is a good area to the north, 500 acres of ploughed land. The sun is streaming down. It's got to be cooking. I'm low again, 1,500 feet, and it's only just working, 0s and 1-ups on the vario. Circle gently. I'm getting a little desperate. I've blown it! 2-up on part of the circles, keep climbing and then it dies. Still, I need all I can get out of 'Sink City' (another American term – they keep creeping in).

I work hard for what seems an age, just holding my own, and then it goes – the whole bubble lifts and I'm climbing fast and smooth, 2,000, 3,000, 3,500 feet, it's fading. The clouds are looking nearer and seem to be building to the east, so I take a chance and pull speed, leaving lift to fly a mile. The hunch pays off and I'm in the best lift for 15 miles, climbing smoothly to 4,000 feet.

Catterick is coming up now. Military camp, with just gliding and parachute drops at weekends. It's really busy. Gliders, barrage balloon, etc, and I'm looking down on it. Not quite at cloud base, I am concentrating on getting there. 5,000 foot cloud base – that's strange – I thought it would be higher in the drier east of the country. Maybe it's the higher wave systems that are about today, pulling the cumulus upwards in certain areas. Richmond is a couple of miles to the north – my declared goal. I'm at 5,000 feet, the North Yorks Moors are to the S.E. in sight now. There's a high performance glass sailplane 3,000 feet below me to the N.E. circling – it doesn't take me long to decide that declared goals are for another day. Let's go get that record back.

Check on the watch – Omega chronograph stopwatch (maybe they'll sponsor me next time?) – and it's late, after 5 pm. I've got to push on now to get the miles.

Full speed to the north to my next cloud, which is building over Darlington. The glider feels very good. It's only my tenth flight in the Birdman Cherokee, and I get there having lost only 1,000 feet or so. Sure enough the cloud is building and the thermal below is strong.

About 500 feet before entering cloud base I decide when I get there I'll pull speed fast to the N.E. to get some miles under my belt while the sky is still good.

I wish I'd had my goggles on as I hit four clouds lined up which were all working, vario reading only 2-down with the bar to my waist in race mode with my eyes streaming. Flying out of the far side I hit 8-down, which I fly for half a mile before deciding to head back into wind to climb back under my last cloud. Maybe I'll wait a while longer as the gap looks too big. Have to fly with a calculator next time. There's a wisp to the north, so I pull out and glide fast cross-wind to meet it at 2,500 feet and steadily climb back in this 'ginormous', very smooth thermal.

On reaching cloud base again, I can see Stockton to the east with its cooling towers and ICI works. The smoke looks to be coming towards me, 'Oh No, not a sea breeze.' From this height (it's 5.50pm) I'm not drifting at all when circling, which leads me to think maybe I'm not going to reach the coast. I've had this idea in the back of my mind for the last 10 miles.

I start to get a little bit worried and decide the best course is going to be, blast on and try and get as many miles into the sea breeze as I can. Maybe making it 40 miles.

I've got the bar way down and flying fast through lift and sink and then I start to slow up as I notice the smoke from the stacks is still drifting out on the light westerly wind, towards the east coast which is now clearly in sight. It's 50 miles to the coast! I've got to make it there.

Just when I need my next thermal, it's there. It's my lucky day and I work it back to 5,000 feet before leaving it once more, pulling speed, straight downwind towards Hartlepool. There's Middlesbrough to the south, Saltburn to the south-east. A cargo boat in the bay, two miles out, Hartlepool straight ahead. No, that's no good. I've got to get more miles so I head up the coast. There's no future in drifting out to sea and missing your spot landing on a cargo boat with no witnesses on board! The blue gap is a beauty, 8-down and it seems only a couple of minutes to being in the middle of a housing estate and looking for a flat landing field.

I'm not going to make it up the coast to Sunderland as I had planned, but instead I am skimming between the lamp posts and land in a perfect flat field by the road. A motorist waves as he passes by and I wave back for him to stop – he has seen me glide in and I have to get my witnesses. It's about the 50 miles mark and he is pleased to sign as a witness. Two minutes past 6pm, I've landed in Hartlepool having run out of land. As I'm de-rigging, I grab a couple more witnesses who have seen me fly in, and then start to think of how to get home. It's taken me two hours to cover 50 miles, using lots of different techniques that I've never used on previous cross-countries. Pulling speed, leaving lift, and flying fast cross-wind. It has all paid off.

The local club around these parts is the North Yorks, and I wonder how good my friends are. Bill Hopkins is one of the most helpful guys around so I ring him with my fingers crossed. Told him the good news and asked for a lift back. Fantastic, I've got friends. We drive back into the sunset for three hours on the winding roads, arriving late at night back in the Dales. The 'hard work' of XC flying. Thanks, Bill.

Looking back on the flight, I suppose I might have blown it six or eight times but each time the decisions I made were the right ones for that particular flight at that time of day. I'm quite sure I could have flown a lot further if (the big 'if') England had not eroded so much of its eastern coastline, 60, 70, 80, 100 miles, who knows? I wasn't all that tired when I landed, just very jubilant and my ears were popping from the descent.

I think it's possible to get the world record and Gold Goal distance in the UK but site and route planning are going to become more a part of hang gliding to do these types of big flights.

Bailey's record lasted through the winter of 1979, and was overtaken in May the following year by Peter Hargreaves making 68 miles, north-west out of the Dales and over the Lake District. Bailey was in the crew car with me coming back from France, having lost that year's Blériot Cup against the French, when we heard that Bob Calvert had taken the record to 79 miles, a European as well as a British XC record. In early 1981, a new pilot, John Stirk, raised the record to 83 miles, again out of the Yorkshire Dales. In the ten years since the first Lilienthal meet, when 196ft was the longest distance flown, British pilots were flying 83 miles … but the Americans were doing twice as well.

Back in 1977, flying a Rogallo (a 'rag-wing') called a Pacific Gull Alpine, an American pilot called Jerry Katz had launched from 9,000ft at Cerro Gordo in Owens Valley, north of Death Valley in southern California. American pilots were to use Owens Valley for at least eight years to pulverise all distance and height-gain records, and Katz was one of the first. Conditions were so rough that Cerro Gordo was nicknamed 'Scareyergordoff!' Katz took four hours and eighteen minutes to fly 103 miles. During the flight a sailplane flew next to him at about 15,000ft, slowed down, and the pilot shouted at Jerry to go down. Apparently he was worried about the altitude Katz was flying at, and some over-development of clouds in the area, foreshadowing thunderstorms.

Rich Pfeiffer, who twice won Owens Classic competitions, described Katz's flight in this way: 'Jerry Katz is flying the White Mountains, getting fairly low when a thunderstorm develops. Its frontal lift saves him from having to land, but he's sucked up into the storm and has to fight his way out of it, swearing to God "I promise to land if I get out of this alive" all the way. When he gets out, though, he can't resist the lift along the front and circles in it. He's sucked back into the storm and has to fight his way down, renewing all his promises to God. The sequence is repeated again and again until fatigue forces him to keep his promise to land. He's made the first official 100-mile flight in a hang glider, a record that stands three years.'

Katz landed 10 miles north of Benton Station in the Nevada Desert, at a brothel called Betty's, where he was made very welcome. In later years, another brothel called Janie's became a goal for competition flights in Owens Valley. The girls there would come out on to the balconies and wave suggestively at pilots as they landed, and cheerfully proposition them too (I don't remember that happening at any British competitions).

Previous to landing at Betty's, Katz had recorded a new world altitude gain record of 9,550ft at the same site. The man he beat for the height gain was then 57 years old, a former Second World War US Navy pilot called George Worthington, who went on to become a legend in hang gliding. Taking on pilots thirty years his junior, over the next few years George – he almost didn't need a surname – held all the major world records, overall distance, flight to a goal, and height gain, on both rigid and 'rag-wing' hang gliders. George had blown the chance of being the first hang glider pilot to fly 100 miles by burning off 11,000ft over Betty's three days before the Katz flight, so he could claim a 95-mile world goal distance record. He always had his own priorities. When he was younger, George held many sailplane records. He was a robust commentator, and competitor, with any youngsters who wanted to take his records from him.

We sent a British team to fly Owens Valley in 1980, and the Americans in return sent us an article by W.A. (Pork) Roecker, telling us what it would be like. The 1979 British team at Owens had not had any success, because one of its members – Bob England, killed a few years later on the normally benign Californian site of Torrey Pines – wound all the others up about the dangers of flying there. I am not sure if Pork ever flew Owens himself, despite the confidence of his stories, but he knew many of the pilots who did. Pork tells a good tale about what it was, and still can be, like at Owens:

> Back in the old days, hang glider pilots were a different breed. There weren't many of them, only a few dozen, so they were close. They flew gliders made of bamboo and rope and plastic sheeting. Some contraptions had no place to hook up a harness – you just held on, weight-shifting between stall and divergency. California pilots in particular had a distain

for helmets or shoes. With the stage set like that, spectators got to see some pretty amazing acts in the sky. I know a pilot who descended 4,000 feet with a ripped plastic sail, another who somehow held his fractured control bar together with his hands long enough to frap into the side of the mountain he'd intended to fly away from, another who ate a piece of Orange Sunshine and launched at night with no harness into a cloud. They all lived, despite the chances they took.

The sport is much safer now, of course. Gliders are load-tested and test-flown by the factories, certified by a national organisation, and harnesses are much more comfortable and nearly up to parachute harness strengths. The new machines perform so much better and are so much easier to fly that they resemble their ancestors in the same way a Mustang resembles a Model-T. Pilot attitudes have changed, too. Most now have jobs and families and a sincere wish to avoid death or injury. 'You can't fly with a busted arm,' says a friend. 'You do something wrong, make a bad decision, and you spend the next few months on the ground watching your buddies fly.' If his attitude seems thoughtful or conservative it is also representative of the new breed who learned to fly on better machines, in more crowded skies.

But a few of the originals, the goforit boys, sky-surfin', 'I bet I can do a loop', pot-partying, flat-spinning, hard-drinkin', womanising, home-growed, philosophising, self-taught artist musicians endure. They still go for it in the White Mountains, sister range to the Sierra Nevada, lying west across the Owens Valley. And 'it' is a hell of a long way. The distance record for self-launched powerless flight is the 100-mile mark. Other records can be picked up along the way, altitude gain, out-and-return and so on. A decent flight for one of these good ol' boys might be a waltz of 60 or 70 miles north-east along the rugged range, with upbeats to 16,000ft above sea level, and one-two-three down to a few hundred feet off the barren valley floor. This circular boxstep, accompanied by temperature changes of 60 degrees or more, is percussioned by 30mph wind changes and sudden reversals. If it sounds bouncy, it is. If it sounds scary, it is. Most pilots won't fly from Cerro Gordo when it's cracking. Cerro Gordo, 'fat mountain'. Lots of weird things have happened at Scareyergordoff. Many of the heavy-duty pilots who flew for competition or for fun there last year said they won't go back again. One will never leave.

Both the Whites and the Sierra rise vertically for more than a mile from the dry baked floor of the Owens Valley. When you fly a hang glider into this cauldron of potential Clear Air Turbulence (CAT to the airline pilots) your first concern is to gain enough altitude to reach the valley and a flat place to land. At the Cerro Gordo launch, you won't make it if there's sink or a head-wind. You'll be forced to land in the 'pits' in the broken foothills. If you can do that without hurting yourself or your kite, you'll either have to launch again from one of the nasty little hills, or shoulder the thing and hike. The Gunther launch site is more forgiving, and was used this year for the official contests. If you can get up from either launch site you'll feel better (at 15,000 feet you'll probably feel inebriated) about having a flat place to land within glide range, but you'll be quartering downwind across desolation row, with little idea of where it will all end or what sort of wind and weather await the landing which inevitably approaches.

Because of the conditions at Scareyergordoff, which only the mealy-mouthed would call adverse, hang glider pilots carry strange apparatus for flying there. The heat in the mid-afternoon valley floor will be a solid 100 degrees F, but the pilots want to fly up to fifteen grand, so they put on heavy thermal underwear, windproof jackets and thick gloves. They carry signal mirrors, snakebite kits, quick-energy foods, smoke-flares and streamers for marking ground windspeed and direction, first aid gear, compasses, windmeters, altimeters, radios and variometers. The truly serious about setting records also carry a large instrument called a barograph, used for authenticating altitudes reached and time spent in the air, a supposedly uncheatable gadget.

'But if you go down in the desert,' says Paige Pfeiffer, current women's world record holder for distance and altitude, 'you've got to take all your clothes off. There's no shade, so you just lie down under your glider and wait for somebody to find you. I always wear my bikini. Being in the air real high is the only good thing about flying there. You can't believe how hot it is on the ground. I hate it.'

Just being on the launch site can sometimes be worse than slow cooking on the desert floor. Dave Beardslee told of waiting with two other ready pilots on the Scareyergordoff launch when they heard approaching thunder. Shortly, the noise proved to be a nasty thermal, turning in on itself so hard it sounded, said Beardslee, 'like a pick-up truck loaded with sheet metal coming up the grade to the launch'. The Beard's glider lay spread-eagled on the ground, so he sat on its nose. Paige Pfeiffer's glider had a noseboom, so she and her mother, a large lady, sat on that. Gary Patnor and Jeff Scott and two others held on to Gary's glider. When the thermal, if that is the right name for it, got on to the Scareyergordoff launch it broke both wings of Gary's glider. It broke both wings of Paige's glider too, and catapulted her distraught mother off the glider's noseboom and almost off the launch. She might have soared, because in a moment it lifted Gary's glider with four men holding it, even with two broken wings. 'You better get off,' shouted 6 foot 6 inch Jeff Scott, ''cos I'm off the ground!'. Jeff let go, and both broken gliders rose and embraced, 'and began to waltz,' recounted Beardslee. A moment after that an empty harness and helmet got up as though they wanted to cut in. When Gary's glider sat down after the dance, it came down on the Pfeiffer's new pick-up, good and hard. It destroyed the Beard's initiative to fly cross-country. He dismantled his Alpine as soon as it calmed. 'I thought I'd come,' he allowed, 'some nicer day.'

Paige Pfeiffer's husband, Rich, had launched with wild man Jerry Katz moments before the killer thermal arrived, but the boys still got a piece of the action. They gained 4,000 feet in three minutes, respectable for a powered airplane, but maybe a mite faster than a hang glider needs to go up. The power that gave them so much lift made Katz so airsick he landed at the first town he came to, Lone Pine. Undaunted, Rich Pfeiffer continued for 60 miles. On the way he saw a hawk working close to a ridge. As Rich watched, hoping to learn something from the bird, a gust smashed the hawk into the mountainside and killed it.

What can happen to a hawk can also happen to a hang glider pilot. White Mountain Canyon is particularly feared by flyers, as they must cross its mouth to continue downrange.

The canyon's maw seems to inhale with violent turbulence and sink. It sucked Brad LaFarr of Seattle back into a place walled with rock where he had to get up to get out. Flying close, in the raggedy heated air, he was also dashed against a rocky face. Another pilot watched helplessly from far above. Later a helicopter retrieved Brad's body.

A few days before, Eric Raymond, 1979 US National Champion, and Jim Handberry, a former national sky-diving champ become parachute manufacturer, headed off down the spine of the Whites. Both pilots flew Fledglings, hot semi-rigid hang gliders steered by rudders on the wing-tips, generally acknowledged to be among the very best machines for cross-country work. Eric was last seen very low between some mountains. Pilot consensus that night was that if Eric wasn't dead, he was crashed somewhere in the boondocks. What happened was that Eric managed to thermal back up out of the valley that had entrapped him. He flew about 50 miles and landed in the desert some way from the town of Bishop. He waited for his friends to come and pick him up. No one came. It was mighty chilly out in the desert that night, Eric said. He needed all his heavy clothes and his sailbag to keep warm. In the morning he walked and hitch-hiked to a telephone. He called the police and the hospitals to tell them he was OK and to see if anyone was looking for him. No one was. Eric hitched to their campsite. It was vacant. Everyone was up flying, and they'd moved to another campsite. 'Talk about going for it,' complained Eric. 'They didn't know if I was dead or what.'

Handberry's flight that day was even wilder. Jim cruised along smartly with his Fledgling at well over 15,000 feet ASL when he encountered monster sink. Later he realised it was the rotor from a wave of high winds coming over the Sierras, many miles to the west. It came down on Jim Handberry like a swatter on a fly. It ripped his hands from the control bar and pinned him against the keel of his glider for the worst drop of his life. He fell, nailed against his wing, for over a mile, 5,500 feet, and it only let him pull out when he was 200 feet off the spine. Handberry had one of his own parachutes, but it likely would have done no good to chuck it into air going down so fast. Handberry claimed he had never been so scared, even while parachuting. He didn't think he'd fly there again.

'You could see the wave clouds that day,' said Eric. 'I don't know why we were flying.'

Brad White had a moment to wonder why he was flying there. A former national champ in rigid wing class, Brad had his glider come unglued. The Mitchell Wing is undoubtedly the fastest hang glider available. It's made from spruce and veneer, just like the real airplanes used to be. In fact, it looks very like the stabilizer off a DC-3, with rudders at the tips. It resembles those ill-fated flying wings of World War Two. At any rate, Brad's wing disintegrated around him in turbulence about the launch. Brad arrived back groundside via his parachute. Bits of the wing came down in lots of different places.

British and Australian teams came last year to compete against the Americans. So did a few Canadians. The British didn't care much for the White Mountains. Maybe it was the landscape, or the turbulence. Most British pilots said they wouldn't be coming back. The Australians and Canadians loved the place. Sixty and seventy mile flights appealed to them, as perhaps did crossing the State line into Nevada. More than one pilot was reported to have landed near the small trailer camps lit up with neon, even in the daytime (brothels, legal in some parts of Nevada, one way some East-coast girls work their way through college). To use the phone, of course. One pilot said this was the only place he'd ever been where you could fly fifty miles across the wilderness without seeing another glider, only to come around a mountainside to confront ten of your competitors, all vying for position in the same thermal. Former Hang Gliding editor Rich Grigsby found the clusters of gliders in the middle of nowhere both funny and disturbing.

'Imagine having a mid-air collision at 12,000 feet,' he said.

There were no mid-airs, but just about every other catastrophe that could happen did. At least three of the hot Fledgling wings encountered conditions that taxed the ability of those craft to remain right side up and in one piece. A Mosquito pilot tucked or was flipped over. The pilot threw his parachute, only to observe his own flying wires sever the shroud lines. The empty chute floated off, but the yank it gave the disabled glider righted it, and its relieved pilot made a safe landing. Competitor Jon Lindburg said that one morning during the Classic contest the pilots voted not to fly after hearing a weather report of winds to 42 knots at 18,000 feet. Butch Peachy and George Worthington, the contest's founder and director, opted to go for it anyway. 'Butch took off and just skied out,' said Jon, 'and we all said *whoa*, maybe we should fly. Then George launched and he got drilled straight into the pits. So we all left. Butch got real high but he couldn't go anywhere. He had to land on top of the White Mountains. He had to spend the night up there at 12,000 feet. I bet he froze his butt off.'

Goforit spirit was probably never stronger than in the Cross Country Classic. Californians dominated the top ten finishers, but pilots from Utah, Arizona, New Mexico and Australia placed there as well. Often competitors had to land in isolation and dangerous winds on the desert floor after an exhausting high altitude flight, a risky proposition. Eric Raymond wasn't one of these. 'I always took safe landing places,' he complained, 'but a lot of guys didn't. They'd do anything to stretch for a few more miles. There was no penalty for totalling your kite.'

The drubbing administered Rich Pfeiffer's pick-up by Gary Patmor's runaway glider must have served Rich inspirationally, because on Sunday, July 15th, the last day of the 1979 Owens Valley Classic, Pfeiffer came from behind Keith Nichols to win it. Flying with a barograph, Rich made 72 miles that day, the goal being a ranch called Katz's farm. Consider Pfeiffer's mileages for the Meet: 45, 21, 17, 17, 33, 35, 72. Not bad for a sport that less than ten years ago consisted mainly of lurching into a shallow glide down a small hill.

In reading Pork's report on the Classic, I should add that he had reasons for feeling the way he did about the British. We had twice gone to the United States, in 1978 and 1979 and – under my leadership – thrashed American hang gliding teams in fair competition, and they were gravely wounded by the experience. But he was also wrong about the British being chicken. Four years later the great Owens Valley Classic was won by an Englishman, Tony Hughes. You will not have read about it in the British media, of course. Ho ho! *The idea.*

By the end of 1981, an American ski patrolman, Jim Lee, had flown an extraordinary 168 miles in a rag-wing, a UP Comet 165. He crossed virtually the whole state of New Mexico, and most of the flight was over flatlands, presaging where future big distances were going to come. Even at the height of its fame and notoriety, Owens Valley appeared to set natural limits on how far pilots could fly. Conditions at Owens to Pork, and the 1979 British team (and most pilots), were awesome during its first few years as a hang gliding site. In 1993 pilot skills had advanced so far, and hang gliders were so developed, that the Americans used the Owens Valley as the venue for the World Championships, expecting it to be a final 'banker' to get them a win at last.

In Britain, we did not pass the 100-mile XC until 1982. The successful pilot, and justly so, was Bob Calvert.

But the tremendous leap in distance flying in the new aviation in just a few short years did not happen in a vacuum. Nor did it happen without opposition, from outside as well as inside hang gliding, to the yearning we had to fly like the birds fly.

Chapter 6

Hang Gliding and Sailplanes

We had a great many problems not long after hang gliding was established in Britain, with sensational coverage from the media. At first we were admired as daring young men (mainly), but as these things happen, responding to the less adventurous spirit of the age, according to *The Sun* newspaper, suddenly we were 'poisonous butterflies'. We had to fight for sites to take off from, to assure worried landowners that we were not going to bleed all over their land or, in American legal fashion, sue them because they didn't stop us behaving in the way we wanted to. It was part of our early training that every hang glider pilot learned the country code; don't climb stone walls, use gates, close them, don't leave litter on a hill and so on.

In a way we are the greenest of all forms of flight. Look at a hill in the morning, and it is all grass and dew. During the day we turn up to fly, cruise around the hill, top-land, have picnics, discuss our flights, make cross-countries, and at the end of the day, pack up everything and drive away. As the light fades, you would not know we had been there. There were no permanent club houses, aside from pubs like that on the Devil's Dyke that did much better business when the site was flown. But the pubs were there anyway. Yet it must be admitted, we all need cars with roof racks.

In the United States, especially on the west coast and in mountainous regions, the size of the country meant flying sites were more formalised. Sometimes tracks were cut to the edge of a ridge, and a platform built to enable pilots to launch cleanly. As the sport expanded, rules grew for sites, fields were selected for bottom landing. In Alpine Europe and parts of Scotland, hang gliders filled a gap left by skiers when the snow melted. We could use ski lifts the way skiers did, and there were numerous good launch sites at the tops of mountains. Everyone had problems establishing sites, but no other country ran into quite the same problem as we did in Britain, with those we might have considered our brothers-in-law, the conventional gliding community, represented by the British Gliding Association (BGA).

Britain is a relatively small island (if 600 miles from top to bottom can be called small) and not long after we started flying there was a clash between the interests of hang gliders and gliders. In general, hang gliders were considered to be alright so long as we plummeted off a hill and 'flew' to the bottom. We got in no one's way, and 'real' gliders could look down their noses and snigger at our foolishness. It was when we started, in a primitive way, to do what they were doing – flying – that the problems arose. A look at their own history would have shown them we were going through an exactly similar pattern in learning to fly that they went through, except for one major advantage they had that we didn't; they didn't have fellow flyers putting the boot in hard at every stage of their learning.

Philosophically, there is a major difference between us and mainstream aviation, especially including cockpit gliders. Historically, aviation has been controlled through landing and take-off sites, and power has evolved in glider fields to the chief flying instructor (CFI). The CFI is able to use that power by banning a miscreant from flying, from having his glider stored, from being assisted into the air through a cable launch or tow aircraft. Glider pilots need more than their feet and a wing to fly. They must spend money on infrastructure – club house, winch, tow plane – and it is a natural instinct, having accumulated resources, to protect them.

Hang glider pilots, by contrast, can turn up on a hill with everything they need to fly. They can put it all together, launch on their own two feet, and fly away. By comparison to sailplane pilots, we are anarchists. We sometimes need help on a launch, a person holding the front wires to steady us, and someone needs to drive away our car (but we can always hitch back from where we have landed to pick up the car ourselves later). You cannot lean on a hang glider pilot the way you can lean on sailplane pilots, because in the last analysis they can just show you two fingers and fly anyway. If they don't respond to peer group pressure, what are you going to do? Shoot them?

The massive growth of paragliders in recent years, in which the aircraft can be stored in a rucksack, 'rigged' in two minutes and launched, compounds this 'problem' in spades.

It is quite possible that we attract different types of people to hang gliding than gliding. We both want to fly, but perhaps we in hang gliding want to for different reasons. There was a spirited debate in Scotland over the issue in spring 1976, when hang gliders were still confined to ridges or to flights off mountains. A pilot called Eric Davis left hang gliding, took up sailplaning, and rubbished the idea that hang gliding was cheaper. Adding all the costs together, he wrote, purchasing a hang glider, harness, helmet, instruments (a parachute was yet to come), and driving to sites to get perhaps five minutes in the air, was expensive. It was much more expensive than joining a gliding club where so much more air-time was available, and aircraft were hired, not bought. The comment among Scottish hang glider pilots that followed could have been printed anywhere in the world … first, Bill Mercer:

> Many times in the past I have felt exactly the same sentiments, but have come to the conclusion that hang gliding beats conventional gliding and powered flight on the following grounds:
>
> 1. One second suspended from a hang-glider to me equals 2 hours conventional flying in excitement and achievement.
>
> 2. The exercise and fresh air in hang gliding can never be equalled in power or glider flying.
>
> 3. The camaraderie on the hills has always seemed more genuine than the airfield clubhouse.
>
> In saying this I am comparing 110 plus hours of powered flying with 12 hang gliding flights totalling no more than 10 minutes. A further attraction is that I have so much to do in the mastery of flying technique, in prolonging my flying time, and in conquering my own innate cowardice.

A second Scottish hang glider pilot, Gordon Bull wrote:

> Eric Davis goes on at great length to explain the actual hourly cost of hang gliding per year as opposed to conventional gliding. He also appears to sneer, ever so slightly, at those who wonder what the wind is doing. Speaking for all the duff pilots who, like myself, happily and in ignorant bliss are content to plod up the hill to fly down again, we may not be too wonderful at assessing what the wind does, where it comes from or where it goes, but if the hill has been checked by an experienced pilot prior to flying, then I'll happily throw my wee body into space.
>
> Last August I paid for a week's course at Coventry Gliding Club, where I flew dual Bocian and Capstan gliders, and this

included a tow by a Chipmunk. The inspector in the glider thermalled us to 7,500 feet above Market Harborough and completed this flight with two loops prior to landing, which I might add I was allowed to repeat next day.

The week's course contained 7 flights, my longest being 1 hour and 6 minutes. Towards the end I can honestly say I was bored and grateful to land.

In my opinion hang gliding is far more thrilling and rewarding than sailplanes can ever be. I do not wish to have certificates to prove to the world how good I am or not. Nor do I need to stay enclosed in a tiny glass bubble, protected by my instruments. All I need is a rag tied to the front rigging to show the exact wind direction.

I have never yawned while flying my low, and slow, Wasp hang glider.

A third comment came from a pilot called G.M. Murray:

It is my experience of gliding at Portmoak that on days when weather conditions limit flying, the majority of club members adjourn to the clubhouse to warm their backsides, while a few of the keen types are left to do any maintenance or repairs. After a few months of this, it was easy to tell the fair-weather flyers who only showed up when the work was done, and the weather conditions virtually guaranteed good flying.

No account has been taken of the money paid to buy a modern sailplane, largely funded from Local Authority grants to the sum of several thousand pounds, nor the necessary upkeep. Costs of the annual Certificate of Airworthiness (CoA) vary with the age of the machine and the work necessary. I have spent months of weekends laboriously sanding, doping and repairing bits of glider with a few more dedicated flyers while the fair-weather pilots stayed at home.

Another factor which has been largely ignored is that sailplanes require some means of launching, either aero-tow, winch, or towing by car. Again, I can only say that if I had a pound for every hour spent transporting, over-hauling and maintaining such equipment, I would be a rich fellow indeed! Eric Davis must have a conveniently short memory when working out 'costs', when he forgets the hours spent coaxing reluctant winches and tractors to life, and trying to repair launch cables on boggy fields, while pupil and instructor slowly turned to ice waiting on the next cable. He should remember that such activities are part and parcel of the gliding scene on virtually all sites, and cannot be reduced to 'costs per hour'.

As regards his remarks of being frustrated at lack of flying, it should be pointed out that when Eric was hang gliding, he only flew the 'syndicate' Skyhook and never owned his own machine. On numerous occasions he declined to fly when given the chance, and seemed content to spectate and assist with retrieving instead of participating in flying himself.

There really is no comparison between sitting in the instrumented cockpit of a sailplane at 3,000 feet over Bishop Hill, and sitting in a hang glider at 300 feet over Tinto Hill. To me, the hang glider wins every time. After all, it's only you, the wing and the wind up there, and gliding just does not offer the same exhilaration or experience.

My first personal experience of the conflict between the two air sports was when I joined Alvin Russell's Long Mynd HGC in early 1975. I could soar by then, seated in a Wasp CB240, a curved boom wing with 240sq^2 sail that I thought at the time was the cat's pyjamas. It could get me up a couple of hundred feet off the Mynd, but if I wanted to turn left and cruise along the ridge, I ran right into the gliding club's area. They didn't want me doing it, nor any other member of our club, and a long, nasty, sometimes astonishingly underhand battle went on between us that lasted for years.

It reached a peak in 1980, five years later. I had become editor of *Wings!* and felt I could discern a deliberate pattern to the aggression that was coming from established gliding clubs. I decided to ask hang gliding club chairmen around the country to write about their personal experience dealing with (or being dealt with by) gliding clubs. I did not ask them to tell me the worst side, just to put their case in print, which I felt had not been heard before. When the letters came in, I published the good with the bad. I was also not actively conscious that others in aviation, such as the Civil Aviation Authority, would read the accounts. But as they unfolded, one by one, they were pretty horrific. We hadn't realised how much the campaign against us was organised!

It transpired that some glider pilots had asked the BGA a couple of years earlier – 1978 – what they could *do* about hang glider pilots. By that, they meant, how could they stop hang glider pilots flying in the same air as them, or anywhere near *their* air. A BGA lawyer, Lionel Alexander, had given disinterested advice, that is, treating glider pilots as clients and looking to their own best interests. It is the sort of advice lawyers are asked to give, and of course it treats the other side as an opponent. We were both creatures who flew, but just by the way that advice was asked for, and given, drew a line in the sand. It created us and them. We had never set out to be a 'them', seeing, naively, all flyers as 'us' and 'them' being people who did not fly.

I wrote an editorial at the time, drawing attention to the legal advice article in *Sailplane & Gliding*, the tone of which was, 'We don't suggest doing this unless it's a last resort.' Lionel Alexander, the lawyer/author, admitted that if tactics he was suggesting were used on conventional gliding clubs, they would outrage his readers. But the substance of the article outlined legal and public opinion weapons to drive hang gliders away. I wrote:

> Hang gliders and conventional gliders have had problems in at least four areas of the country. The relationship at club level between the two air disciplines at Dunstable, Long Mynd, Sutton Bank and Frocester near Stroud, can only be described as dreadful.
>
> At one time or another, a gliding club's personnel have informed the press we are a 'death threat'; gliding clubs have held parties to sweet-talk local landowners and councils into banning us access to take-off sites; in extreme cases, as Paul Bridges describes about relations on the Long Mynd, and Gerry Stapleton confirms on Sutton Bank, glider pilots have 'beat up' hang gliders in the air to try and scare them away. They have even called the police (80 times in one day!) in the mistaken belief that the police can ban us flying.
>
> If there is any anti-hang gliding lobby, it exists at the professional club level in some gliding clubs. Not at the top of the BGA, nor among ordinary glider pilots, but at this specific level. Were I a glider pilot I would be ashamed of the behaviour of some of my representatives, who appear to have forgotten that we too are the inheritors of Lilienthal and Pilcher and Chanute.
>
> Unless the so-called 'Dinosaurs' – as one glider pilot described them – have their behaviour brought to public

attention, we will continue to face evasions, half-truths and even outright lies about ATZs (air traffic zones) and 'rules of the air' in the efforts of some people to keep us away from 'their' hills and 'their' air, even if they have to destroy an air sport to do it.

The most significant of the articles I published from the clubs was the first, because of the meticulous attention to detail of the local hang gliding club chairman, Paul Bridges, whose mild appearance belied the formidable way he coped with the threats:

The Long Mynd is our Club's prime site. It faces west to north west and is about 3 miles long. We started flying from it as a Club in early 1975 on our sturdy standards. One flying site was near the south end of the hill, and the other 200 yards north of the Midland Gliding Club (MGC). Our early flying was tremendous fun, and we had all heard of someone who knew someone else who had actually soared above the hill! None of us had heard of the Air Navigation Order of 1974 (ANO).

The MGC informed us of the ANO in a letter on 4 August, 1975. We were told that our hang gliding operations were dangerous to them and violated their air space, as defined in ANO 1974. They regretted, therefore that our hang gliding operations at the Long Mynd must cease immediately. No one in the Club doubted the legality of the MGC's information. But what we did find intensely annoying was the arrogant tone of the letter, and the fact that no attempt at all was made by the MGC to suggest a workable solution, or a meeting to find such a solution. It was just, 'sod off!'

Alvin Russell, our club chairman then, decided that without the Mynd the Club may as well not exist. But with the mushroom growth of hang gliding at that time, our fear was that if we didn't fly and attempt to control hang gliders on the Mynd, things would get out of hand and this would help no one.

Investigations were made and the CAA contacted. 'They can't do it,' Graham Driscoll was told by a stern-sounding official at the other end of the phone, somewhere in the corridors of power. Our own reading of the ANO and further contacts with the CAA made us realise that the law was not as clear-cut as the MGC would have us believe. Alvin Russell was told that if the MGC had an ATZ – Air Traffic Zone – this did not entitle them to ban other air users, such as us.

I think that Alvin's thinly veiled threat of uncontrolled hang gliding on the Mynd was the real force behind our agreement with the MGC, that we soared only the south end of the Mynd. Eddie Bowen, a local farmer who owned the land we took-off from next to the MGC, was (and is) our club's president. Flights from the top to the bottom from Eddie Bowen's land near the MGC were outside their ATZ, since we were flying below the surface level of their gliding field. The MGC told us not to use the track along the top of the hill through their gliding field to the south end of the hill. But since we had acquired an Austin Champ 4WD for transport purposes, we could easily get up the steep rough track to the face of the hill. Otherwise we would have to walk up, carrying all our equipment, which was physically extremely tiring.

During the Spring of 1976 some of us shed our bog-rogs and started to fly the new super hang gliders of the day. We could now soar in much lighter (and higher) wind speeds, and previously unheard-of height gains were common. Our soaring was still kept to the southern end of the hill, well away from the MGC airfield. On August 28 we received another ban from the MGC.

In this letter the MGC told us that since we were now soaring to well in excess of 1,000 feet above the hill, and thus well into their normal operating heights, they considered it dangerous for us to mix. Therefore, they wrote, in the interests of safety their concession to us to enter 'their air-space' was withdrawn. Again, this letter did not offer to discuss the 'problem' with us, or suggest any solution. After much effort we eventually had a meeting with the MGC in their club house on October 24 (two months later), and attempted to educate them as to the true nature of hang gliders. We left the MGC to discuss the matter among themselves. Not until January 23, 1977, were we able to arrange another meeting, which ended in an agreement to fly again, under virtually the same rules as we had before. For five months no hang glider had soared the Mynd when the MGC was operating. That says a lot for the responsible attitude of hang glider pilots. But was this delay, or even the ban, really necessary? I think not.

In the meantime we were still trying to discover the full legal position vis-a-vis glider launching sites and ATZs. Anyway, we were flying again, but there was a lot of bitterness over the lost flying time. Our only consolation was that we had behaved responsibly, but we were determined not to be pushed around so much in the future.

There then followed a period of goodwill between us, and increased contact between flyers from each club did much to improve relations. In the meantime, we had had to get rid of the Austin Champ and we resorted to climbing the 600 feet to our soaring site. We were also learning from local knowledge, and discovered that we could, as of right, use the track through the MGC gliding field to get to our southern flying site. The agent for the landowner of the south end assured us that we had rights of access, as did other local farmers, and members of the parish council. Armed with this backing we started to assert our rights, and were met with a confused reaction. Then, eureka! The CAA laid down a clarified ruling which stated that ATZs of airfields (other than military or those controlled by the CAA or having ATC or AFIS units) could be entered without permission.

Did we soar the gliding club hangar roof or do beat-ups of their bungee launching point? No. After brief discussion and almost unanimous agreement we decided to continue flying as before, provided we could drive to the south end of the Mynd unhindered. Soaring would not take place at our northern site next to the MGC without their approval. It appeared that now we were making concessions to them, and not them to us.

However, as time passed it became clear that the MGC were getting increasingly unhappy with us driving through their site – we disagreed on the scale of this inconvenience. The MGC don't like people to disagree with them and there were a number of stupid beatings-up flights by sailplanes. Their respect for air law seemed to be cracking!

In December, 1978, the MGC told us they would not allow any vehicles connected with hang gliding to cross their airfield. Our reply to their letter was that we did not accept their right to prevent us access to the south end of the Mynd, nor that the scale of inconvenience to them was as great as they suggested. All previous agreements between us were now at an end, and we reserved the right to fly the whole of the Mynd. Also, what about the near miss on September 17? Such incidents made a nonsense of their fine words about safety and 'spirit of the agreement'.

On March 4, 1979, the gliding club blocked the track – a public right-of-way 'to make a point', according to the MGC chairman. This was, the Salop County Council tell us, an illegal act. Again, so much for the MGC respect for the law when the boot is on the other foot. On March 8, we received a request for a meeting the following weekend. The MGC can move fast, it seems, if it is in their interest to do so. Unfortunately, we could not meet that date.

The next good soaring day was on March 31, and we 'made a point' by soaring at our northern flying site by the MGC. We were now ready for another meeting with them.

At that meeting the access problem was discussed, and we were left in no doubt that the MGC had gone into the legal aspect very thoroughly. They claimed the land agents backing for us was very wrong. Despite this, temporary permission was given for us to use the track to the south end of the Mynd, but we were careful not to state that we would not soar the north end of the Long Mynd by the MGC.

It took a high-powered meeting between our respective clubs, the BHGA and the BGA, to get us to agree not to soar near their clubhouse, while protracted investigations into an alternative access to the south end continue. These investigations proved fruitless, and a MGC letter gave a deadline for termination of permission to pass through to the south end. We went back to soaring near their club again.

It seems tragic that the MGC could not let the old soaring agreement stand, and allow us to go quietly through at the beginning and end of those days when we needed access. As it is, our solicitor has been briefed and I have no doubt that in the fullness of time our right of access will be proved. If that day dawns, as I believe it will, the MGC will get the same sympathy from us as we got from them. It will be no use their pleading that it was all an unfortunate mistake.

Another significant point concerns their insistence that we must not fly anywhere near their circuit pattern. This argument sounds very good, but the CAA in their letter of March 30, 1979, to both the BHGA and the BGA, state their opinion is that hang gliding sites are also aerodromes and also have ATZs. The MGC do not respect our take-off and landing areas in the way they expect us to respect theirs. They are not afraid to fight us. We must not be afraid to fight back. In my opinion, reluctance to do so will be traded upon.

In terms of an immediate effect, I do not think I published a more important article than Paul's account. The response was amazing. Other clubs said, 'but that happens to us, too, and we thought they had the law on their side'. The other effect was that Paul had learned what our rights really were, and other hang gliding clubs started to use the knowledge he had so painfully gained. In Sutton Bank, we heard of glider pilots urging landowners to ban us from their land, and the Frocester Club briefed the media, privately, that we were a 'death threat', to such effect that the slur was printed first and then, as an afterthought, a comment was sought from us. So much for modern British journalism. At Dunstable, the London Gliding Club (LGC), the oldest BGA club in the country, concluded an agreement in 1975 with a just-formed hang gliding club when we were flying little better than steerable parachutes, confining us to within a height of 100ft, and a limit of 150ft out from the ridge, as if in a cage. There was a total ban on so-called 'high penetration hang gliders'. As hang glider performance improved, the LGC insisted hang glider pilots comply with that agreement, which became the basis of a Bedfordshire County by-law.

I think the airing in *Wings!* was healthy, just by showing that the divisions were very deep. It is fair to say that others, such as BHGA president Ann Welch and BGA chairman Roy Hill, both with gliding backgrounds, thought otherwise. As is obvious in Paul Bridges' account (and the others), hang glider pilots understood the rights glider pilots were defending. We just wanted to talk about how to live together. And we absolutely hated, as any Englishmen might, living under constant threats all the time.

There was a reply of sorts from the BGA, by the same Lionel Alexander who wrote the notorious guide for gliding clubs in the first place. Very few of the specific points brought up by the hang gliding club chairmen were addressed directly. There was no comment on the pressure brought on landowners, the snide briefings to the press, the unwillingness to talk.

Mr Alexander emphasised that we were all subject to the law, and said he kept his members up to date with changes in ATZ rules. He asked for sympathy to tackle the problem of 'self-discipline', but went on to say, piously, that the air was free to all. He suggested that we learn how the law operated, so we could meet CFIs at their level, and 'if he is wrong, see that you are well-informed and put him right' but don't think of him as malevolent.

He told us to mind our manners, and suggested that the BGA had won many freedoms for pilots, and we should recognise this. Mr Alexander highlighted the power of a chief flying instructor in a gliding club, and suggested we adopted the same structure.

There was a veiled threat, a very lawyerly threat, about our outraged language, especially over the allegation of hang gliders being beaten up in the air. Mr Alexander made the point that the (woman) editor of *Sailplane & Gliding* had much higher standards than us ...'faced with an allegation (April, 1980) Wings! that another flying machine had been deliberately "beaten up", (she) might be told by her legal advisers that such an allegation, amounting as it does to an accusation of dangerous flying, not to say attempted murder, constituted actionable libel'.

On that last point, Mr Alexander was not saying the beating up did not happen. He was saying that if we say it happened, it could be a libel. A miserable little lawyerly point. But, significantly, the *case* was never taken any further. Neither the Midland Gliding Club, nor Sutton Bank, ever challenged us to prove it. On one day the police asked the hang gliders to stop flying for an hour while they went down themselves to talk to the Midland Gliding Club, because they were concerned at the aggressive tactics of the sailplanes in the air.

Finally, Mr Alexander admitted, somewhere in the middle of his article, that 'I cannot deny that in one, or perhaps two, instances, relationships have become so soured and attitudes so entrenched (though I am not apportioning blame), that there cannot be, in the foreseeable future, a happy mix of gliding and hang gliding.'

It was all a long time ago. It hurt then, and revisiting the issue years later, it hurts now. We, of course, are not bound by the same lofty and disinterested standards as Mr Lionel Alexander.

Years later, when 100-mile hang glider flights were common in England, indeed, part of normal competition flying, there seemed to be a much different attitude on behalf of glider pilots. Two pieces were published in *Cross Country magazine*, the best chronicle of the new aviation. One, written by Christophe de Cassan, a hang glider pilot who took up gliding, outlines advantages and disadvantages of both flying disciplines:

Gliding – Advantages

- offers good long distance flight
- flies fast and makes quick transitions (speed vs height)
- classy-looking apparatus – established radio frequencies
- take off and land in the same field
- first big flight with beginner's lessons
- grant possibilities
- structured sites and organisation

Gliding – Disadvantages

- cumbersome and difficult to store (hangar, trailer etc)
- tedious mounting and dismounting
- high cost of apparatus
- high cost of schooling and maintenance (time and money)
- emergency landing constraints
- binding regulations

Hang Gliding – Advantages

- easy to store
- autonomous take-off
- low-cost usage
- reasonable price of equipment and schooling
- possibility of landing in small area (soccer field)
- freedom from regulations
- quick to very quick schooling
- offers sporty flying
- easy practical usage and maintenance
- takes thermals much more easily

Hang Gliding – Disadvantages

- slower speed, and more difficult in transitions
- rigorous classic schooling
- necessitates frequent retrieval assistance (a car/driver)

- costliness and difficulty of reaching launch sites
- no legal radio frequency

One might add since that new methods of towing have been perfected, and hang gliders can set up in any field and be towed up by a winch small enough to leave in a garage, or get towed into the air by microlights, even two at a time! I recently saw a rag-wing microlight, direct descendants of those nasty Rogallos nearly strangled to death by some BGA clubs, towing up a conventional glider! But all that was in the future.

The second article in *Cross Country* was from William Malpas, and seems to be a plea for gliding to recognise the boom in youth in hang gliding. It was first published in a sailplane magazine:

On July 3rd, 1990, after a departure from an airfield in Hobbs, New Mexico, Larry Tudor succeeded in crossing four States and landed at his goal, Elkhart, for a straight-line distance of 487 kms.

You might well ask what is so special about that? After all, 55 years earlier, four German pilots took off from the Wasserkuppe and flew 500 kms, and the best glide angle on their machines was about 20:1. The answer is that Larry Tudor was flying an HP/AT 158, a hang glider with at best a glide angle of about 10:1! It was a world record distance for a hang glider, which this remarkable young man will, no doubt, exceed himself, if he is not beaten to it by another of the many determined young men and women in which their sport abounds. We could do with a few of them moving up the performance scale on to modern plastic gliders. We might learn quite a lot from them. I have noticed, reading their magazines, that they have the will to learn from us. They read books which were originally written with high performance gliders in mind. They have blown the dust off micro-meteorological studies which were made by our own comrades, and adapted them to their own special needs.

All this is leading to the question, why is there no 'entente cordiale' between the older gliding movement and the young branch of the same sport? Perhaps it exists somewhere in the world. If so, let's hear about it.

Objectively, there seems to be only one major problem. We tend, either collectively or individually, to be heavily invested in equipment and real estate whereas hang gliders and paragliders are much more mobile. They don't need club houses and probably don't take kindly to rules, regulations and club politics, and their sport is much more compatible with a young person's pocket. However this seems a petty problem compared with the advantages that a close collaboration might bring to both groups. The first and most obvious result would be a more harmonious use of air space, especially along the face of popular ridges. If we knew more about each other's techniques and practices, we would feel much more confident about close encounters.

For hang glider pilots, access to higher performance machines would be simplified, and the natural progression towards other forms of aviation would follow the same routes as for ambitious glider pilots. It might also help them to shed the public image of an unacceptably high accident rate in the early days. Unfortunately, some of us still believe that to be true, and we should congratulate them on putting their house in order.

These chaps are masters at the exploitation of special micro-climate situations, sometimes in difficult areas where we fear to tread. We can certainly learn from them. If we can persuade them to build on their experience with low-performance machines by moving on to ours, what a rich source of recruitment! If we could only harness a fraction of that great pool of energy, skill and determination, what a boon!

Reflect for a moment on the new 'World Class' gliders which we are shortly to see in vast numbers in our hangars. Who is going to fly them? Probably not the old and bold pilots incurably hooked on glide angles of 45:1 and better. Plot a graph if you are unconvinced. Put age of the pilot on one scale and the glide angle of his machine on the other. Correlation with a straight line should be significant! So who is going to take the first step?

While William Malpas has written a lovely article, I am not sure he has quite grasped the sheer scale of the revolution that is the new aviation. There will always be some cross-over point between hang glider and glider pilots, as there have always been siren singers for rigid wings and three-axis control in hang gliding. But the Rogallo revolution introduced a quite different flying experience over the past twenty years, and it remains the mainstream of our new way of flying. *We are the wing* in a way that a conventional pilot is not. It is not just about performance. Being stuck, baking, under a canopy, cut off from the air, may give a pilot a great many kilometres, but the cost is something many of us do not want to pay.

Ironically, the conflict between gliders and hang gliders was mirrored twelve years later in Britain when paragliders began to crowd ridges. With some Rogallo pilots, there was scorn for the paraglider's performance ('Woossie PGs!'), and they too felt threatened by so many wings in the same air. Originally, gliders doing 80mph felt obstructed by hang gliders doing 30mph. Now hang gliders can do 60mph, and they are obstructed by paragliders doing 20mph. Our solution, though, after pained debate, and learning from the deep wounds inflicted on us by those dinosaur gliding clubs back in the 1970s, was to merge with the paragliders, which are now called class 3 hang gliders. They are yet another part of the extraordinary exploration of the new aviation.

Chapter 7

Competitions – How they Evolved

Sport used to mean hunting, shooting and fishing, an ethical equation where the 'fair play' ethos was developed. Nowadays it is the comparative measurement of physical and mental excellence. We can look at a pilot and say, he is a good pilot, but how good is he? We know that Rich Pfeiffer is a good pilot, but is he better than Keith Nichols? Is Larry Tudor better than John Pendry? Graham Hobson better than Bob Calvert? Manfred Ruhmer better than Tomas Suchanek?

The only way hang gliding is a *sport* is through competition. This is an obvious statement, but in the thirty years since the first Lilienthal meet, there has been a constant whinging about competitions. Critics say they detract from the true spirit of flight, and that we should all fly like the birds do (as if birds never competed with each other).

The amazing developments in equipment, changing wings from steerable parachutes capable of flights of 196ft to sophisticated wings, still clearly Rogallos, which Larry Tudor flew nearly 500km, all came through competition. Pilots demanded better wings to beat their opponents. Manufacturers responded, or they went under. Lots went under, and deserved their fate.

In 1975, the first World Championships at Kössen in Austria gave enormous prominence to spot landings, much as parachutists do. The following year, the competition divided points 50/50, with half going on duration, the time you could stay in the air, and half being awarded for a spot landing. Crucially, if you failed to make the spot, or fell over on it, you got a zero. It was scarcely a test of flying when everything could be lost so easily on a landing … just touching a control bar on the ground constituted a fall-over.

The wings we used then could just about be called wings. We had recently graduated from seated harnesses that were barely more than a short plastic plank, like a child's swing, with two ropes leading via a spreader bar to a carabiner; the pilot had a strap across his lap and under the plank.

The Wasp harness had two leg straps rather than a seat. It was known as the nutcracker, and other pilots were kind to you if you spoke in a squeaky voice for a while after landing. We had helmets but no instruments or parachute.

Skilled pilots flew prone, but no one was quite sure what the best type of harness was. In some, with knee-hangers, it was disconcerting to be picked up by the knees, like having your legs swept away and forced into the prone position. We graduated on to aprons, with stirrups to hold your feet after take-off.

Wasp made me a special harness during this period, when I wanted to have a go at the duration record. In theory, the harness would allow me to fly seated, prone on my front, and supine on my back, and be able to change all these positions in the air. On paper it looked good, and in factory tests, but I tried it first off the 600ft southern end of the Long Mynd one quiet evening. What was wrong was that I did not have a strap to attach me to the seat during those fraught moments when I was committing aviation, and I found myself held up by the harness, but only because bits were caught between my legs, and in an exposed vertical position where the control bar was above my head. In this manner I descended 600ft, barely able to steer and in great discomfort. I was lucky I hit a big field when I came to the ground and I lost no more than a broken upright. At that time I was not yet the father of a daughter, and I could quite easily have missed the chance.

There was, naturally, a revolt against the Kössen values. In Britain it was started by Ken Messenger, by now an established manufacturer. In a brave gesture, because he was risking the reputation of his own gliders with no guarantee he would win, Ken invited other manufacturers to nominate a team of three to fly in a manufacturer's competition called The Birdman (in fact his wings came fifth of eight). It took place in March 1976, and revolutionised our thinking about competitions, as Tony Fuell explained at the time:

> If ever an event took off with all the omens against it, this one did. When Ken Messenger issued his challenge to other manufacturers to come and put their latest machinery on trial, and fly it against his own new machines, he received a fairly lukewarm reception. Several manufacturers didn't show, and those of us who had experience of organising events in the past felt that there was every likelihood that either the organisation would fall down completely or the thing would come to pieces in an orgy of bitching and mutual recriminations. Against this background, it was very pleasant to see the whole event run

like a Swiss watch, and experience the helpful, friendly and good-humoured attitude of everyone there.

The secret of the success of the event lay in three things. Firstly, the number of competitors was so small that briefings, performing the task and scoring was made very easy for the controllers. This gave a good deal of flexibility, and scope; if the weather went wrong on a particular task, it was easy to up sticks and go somewhere else.

Second, the organisers pulled a very shrewd move in getting BHGA Secretary Chris Corston, and pioneer Nick Regan, to act as judges/taskmasters/scorers. Both are very experienced and completely impartial. Chris is a conscientious, hard-working personality who shines as a mediator in trouble. Nick has a mischievous streak in him which delights in getting people into situations bordering on the impossible – he arranged most of the landing areas!

Thirdly, the fact that all the pilots and machines were extremely good allowed the use of sites and a choice of tasks which would be impossible for the average event. I never realised the vast gulf which is beginning to open up between the people who fly every day for a living, and even the best of the weekend aviators. To see Brian Wood vanish behind a line of trees in a screaming banked turn, whistle through a gap in the trees still banked, immediately bank the other way less than 30 feet high, pop out of prone, skim the grass for 20 feet and come to a perfect landing within the area that even other experts were having trouble with; all you can do is scratch your head and think – 'Gee whiz!'

And this was the other secret – there was nothing very difficult to do in the actual scoring. For example, when we flew the Blorange near Abergavenny on the second day, the landing area was a fair-sized field. But to get there you had to do a cross-wind 20 mph take-off at 1,500 feet, out of sight of the landing area, fly around the end of the mountain, do a 2-mile downwind leg avoiding a housing estate, cope with huge thermals, windshear turbulence and general in-flight nastiness, eventually make a 180 degree turn and lose height into the designated field which had a row of houses causing rotor upwind of it.

But judging was easy. You either made the field, or you didn't. Scoring was an all-or-nothing business; 100 if you made it into the field, nothing if you didn't. Yesterday there were impossible tasks, today's are bad, tomorrow may be worse. No wonder the pilots were feeling the strain a bit. Nevertheless, the tasks were obviously set at exactly the right level of difficulty, as the team prize result was in doubt right up to the very last flight of the competition.

Just a brief description of this task might make you think a bit. Picture the site at Tredegar – a good soaring slope, a wind blowing variously at 14–25 mph. A road at the top, gradually descending the contours to a junction on a slight slope about half a mile away. The task – take off, get down to the road junction, turn, penetrate back upwind and come in for a top-landing. Simple, yes? Just try it. Oh, and by the way, you've got six minutes to do it. And as you come in for a top-landing in difficult conditions, you've got two sticks, six feet apart with a tape stretched between them, at a height of 3 feet. Just break that with your feet, that's all.

Robin Haynes, flying his new model Wasp with what has to be the most beautiful sail yet seen in England, made a valiant try. After nearly going upside down at one point, he eventually made it to the top-landing and missed the tape by about six feet. So very sad, as if he had made it, it would have been a Wasp–Hiway tie requiring a further fly-off. All in all a very nice experience all around, and thanks a lot to Ken for making it happen.

At the BHGA Nationals later that year, only one of the pilots who featured in The Birdman – Tony Beresford – placed high enough to be selected to go to the World Championships. Great pilots like Brian Wood, Bob Calvert and Graham Hobson, all Birdman competitors, failed to get selected, while pilots of much less ability, such as Bob Wiseley, deemed national champion, and myself, second in the Nationals, made it through. It was obvious the Nationals were not a significant test, like many tests that were being run then. I did not see myself as the second best pilot in the country, nor Wisely the best, even though we both scored maximums in the final. So I asked to be nominated for, and became, Chairman of the Competitions Committee, to change things. This had always been considered a nest of thorns.

I immediately ran an extra competition for top pilots from the Nationals, with an invitation to Calvert and Wood to compete, in the hope we could find an intellectual reason to select them. They did not score well enough on Kössen's silly rules, but I did badly enough (not deliberately) to be able to drop myself and send better pilots like Keith Cockroft. Bob Wisely went to Kössen, sprained his knee on the third flight and retired hurt, though he made an amazing recovery at the dance at the end of the competition. He never competed at national level again. Our best pilot in the most hotly contested class 2, high-performance Rogallos, was Lester Cruise, in twenty-first place, in a competition won by a New Zealander, where a Canadian was second and an Australian, Bill Moyes's son Steve, was third. Johnny Carr placed tenth in the rigid-wing class, while Tony Beresford was sixth on a 'bog-rog'. Brutally, Britain came nowhere.

At the British Open Championships in Mere in Wiltshire that August, Bill Moyes turned up with his Australian circus, and his pilots were a dominant group in distance flying and competition. As always, Bill was kind to us British, but only because he walked off with most of the prizes. We ran tasks where pilots slalomed around a course like skiers, and landed on a spot. Five tasks were completed despite rain and fog, to general applause, but the rigid-wing class 3 turned out to be absurd; supposed to be about moveable control surfaces, the first five places were taken by Australians who used their best Rogallos with bits of string tied to trailing edges of the wings, allegedly to control the wing. Technically, they had moveable control surfaces, but the tasks, for which I was responsible, were naive.

The main competition was in class 2, high-performance Rogallos, as we were all losing interest in class 1 bog-rogs. It turned out to be a superb battle between Steve Moyes and Brian Wood … and Wood won! So we had the pilots, what we needed was the competition. I was also absolutely hacked off with different classes of hang gliders, and determined not to bother about them much again. We had to concentrate on where everyone wanted to go and get the best weight-shift machines we could.

Moyes' visit and the latest changes to wings caused all British manufacturers to go back to the drawing board. The turmoil, as I said earlier, produced new machines like the Moonraker (which I flew despite Alvin's death on one); the Hiway Scorpion, and Skyhook Sunspot. All competition pilots now flew prone, and the first instruments were appearing on control bars, starting with the essential vario, which told us how fast we were climbing or sinking. Up high, you just cannot tell with the naked eye.

In driving forward competitions, there is one influence I must explain; it is difficult to understand what happened without knowing about it. Back in 1969 I was one of six journalists expelled that year from South Africa, possibly (I was never told) for writing pieces for foreign newspapers that mocked the workings of the racist political system *Apartheid*. The South

African Special Branch came around the evening that I and my fiancée, Fiona Campbell, were writing our wedding invitations. It is now considered a good thing to have happened to me, but at the time, matters were fraught; Fiona's mother was South African and she was due to become my mother-in-law! You can imagine how Mrs Campbell felt.

But I was not a doctrinaire politician. I just didn't like racism. I agreed with Peter Hain's campaign against sporting ties with South Africa, and said so when I heard from BHGA chairman Martin Hunt that the 1977 World Championships were due to be held there. 'Don't whinge,' said a BHGA council member at the time, a former RAF wing commander called Reggie Spooner, 'if you feel strongly, get on [the] Council.' So I did. I took over competitions because they were manifestly unfair, but sooner or later there was going to be a row about sending a team to South Africa, and I would be in the middle.

Among those I was going to be at loggerheads with was the British aviation establishment itself, where the BGA in particular did not want to see the intrusion of 'politics' into sport. Their view was that Apartheid was a domestic problem for South Africa, and should have no effect on whether or not we competed against them. BHGA p resident Ann Welch, a former BGA luminary, felt this strongly (as she also felt that gliding and hang gliding should *not* be an Olympic sport, because of the racial and other politics in the Olympics).

The 1977 World Championships in South Africa were cancelled. One factor was a letter I published, with the agreement of BHGA chairman Martin Hunt, putting the case *against* going, while he was supposed to put the case *for* going. We would then have a debate, and go to a vote.

The resolution not to go to South Africa passed 5-2, despite my lack of taste. I made more enemies. We did not offer an alternative competition, being too busy with the League. It was not an issue that ever went away, and came back to haunt me more than once.

Like most pilots, I wanted to fly. I did not want to talk politics. But if we were not to go to South Africa, what other goodies could I offer instead? I felt that choosing a champion on one competition was so likely to go wrong that a League was necessary, where a pilot could choose the best five of six competitions as his score, each competition worth 500 points. I proposed the idea, and collected together the best pilots in the country to become my competitions committee (and cover my back if, as happened, things went wrong). The first committee, destined to become the most powerful and active in the BHGA, included Johnny Carr, Brian Wood, Alvin Russell, Ken Messenger and Len Gabriels. We were soon joined by the BHGA treasurer himself, Derek Evans, the man who became my bank manager, colleague and successor. My committee was made up of almost all active competition pilots, and I wanted them with me to draft rules.

Who wanted to fly in the League? I asked for volunteers; fifty-four pilots applied, and on the grounds that all previous competitions had been poor so we had no way of judging who was good or bad, we took them all. Pilots paid £21 each, so I had a £1,100 budget to run it in 1977. I was one of the flyers, which meant that when we came to choose death-defying tasks, as we did, pilots were comforted by knowing I had to fly them as well.

By comparison to modern competitions, we were so amateur. Ken Messenger, in deference to his experience with the 1976 Birdman competition, organised the first League competition in South Wales. We had five tasks that, for the time, was very good. The flying was superb, but I had not thought through the scoring, which became a headache. It caused a major clash when five pilots from the Southern Club wanted to talk about the scoring while I was running a competitions meeting. By some accounts, they 'crashed' into the meeting. Ken Messenger took great offence, and said the next day he wanted them banned from the League. The implicit threat was that he would call an end to his competition there and then, and the League would die before it had lived three days. I went to a committee meeting, got a unanimous vote to back Ken, and the case became a *cause celebre*. The banned pilots were known as the Abergavenny Six (Graham Slater, Chris Johnson, Ray Sigrist, Dale Clothier, Peter Day; the sixth was Tony Fuell, who had written so approvingly of Ken's 1976 competition, but asked to be banned in sympathy).

I think, on reflection, the clash was between two cultures, the cheerfully aggressive, competitive, egalitarian values of the Southern Club (where Tony Fuell was chairman), versus the rather more genteel atmosphere surrounding Ken's West Country clubs. After a gigantic row involving the BHGA council and an AGM, the pilots were reinstated, but lost the scores they were not able to make through being banned on the final day. This was despite Tony Fuell's brilliant and passionate defence. I kept the competitions committee together, which was my major aim. Ken had second thoughts and never really recovered his position in competition hang gliding. At least one of the banned pilots, Graham Slater, went on to become among the best in the world, and a competitions committee member. All suffered a major injustice. I bore a large responsibility for that injustice. I am sorry that it happened, but I also do not think at the time I could have done anything else. The League survived, as everyone wanted it to, including the Abergavenny Six.

By the end of the year we had run the first open-distance XC task, over the back in free air, won by Calvert. And we had a system where those acknowledged as the best pilots in the country were actually found to be so, confirmed by the League's scores. Brian Wood won, Johnny Carr was second, Bob Calvert third, then Graham Slater, Bob England, Graham Hobson, Tony Beresford, Lester Cruise and Mick Evans. No one questioned these rankings, as I had questioned my own ranking as so-called second best in the country the previous year. We dropped the bottom 25 per cent of pilots, which included Paul Maritos, who wrote so beautifully about flying from Snowdon with Hobson.

We also established some principles, that *we*, the competitions committee, were in charge of competitions. The BHGA council tried to impose a made-up score for the Abergavenny Six, which we rejected absolutely. Later that summer, I made the case that we would select teams to be sent to overseas competitions, and the BHGA council would endorse our selection but not be involved in it. If the council had no confidence in our decisions, then we would resign. As selecting teams was one of the perks of being a council member, this was another fraught moment, but the case went through when we got down to the details ('Tell me Bob Calvert's strengths and weaknesses!'). The principle for which we fought turned out to be the most important in competition hang gliding, and had a crucial role in our success later. At the time I was viewed, once more, as just bloody-minded.

We decided to make one of the 1977 League competitions the Scottish Championships, held at Minto Hill south of Edinburgh, though weather and a culture clash with Scottish pilots meant we dropped the idea before the competition began. Nevertheless, many League pilots went to the Minto Hill competition, sponsored by Glen Grant whisky. Scottish pilots were used to seeing perhaps four hang gliders on a hill, after which it became 'crowded'. They had a whistle system to bring down the extra wings. Seeing thirty hang gliders in the air as the League 'animals' soared around caused consternation and frenzied whistle-blowing.

It rained and rained on Minto Hill. Every day we slogged up the hill carrying our gliders, and then flew around slaloms and landed on spots and other Mickey Mouse tasks that were all we really knew then. But then the word went around that Bettina Gray was on the hill, that she had come over from California to take photographs! We were all thrilled, but we did not at first believe it. For us, it was like David Bailey being there. Bettina was one of the official photographers for the fabulous *Hang Gliding* magazine in the US, and she was going to photograph us! We were going to talk to her, and more importantly, she was going to talk back. She could tell us about American flying! Bettina had been at the 1971 first Lilienthal meet, and her son, Bill Liscomb, was one of the original fourteen young men who flew there.

Her first words when I met her were, 'Oh I'm so glad to be here. Last time I was photographing hang gliding I spent most of the time dodging rattlesnakes!' She was small, blonde, bright, wrapped up against the rain with cameras slung across her chest, and she was absolutely full of life. In her youth she had been a beautiful Hollywood actress and married three times, once into the fabulously wealthy Bancroft family, which owned the Dow Jones Index and the *Wall Street Journal.* We were used to rain and hassles and walking hills bent under our gliders, but she never complained at the physical discomfort.

Bettina said later that she went back to America and bubbled over with enthusiasm about British flying. She told them we had some brilliant flyers like Calvert and Wood and Carr. 'Yeah, yeah', was the general reaction to the news, 'ho! ho! ho!' Miffed at having her opinions rubbished and counting for so little, Bettina returned for the 1977 British Open, which was the last such competition Bill Moyes came to. Plagued, as ever, by the weather, it came down to the last day, with responsibilities to the sponsors, Long John whisky, and BBC TV's *Grandstand.* I had to get 700 flights off in a day, more than Heathrow Airport, and scored, including a distance knockout, duration/spot, and slalom/spot. Bill Moyes said he would have to think for a long time before coming to Britain to take part in such competitions again, though his boys again took the top three places (I was fifth, and I could have won if I hadn't cartwheeled across the landing spot after a successful slalom). Moyes was as good as his word, and never again visited the League competitions, so I was not to see him again until the 1979 American Cup, when we had changed beyond any of his expectations.

Again, Bettina was a big hit with the pilots, and she remained impressed with the flying despite the Mickey Mouse tasks. On one of the non-flying days she gave me tea, and phoned Tracy Knauss, publisher of the other big US hang gliding publication, *Glider Rider.* Tracy worked out of Chattanooga, Tennessee, on the east coast of the US, and his magazine was printed in newspaper format.

Because of Bettina's introduction, I got into the habit of calling Tracy from time to time, looking for information on American flying. When the first year's League was over, I wanted to send British pilots abroad to see how good they were. I thought they were good, but was I right? The European Championships were to be held in 1978, and we were tickling money out of the Sports Council for a programme of foreign competitions. What competition was there in the US? I asked Tracy during one phone call, where should we send British pilots? Should it be the US Nationals, the US Open or the US Masters of Hang Gliding? And could we get an invitation to these awesome events? I thought that sending an official team to the US would be good publicity, for the Americans as well as us.

Tracy had just bought himself a hang gliding site on Lookout Mountain, Tennessee, where one of the most famous and bloody battles of the American Civil War had taken place in the 1860s. He had two partners, the legendary Bill Bennett, owner of Delta Wing Kites, and Larry Newman, owner of Electra-Flyer, a hang glider manufacturer; Larry was the only survivor of the three-man team that first flew a balloon across the Atlantic.

'I could put you on a competition,' said Tracy, and in the next ten minutes we agreed on a team contest, based on yachting's America's Cup. That is what we called our competition at first, until threatened with legal action by the New York Yacht Club, which still had the original trophy nailed to its sideboard. We then settled on the American Cup.

I knew quite a lot about the yachting race, and this influenced the challenge; how a yacht from New York called *America* had sailed across the Atlantic, and in 1851 won a 100-guinea cup in races in the Solent and the Isle of Wight. How *America* had sailed back across the Atlantic with the cup, and said, in effect, come and take it from us. There had been numerous British challenges for the America's Cup, at the cost of millions of pounds, which had all failed. Now every nation that could afford to was having a go, and it was still in America's grasp (where it would remain until the Australian Alan Bond won it in 1983).

Tracy Knauss and I agreed a team competition, eight flyers per nation, and settled later on four teams, from the US, Canada, Japan and Britain. We closed the door then, because we thought that was enough. Canada had issued a challenge as soon as they heard about the American Cup, and Japan was included, I think, for commercial reasons. We knew Canadian hang gliding was strong, but Japan at that time had no form at all. In any case it was about us and the Americans.

We took a conscious decision to imitate history, with the British having the original role of the yacht, *America*, so it was all in reverse. We agreed to go to the US, to fly their hills, in tasks they devised, with their officials ... and beat them (or try to). Tracy and I struck a side-bet of $5 each, partly for publicity, but partly to emulate two other famous British yachtsmen, 'Blondie' Hasler, leader of the wartime 'Cockleshell Heroes', and Francis Chichester, later Sir Francis, who raced each other single-handed in yachts across the Atlantic in 1960 to settle a half-crown bet ($5 took account of inflation). I had my $5 bill encased in a plastic block.

The unique part of the competition was that it was for teams, not individuals, so while it would be nice to have the top-scoring pilot, this competition was to test a country's pilots in depth. Pilot number 8 would count as much as pilot number 1. The competition would, suggested Tracy, take place in October 1978, at his site in Tennessee; he would be responsible for raising the $5,000 first prize for the winner. Winner takes all inevitably means loser takes nothing.

The risk to us, in public ridicule, was considerable, but at the time I seem not to have considered it. I really knew nothing about American flying, except that when any US flyer turned up in England, we always put them among the top three seeds. I wanted to tackle America head-on. So far as I could judge, we had some brilliant pilots in Britain. Why should they not be the equal of the Americans? You can imagine the reaction of the BHGA competitions committee when I broke the news. They were half-thrilled at the size of the challenge, but the other half was appalled at the beating we were going to get. Most people, not only in Britain but also in other countries, thought we were going to get creamed. Paradoxically, my competitions committee then decided to go for broke, led by a normally cautious member, John Hudson, who was intensely patriotic and ran the biggest glider supply shop in the country as well as being a League pilot.

'Let's do it on British kites!' he proposed.

In the 1977 League, 25 per cent of the gliders used had been made overseas, in either America or Australia. This proportion dropped to 20 per cent in 1978. Our 1977 champion, Brian Wood, the man who taught me to fly, won on an Australian Moyes Maxi, and he continued to fly a Moyes wing in 1978. If Hudson's proposal went through, strongly supported by an ex-Abergavenny Six member, Chris Johnson, also on the committee, Wood could only be selected if he moved on to a British glider. The debate was intense and passionate in an upstairs room in the Black Bull Cafe in Hawes, Wensleydale, where tea was served by 18-year-old Pat Kirkbride during a rained off League day. It came down to this; if we were going to be thrashed, let us be thrashed on British equipment and match it up against American hang gliders. But if we could win, what a boost that would be for British hang gliding! There would, we thought, be no excuses. The vote went 6-3 for John Hudson's proposal, and we were committed.

Throughout the 1978 season I was asked continuously (by Hudson more than most) if I could water down the terms of the challenge so we did not look such fools at losing. I could not see a way to do it. We received news from America from time to time, pledges of sponsorship to make the competition work, and Tracy's magazine set about making it the most prestigious international competition of them all. We heard the American team (including the reserve) was to be selected from the first three pilots at the US Nationals, US Open, and US Masters of Hang Gliding, the three competitions that we had looked at wistfully from afar and, in moments of delirium, dreamed we could compete in.

Meanwhile, the League was forcing changes in British kite design. Johnny Carr and designer Miles Handley used a freezing day in Wales, between tasks, to lay out the design for a radical machine, the Gryphon III, later manufactured under licence by Waspair. This wing had no cross-boom, normally a draggy item in hang gliding, and was later buried inside double-surface wings. Instead, Miles extended the keel forward, and held the leading edges apart by a wire around the extended boom. A lot of League pilots flew the Gryphon III.

Hiway Scorpions gave way to Superscorpions, perhaps the single most successful British hang glider, a clone of the Moyes Maxi that Bill had brought to the 1977 Mere Open. Birdman came out with the Moonraker 78, Skyhook produced the Safari, and Paul Maritos went into production with his Vector. We all had varios, altimeters and parachutes now; some even carried air maps to avoid restricted air space on cross-countries.

The 1978 European Championships were quite a success. We sent a strong team, including six of the ten-man squad who went later to Tennessee. A great French pilot, Gérard Thevenot, won the main class 2, but Bob England placed second, and Johnny Carr claimed fourth place. In class 2, Mick Evans came second. Better than sixth and tenth two years earlier, but still, not a win.

Without going to the membership for money (too many strings), and through judicious use of Sports Council funds, plus the luck of landing a sponsor for the League final – Atlas Express – we had money to back our 1978 teams, first to the Europeans in Kössen, and then to go to Tennessee.

When it came to selecting for the American Cup, the most painful decision was not to pick Brian Wood. He deserved selection, because he came fourth at the end of the year, but he did not think we were serious about sending pilots on British wings and did not want to leave his Moyes wing behind. By the time he reluctantly agreed to fly a British wing, we had the bit between our teeth, had already made our selection; he was automatically excluded. We could not go back and de-select one of them when Brian, too late, changed his mind. We also failed to select the pilot who came seventh that year, Geoff Snape, but I cannot remember why.

Our squad of ten, from which we would choose eight in Tennessee, was Keith Reynolds (1978 British champion in his first year in the League!), Bob Calvert, Robert Bailey, John and Jeremy Fack, Graham Slater, Bob England, Graham Hobson, Mick Evans and Mick Maher.

Derek Evans went as manager, Keith Cockroft as coach, and I went as non-flying captain, as in eventing, a position we later gave to an actual competition flyer. John Hudson organised a large contingent of British pilots, including future BHGA chairman Noel Whittall, to fly there, cheer us on and wave the flag. Hudson had been in line to be one of the team managers, but said (wrongly) he did not feel he was up to the job and he would pay his own way. Thirty-nine of us arrived in Chattanooga. We had flown together throughout the year, knew each other well, and were united in wanting more than anything else, to win.

We played to Tracy Knauss's publicity game right from the start, emphasising our Britishness, quite willing to be cast as historical villains. Derek Evans had spent some money on clever details. All our T-shirts had the slogan 'The British are Coming!' on the back, an echo of the alleged cry by Paul Revere back in 1776 arousing Americans to rebel against King George III (in fact, Revere shouted 'The Regulars are Coming!' because, of course, they were all British back then, including the rebels). We stuck well-produced notices on our van, such as 'UK pilots stay up longer!' We all had uniformed flying suits, jackets and badges. We looked like a team.

The British arrived in Chattanooga before anyone else, took the book of rules hot off the presses, and rushed off to see the sites. All the squad rigged their gliders and flew Lookout Mountain, soared it for a while, then landed in the official landing area. We went through the rules quickly, then slowly, then word by word, until everyone knew what was expected of them. And wherever the wind was on a site, we flew, from not long after dawn in those autumn days until close to dusk. I think, to onlookers, we were rushing everywhere and talking all the time, trying to understand the rules and sites, and share our knowledge. Perhaps it was me talking all the time.

Tasks were simple, and designed for safety and spectator appeal. If it was marginally soarable, a pilot flew straight through the lift band off a 1,000ft hill and raced to a gate in the landing field 1 mile away, with 360s right and left, alternatively, twice. Once through the gate, he made a figure-of-eight, and then had all the time in the world to land on a 400ft target. If it was not soarable, pilots had to stay in the air as long as possible, timed through the gate, and land on the target (if it was really soarable, there was a 20-mile race to Lookout Point and back, but it was never called). The format was 1-on-4, one pilot from each nation, and a strict time limit between the first and last pilots in a heat to ensure they had roughly the same conditions. The speed run tested pure glider speed, but the 360s and figure-of-eight were added to ensure the kite could handle turbulence, and a pilot's nerve was tested in how much height he was prepared to lose to get speed and still make the gate and landing area. As for the duration task, out-sinking opponents is a classical hang gliding game.

Our pilots were instructed not to worry about the spot landing, so long as they landed safely on their feet in the landing area. We concentrated on beating the others in the air before going through the gate. Landing in the crowd cost 100 points, and on one day gave us a near heart failure as Mick Evans floated over the landing area and headed for the spectators, but managed to land, just, short, by stuffing the nose of his aircraft into the ground.

While we were running up and down hills and reading our rules, the Canadians arrived and showed us how brilliant they were at flying. They disappeared into the sky in soaring conditions, cruised for miles in thermals, and rather looked down their noses at our activity. This was, they then told the media, a two-nation competition; *they* were the other nation, so pay less attention to the British, please. The Japanese turned up two days before the meeting, absolutely jet-lagged, and had barely rigged their gliders when the competition began.

The American team arrived in ones and twos, looking just like their photographs. All seemed to have been cloned in California, with beach boy clothing and large, gas-guzzling estate cars with their wings on top. Their names still resonate down the years, Rich Grigsby, Sean Dever, Dennis Pagen, Michael Jones, Rodríguez, Huss, Cocker, Pollack, flyers who had creamed the best in the US and were set to cream us. The great Keith Nichols, the famous bearded vagabond king of hang gliding who toured America in his large combi, kites for sale on his roof, Kerouac in his bookshelf, a case of French wine under the available double bed, and a lady in every city, turned up as coach. My sister-in-law Jeanie immediately fell for him. The Americans had nominated Tom Peghiny, the man so awesome Johnny Carr couldn't speak to him in 1975 (just three years earlier) as a wind dummy, merely to test conditions! They were so laid-back and confident. We eyed them warily and wondered what to do about that confidence.

Every evening the British team met in the Chattanooga Choo-Choo hotel, official centre of the competition where every team had rooms, and discussed tactics. Two emerged. Derek, a keen golfer, told us about Jack Nicklaus's strategy in a four-round game. 'He plays the first three rounds very carefully, not taking any risks, going for the percentages,' said Derek.

'Then, if he's in a position to win, he goes balls-out on the last round.' We decided that is what we would do. Let them make mistakes. We would go for percentage hang gliding, play safe and take no risks at all.

The second piece of advice was mine. 'I don't care what you do, just do it better than them. When they come down for breakfast, I want us to have finished ours and be on the hill. When they get to the hill, we're in the air. If they meet us in the air, get on top of them and stay there. Challenge them to races, and beat them even in free flying. Especially in free flying. When they come back to the hotel, we should still be flying. In the evenings I want them to see you in every fashionable bar they enter, a woman on each arm and the beers lined up. I want them to go to bed and see you still partying, and when they come down next morning you're back on the hill, flying or ready to fly.'

Hang gliding competitions nowadays demand a very high level of physical fitness and stamina. But in 1978, even with four flights a day, it was just like sprinting. What gave the American Cup its unique flavour, especially in the Tennessee competitions, was not the quality of the flying but the wild partying that went on.

Eventually, the Americans became concerned about our aggression. Bettina Gray, official hostess to the American Cup, was telling them (when they finally listened) that we were serious and some of us could fly. Biff Huss, a US Navy pilot as well as a top US team hang glider pilot, took to flying with us when he could. I remember a day on Crystal, considered a tiny site in the US but at 800ft, pretty high to us, where we were practising duration/spots. Keith Reynolds had been particularly keen on pursuing my tactical advice the previous night, and one could almost cut his hangover with a knife. We rigged his wing for him, put him in his harness, and pointed the way to take-off. Biff suggested a competition, longest in the air then closest to a tyre, which made a target. Keith sleepily agreed, and they both ran off.

There was little to stay up on, puffs of wind, heat off some rock faces, bubbles here and there. It was the most delicate and skilful of flying, like ballet, trying to maintain height on virtually nothing. For a while it was even, but eventually Biff was driven down, fighting all the way, until he broke off and headed for the spot. It was a good landing, just 3ft away, a stand-up. We were prepared to concede him the spot so long as Keith won the duration, because we were not sure Keith *could* stand up. But then, minutes later, Keith came in on his Gryphon, not a spot-landing machine, and planted both boots actually inside the car tyre! He held his position to establish a landing, then slowly collapsed. We carried him off – a bit ostentatiously – laid him out to sleep, and de-rigged for him. Biff gritted his teeth.

We dropped John Fack from the squad (half blinded by a twig in his eye on practice), and Bob England, after assessing all the tests we ran on Lookout Mountain, in choosing our final team of eight.

Of the competition itself, there was a lot of razzmatazz, bands playing, flags, an excited commentator who knew Bill Moyes and went by the name of 'Barefoot Stew' Macdonald. He turned up at the official dinner in a splendid dinner jacket, bow tie and bare feet. Meet officials were confused about the rules, and marked duration from take-off to landing, rather than through the gate, so at the end of the first day it looked like the Americans were ahead, the Canadians second and us third. As we left the landing field they played that song, '1814', which went, 'Oh we fired our guns and the British kept a'coming, although there wasn't nigh as many as there were a while ago, we fired once more and they began a'running, down the Mississippi to the Gulf of Mexico ...' It was a celebration of the stand-off war between Britain and the US that started in 1812, and the only time we heard that tune on the trip.

That night, having discussed the rules with the organisers, and agreed with Keith Nichols the actual timings from take-off to gate, the official scores were adjusted to reflect the rules and we found ourselves lying first, with Canada second and the US third. The Americans won the second round, we won the third, they the fourth, and then we beat them over the next five rounds. The Canadians, in shock, lay third after seven rounds, and began a storming comeback from there for the last two.

When the smoke cleared, British pilots were in six of the top seven places. Graham Slater had won eight of his nine heats, and was second in one. Keith Reynolds had won seven heats, with a second and a third. Then it went Hobson (GB), Bailey (GB), Pagen (US), Calvert (GB), Evans (GB), Chernoff (Can), with the great Rich Grigsby (US) in ninth place. Micky Maher placed twelfth, and Jerome Fack twentieth. In layman's terms, we had beaten the USA seven rounds to two, a victory so complete that I think it was beyond comprehension; that is, one could not get one's mind around it. Many Americans who were not there managed to convince themselves we had been lucky.

Graham Slater dominated the competition, but missed out on the Francis Rogallo Trophy, actually presented by the great man himself to the best pilot at the meet. Instead of giving it on scores, the organisers went to a vote, so popularity counted. No one knew who the British were anyway, especially the Japanese – who were otherwise very courageous, despite being hammered every flight – so it went to the most well-known pilot, Rich Grigsby. Rich, one of nature's gentlemen, looked suitably embarrassed.

In Europe, the victory was seen as a *watershed*, to use the words in the editorial in France's *Vol Libre*. The American myth of invincibility was shattered. We should have been absolutely trounced for our cheek. Instead, we won convincingly. One American commentator was more thoughtful in his assessment of what happened that October in Tennessee:

The Grand Delusion – by Michael Jones

There is a curious attitude in the United States that tends to label nationalistic feelings as being naive and unsophisticated. Perhaps as a result of the growing corporate control of American politics, or just post-Watergate fallout. Whatever the case, being an American just ain't what it used to be. Or, at least that's what some people would have you believe.

And, being an American hang glider pilot certainly ain't what it used to be either. The British proved that at the first American Cup and now we have to live with that reality.

We are no longer the undisputed leader in hang gliding. Not in pilot skills. Not in glider design. Not in competitions.

Until the American Cup, world competitions could easily be pooh-poohed by critics who felt the tasks were outdated and the competition unrepresentative of modern trends in hang gliding. And, indeed, these observations were absolutely correct … until now.

The international team competition at Lookout Mountain for the American Cup changed that and opened the eyes of all who were present to the phenomenal abilities of the British.

It also opened a lot of eyes to the organisation of their competitive system and team participation in international events. With the British, national pride has a lot to do with their success, as does a precise, well-run organisation.

They look like a team. They act like a team. They think like a team, and it pays off.

American pilots, however, love the 'laid back' image and go to great lengths to prove to the rest of the world that they are individuals. Basically, this is all well and good since our country supposedly functions on the concept of the citizen as an individual.

But functioning as individuals in a team effort just doesn't cut it. Unfortunately, these attitudes may not be something we necessarily agree with, but are an outgrowth of the certain non-competitive nature of our sport. The members of any American hang gliding team cannot be held responsible – there are just too many negative factors to overcome.

As competitors on a world scale, Americans are hopelessly unprepared for winning. As a member of the World Team to the European Championships, it was a demoralising realisation that we, as representatives of the country that has for years been the driving force in hang gliding, are the least capable of capturing a world title.

Why? The answer comes in two words – attitude and organisation. First of all it is difficult to take anyone seriously when you show up at a world meet looking like refugees. Not so much that uniforms will make the difference in flying ability, but it is disheartening to think that no one back home cared enough to make sure that the United States was represented abroad in the best possible light. Thankfully, we at least had uniforms at the American Cup.

Nationalism and patriotism are feelings not often put to the test until you're competing in a foreign country. Suddenly, you want everyone to know that you're an American. In Kössen, for lack of anything else that physically typified us as team members, we were forced to buy coloured tape in order to have the letters USA on our helmets. It was obvious that cultivating team spirit at the last minute was, quite literally, a losing proposition.

It was also apparent at the American Cup that the winning attitude of the British was a direct result of their organised approach to competition. The team arrived together, practiced together, and received tremendous support from an entourage of formidable proportions. Scores were recorded and double-checked. Radio communications kept team pilots informed of the prevailing conditions over the course.

One of the English pilots, Mick Maher, made an interesting observation when he noted that the British, at one time, also had a very casual attitude towards competition until they realised that the only way to win was through careful planning and organisation.

144

The British League competitions have seasoned the English pilots well and have provided them with an opportunity to hone their competitive skills. In doing so, these pilots have become a study in consistency, gaining the competitive experience necessary to keep from beating themselves.

Beyond that, there is a very obvious camaraderie and support that exists within the team framework. They are used to pulling together as a team and it shows.

If it had not been for Keith Nichols, who donated his time as manager of the USA American Cup Team, the final score might have been even more humiliating. Keith managed to borrow several CB radios to help negate the British advantage, kept careful score, and brainstormed during several much-needed strategy sessions.

Compared to the well-planned British, Keith's eleventh-hour efforts were just too little, too late. But it was apparent that his leadership made an important difference.

The point is that in order to keep from embarrassing ourselves in international competition and to restore our number one position in the hang gliding world, we, as Americans, must develop a supportive attitude towards our national teams. Whether this is the result of efforts by individual pilots, or action of the USHGA, the outcome will be a positive step for the sport.

The loss of the American Cup has put the American hang gliding world on its ear. The grand delusion is over. Perhaps we will finally realise that it takes more than just saying we are the best pilots – because now we have to prove it.

The Americans were very generous in defeat. Outside the League, there was amazement within the British hang gliding community. We might have had a better public image, skilfully exploited, but unfortunately I spoiled it all by plummeting out of the sky from 250ft on a powered hang glider two weeks after our return, right in front of BBC *Nationwide*'s TV cameras. By any measure I should have been killed; by the fall, or by being hit by bits of the glider, engine or propeller that fell with me. But I plummeted into a just-ploughed field, it had rained the night before, and, anyway, I didn't die. Parts of me were broken, but not seriously, and other bits needed sewing up. I was out of hospital in three days, in time for the annual Royal Aero Club reception, the first to which I had been invited. I turned up with the right side of my face and body blackened by bruising, stitches under my chin, right arm in a sling, and left wrist in plaster.

'Your Highness,' said our host, bringing Prince Charles over to see the British team, 'may I introduce you to the British hang gliding team captain ...' Prince Charles said hang gliding was the only flying sport he hadn't tried. I was hardly an advertisement.

I thought, 'If your mum saw me, she wouldn't let you near a hang gliding wing.'

You can see 'The Fall', captured by BBC TV on film, as part of a marketing video when, with Keith Reynolds – placed second at the 1978 First American Cup – I set off to try and fly a microlight – a powered hang glider – around the world in eighty days in 1998, twenty years after it happened to me. (http://www.youtube.com/watch?v=06KgKh9PwDU).

The Sports Council was pleased with our success, and we found access to other sources of money to back our teams, though no commercial sponsorship for another two years. We sent teams again to the 1979 Worlds; Johnny Carr came second in class 2 and was a favourite with French commentators as 'Jean Icare'. Josef Guggenmos of Germany, 40 years old, became world champion, and Gérard Thevenot of France placed third. Johnny could have won had he not gone the wrong way around a pylon and dropped, after that, to forty-sixth place, from which he had to claw his way back to the top. He showed immense character in never giving up.

The League, now in its third year, was very competitive, though Brian Wood dropped out and moved abroad. He hated not being champion, but I think not being selected for the first American Cup was deeply wounding. In the early days it looked like Graham Slater would win, but after five competitions, it came down to a struggle between Robert Bailey of Yorkshire and Bob Calvert of Lancashire, which Calvert won. It was to be the first of four British Championships he won, more than any other pilot. We ran the last competition in heats, one-on-five, which gave us flexibility and nullified the rotten weather, but whenever we could, cross-country – XC – tasks were called.

Gliders were also getting better, now called the fourth generation, which started with the Australian Moyes Maxi, continued through the Hiway Superscorpion, and reached its peak with a French glider, the Atlas, made by La Mouette, a company owned by the European champion and World bronze medallist, Gérard Thevenot. The best British glider, fast as well as with a good sink rate, was probably the Chargus Cyclone; Johnny Carr never felt a performance disadvantage against Thevenot in the Worlds, but its handling was never as sweet as the Atlas. Johnny never cared much about handling, and could fly a plank. The Atlas sold all over the world, and became a favourite with top British pilots like Bob Calvert.

Choosing the British team to send to Tennessee in 1979 caused a tense row within the competitions committee. The man who had acted as chief marshal for the League almost since the beginning, Roy Hill, also managed the British team in Kössen, and was very unhappy about Calvert's performance. Calvert, brilliant but sometimes given to 'moods', threw away a lot of points when he saw he was not going to win individually, despite Britain being in contention for the team gold. Calvert set out again on the course with 25ft only in height, absolutely certain to land out and score a zero, and mumbled afterwards that he had to take any chance, even an absurd one, to win.

Roy rightly felt upset about this, and in the debate about choosing the American Cup team, spoke strongly against Calvert being chosen, though Calvert was on the verge of becoming that year's champion. Roy felt Calvert needed to be taught a lesson. When we came to a vote, we had a ten-man squad and the eleventh man was Calvert! I refused to accept the vote. It was arbitrary and high-handed, but I could not take a team to the US without Calvert. It was one thing to teach Calvert a lesson, quite another to remove the most brilliant pilot we had when we were going up against the Americans, Canadians and Australians in this year's American Cup. A pained debate followed in which I promised to write Calvert a disciplinary letter couched in blood-curdling terms. On taking a second vote, Calvert was grudgingly selected, in tenth place.

Bob Calvert told me later that when he received the letter I sent him (copy to Roy Hill), he spent the whole evening sitting by the phone, telling himself to pick it up, dial, and tell me to take a running jump at a walking doughnut. In the event, he did not pick up the phone, and went to Tennessee.

Bill Moyes turned up in Chattanooga with his brilliant circus, including his son Steve, and Peter 'the Black Death' Brown, a pilot of formidable ability. Brown got his nick-name from Graham Slater at that year's Owens Valley competitions, because he flew a large Black Moyes Maxi, and Johnny Carr used to emphasise it by calling out, 'It's the Black Death, chaps!' whenever Peter Brown appeared. The name stuck. Even the French used to write about 'Le Black Death'. As a wind-up ahead of the competition, Brown flew 81 miles from nearby Sequatchie Valley, easily the longest XC ever flown in the area.

There was amazing tension in Tennessee before the competition began. The US had not liked being beaten in 1978, and nor had the Canadians. The

Australians had never been beaten by the British. And of course, we were four of the central nations of the English-speaking world.

We lived in the same hotel, flew together by day and socialised by night. Again, the British team were under instructions to out-party the rest, which they set to with a will to achieve. The night before the competition began we all met for a barbeque, but such was the supercharged rivalry that we retired to a nearby lake full of pedal boats and decided to re-enact one of the events of the 1812 war; a splendid battle occurred. As dusk descended, you could hear the cries, grunts and splashes and shouts as paddle boat rammed paddle boat and protagonists fell struggling into the water. I was one of the first in, locked in combat with Keith Nichols, both of us having agreed to chuck the umpires in first. Semi-naked figures appeared out of the gloom looking for missing clothing and a beer. Phil Matthewson of Australia, a transplanted Scot who had won the 1977 British Open, appeared out of the gloom having no clothes on at all. Tom Price had removed Matthewson's briefs and was displaying them like a wet scalp. The Scottish–Australian was unabashed by his nakedness, but one or two of the local Tennessee dignitaries looked as if they had swallowed bees. Sadly, we were never invited back.

The actual hang gliding competition was marred by relying heavily on judges for some tasks, to judge, would you believe, the 'quality' of the 360s! A pilot had to fly straight for two seconds before and after each 360, and was penalised if he didn't. My pilots flew six seconds straight before and after their 360s, yet the judge allocated to us was responsible for eleven of the twenty disqualifications. We suffered, not, I have to say, in total silence, until an independent test showed his interpretation of the rules was way beyond anything the organisers had intended, and he was dismissed, although his 'disqualifications' stood. Despite this, Britain won again, with the Americans staging a late rally after a disastrous start to finish second equal with Canada, and Australia falling into unaccustomed last place, having led the competition through the early rounds. Top pilot in the competition, by a whisker, was again Graham Slater.

Bliss it was to beat America, but to beat Australia was heaven! Bill Moyes gave me a mounted set of teeth, claiming I protested too much about the disqualifying judge. He was not a happy man, but our margin of victory would have been even bigger had we not had so many absurd disqualifications.

'I always knew I was going to have trouble with you,' he said, 'ever since I met you.' I took that as an Australian compliment, which of course, it was.

Bettina Gray was once more a key element in the American team's performance, restoring their morale after dreadful opening rounds. She took them all out to dinner, and paid for the whole squad to dress up in top hat and tails at the competition dinner (the British team's official dress was a striped blazer and boater), trumping our one-upmanship games. I am certain she encouraged the wilder elements on her team to corrupt the British later that evening.

This time, reaction at home was less amazed; British hang glider pilots were getting accustomed to winning. Prince Charles gave me the highest award in British sporting aviation that autumn, the Prince of Wales Cup. I had an invitation to Downing Street, not long after Mrs Thatcher was elected PM, to a reception to see the English cricket team off to Australia. At that time, less than a year in office, she was small and 'peaches and cream'.

Also at that time the official BHGA magazine, *Wings!* was edited by Jeannie Knight, who thought too much attention was paid to international competition. Her predecessor, Garth Thomas, had felt the same. I wrote a paper critical of *Wings!*, and as these things happen, became editor myself. I was now competitions chairman, editor, BHGA press officer, a League pilot and on the governing council, at the same time working full-time as a freelance journalist on BBC Radio London as the only breadwinner for a young family. On top of that, I was the only one working seriously to raise sponsorship money to pay for all our overseas competitions. Had I not been so absorbed in what I was doing, which I thought was to get Britain to the top of the competition tree, I would have seen how exposed I was.

We were keen on sending teams anywhere to get experience, not just for the top ten pilots but for those further down the League who needed the glamour and toughness of flying for their country. It forced them to be better than they thought they were. We sent a small pathfinder team to Japan, ahead of the 1981 Worlds there. We also put aside funds to send four pilots to Owens Valley, where the Americans (including 'Pork' Roecker) were saying it was OK to be beaten in Tennessee, but *real* men flew Owens Valley, and where were the British when that was happening? We could not have *that* state of affairs at all, said John Hudson, rightly, volunteering to lead Keith Cockroft, Jo Binns and John North off to Owens.

In Europe, we saw the French as our biggest rivals, and wished to learn from them and more importantly, to stay in touch with their development. They may have felt the same way about us. This led to the founding of the Blériot Cup in 1978, for a long time the oldest annual international competition in the world. Like the American Cup, it was set up to test talent in depth, usually teams of eight, and because of the small number of competitors, it was very flexible. The challenges between the two teams were light-hearted, but contained a certain amount of frog/rosbeef bigotry. My challenge ran:

> Sir, because of what your nation is doing to good English lamb, because of Agincourt, because of Waterloo, because of the extraordinary things your so-called Golden Delicious apples are doing to our honest Cox's Orange Pippins, because of the EEC Farm Policy and those butter mountains, because of garlic, because of some of the nasty things your M. Gisgard d'Estaing has been saying in private about our lovely Mrs Thatcher, we say ... ENOUGH!
>
> You, sir (that's all of you) have cast a stain on our escutcheon and the only way we can remove it is by a duel.
>
> Hang gliders, sir, at 10 paces!
>
> We resolve that, flying British hang gliders, we shall send a team of 8 trusty pilots to France in August to fly against 8 such pilots as you shall find, flying French hang gliders, and that at Lachens Mountain in a cross-country hang gliding duel, we shall remove that stain from our escutcheon.
>
> So, sir, look to your hang glider!
>
> Blériot knew a thing or to when he left France and set off for England, you know.

The French reply was in the same vein:

> Monsieur, we are well aware of your detestable British arrogance, so we are not offended by your bitter words. No English person in France has ever been ill eating a casserole from Lorraine or Toulouse, or even a good fricassee of frogs' legs or snails. We cannot say the same for the hundreds of French schoolchildren who go to your country to improve their English, and we will not waste our time describing their faces, bloated and pale from the assault of your wobbly jellies ('jellies tremblotantes'), your haggis and your sickly baked beans.
>
> We accept the challenge which we are certain is solely the result of your blind vanity, but we reserve the right to choose our kites, regardless of country of origin. Such a duel

is one for pilots, not machines. Nevertheless, even if we fly handkerchiefs, we will win.

So, sir, to your wings, whatever they are. At the Mountain of Lachens on August 18–23, we await you with every confidence … etc

We had reached a crucial stage in kite development in every country in the world at the beginning of 1980. Theory said that we had to bury the cross-booms, a major source of drag, inside a double surface. Two double-surface machines had been in production. One was Bill Bennett's Mariah in the US, the other was the La Mouette Jet, predecessor of the Atlas; Thevenot had won the European Championships on a Jet. The problem was, a lot of pilots were getting killed flying both these machines, fifteen that I know of by the Jet alone, French and Italian flyers.

The 1980 League concentrated on pilot skills, rather than force-fed glider development. That meant we favoured tasks where pilots stayed in the air, 1-on-5, rather than on racing. These task required delicacy rather than strength and speed. Our task-setting favoured gliders like the Atlas, and the ubiquitous Superscorpions, and the Birdman Cherokee, virtually a clone of the Superscorpion. It did not favour the Cyclone, our fastest machine, flown by Johnny Carr, which was never developed and which must have had some effect on the company folding.

In California, by contrast, now with two humiliating defeats under their belts, there was a steely resolve not to have it happen a third time. American development went into a crucible, and competitions began to be about 'climb-and-run', in which speed was all-important. UP – Ultralite Products – run by a tough man called Pete Brock, employed the young genius who had placed third in Kössen in 1975, Roy Haggard, whose UP Dragonfly was so many years ahead of its time.

Haggard discovered what we had been doing wrong with double-surface machines, and why they were killing pilots. At certain angles, often turning on the way in to land, the bottom surface, instead of remaining flat, billowed out and became concave. The wing ceased to be a classical wing, curved on top, flat on bottom, and the glider tucked and dived into the ground. But if straight battens were put into the bottom surface, this did not happen. As a result, Haggard could bury his cross-booms, even float them instead of attaching them to the keel, and really build a fast, taut wing.

Rumours began to reach us in Britain in the middle of 1980 that the Americans had a superkite, called the Comet. It was only rumour, but it persisted. I received two personal letters, one from George Worthington, whom I had met, the other from Peter Brock, whom I hadn't, each telling me how much the Americans were going to thrash the British at this year's American Cup. I was not quite sure what to make of the letters, they could have been bombast, and I was just too busy anyway.

I took the British team to Lachens in the Alpes Maritimes for the Blériot against the French, and we lost. We were beaten so badly on day one that we could not pull back, despite winning every other day. Tactics for the French were worked out by Mike de Glanville, their top pilot, who in other circumstances could have passed for an Englishman (because he was one, just domiciled in France). Then our team went to Owens and, despite flying their hearts out, were completely pasted. Our highest position was twenty-first, and the man who won was a small aggressive man called Rich Pfeiffer, of whom we will hear more. He was, if you remember, Page Pfeiffer's husband, the man who launched into a killer thermal and watched a hawk get smashed against a cliff. And, he flew a Comet.

But Roy Hill took a British team to the European Championships where, for the first time, we became official team champions. Thevenot was again individual winner of the popular class 2, while Mike de Glanville led class 3, but we had the best team in depth. The competition was particularly painful for Roy Hill because the organisers had invited the South Africans, and I instructed Roy that we were not to fly if they were official entrants. Roy was chairman of the whole BHGA by now, and a close ally of Ann Welch; both of them, president and chairman of the BHGA, hated and resented this sort of thing. We would, in passing, have lost all our Sports Council grants had we not done as I instructed, but in any case, there was a moral point to make that went right to the core of why I was on the BHGA council in the first place. In the end, the organisers did not accept the South Africans as official entries, and we were able to compete. Both Roy and Ann were scarred by the experience, and understandably not very happy about the man who had caused it.

As the American Cup approached, it was, I suppose, a great compliment to learn that Pete Brock would not, under any circumstances, sell a Comet to an Englishman until after the American Cup was over. Robert Bailey tried to buy one at the Grouse Mountain meet in Vancouver, Canada, and Bob England even tried to build his own version of one, called the Demon. But the boycott was complete. I did not see a Comet until I got to Tennessee and watched the American team – coached by Pete Brock – go through the painful process of selection by elimination that we first used two years earlier. The nine-man squad, from whom six would be chosen, were kept away from us as much as possible, so we were not able to judge their kite.

Rumour said it was brilliant, a whole new generation. Rumour turned out to be right. When the American team was selected, Brock ordered them all to fly Comets, and they did. He wanted a win just as much as we had in 1978, and managed the team quite ruthlessly.

Two of the American team, Rich Grigsby and Malcolm Jones, were part of the 1978 American team so comprehensively beaten by us, so their anticipation of victory was sweet. Rich was also there for the loss of 1979, as was the man setting the tasks in 1980, Sean Dever. Tasks were still quite Micky Mouse, speed along the ridge around pylons, sink rate, and the option of double-points scoring open XCs. But for their day, they were radical.

We tried to wind the Americans up by sending almost the whole British team off XC one day, and smashing all the site records for distance. Looking back now, that probably made it even more unlikely that open XC would be called.

The Americans dominated from the start, despite a Brazilian team with great individual talent, like future world champion Pepe Lopez, who were also on Comets. The British, along with France, Canada, Brazil and Australia, were beaten comprehensively. The Americans were quite as single-minded as we were, more so because they didn't go partying as we still did, until they were sure of victory. Right at the end, when our only chance was an open XC, scoring double points, one was nearly called. Each member of the American team, wearing their harnesses, walked up to an English pilot and brandished their carabiner. By this smiling demonstration they were mutely saying, if you go XC, we will mark you man to man, never mind what the other nations' pilots do. It would be as if they were connected, physically, one to one, with our pilots, to nullify any advantage we might gain. In the event a cross-country task was not called. The Americans achieved a brilliant win.

Yet, against the odds, the top pilot in the competition was Britain's Graham Hobson, that same Hobson who did not quite know, just three years earlier, what a thermal was. With superb and intelligent flying on his outclassed La Mouette Atlas, Hobson reached the top of the greasy pole and stayed there, despite strong efforts by the Americans to displace him. Rich Pfeiffer had been so confident of beating Hobson on a speed run that he had sailed past making gestures (typical Rich!), but then got so low he had to circle desperately to gain height, and like the tortoise and the hare, Hobson passed him and won. Grigsby said later, ruefully, 'Next time, Graham …'

In the competition, we placed second, France third, Canada fourth, Brazil fifth … and Australia sixth! Thereby hangs a tale.

Peter Brown was a rather solitary man. He was at home among pilots where he was acknowledged as brilliant. At the 1979 American Cup, he met a girl in Tennessee, and they had an affair. It lasted a while, but as Bill Moyes told me about it later, for her it seemed to be of less importance than it was for Peter. Earlier in 1980 the affair came to an end.

The month before the Tennessee competition, Peter was a finalist in the US Masters Competition on Grandfather Mountain, with $5,000 in prize money. The 'Black Death' had come second to Steve Moyes, and won $1,500. Looking at the photo of him standing, smiling, between Moyes and third-placed Grigsby, you would think he had not a care in the world, except to wonder where the next meet was going to be so he could win some more money.

'I should have seen what Peter was up to when he started clearing off small debts and putting his affairs in order,' said Moyes, when the news of what Peter had done came through. 'He seemed to just go around closing bank accounts, paying debts, and making sure there was nothing outstanding.'

Peter cried off the American Cup, despite passionate pleas from Bill and Steve Moyes, and went to California. There, in the middle of the American Cup, he got on to a motorbike, revved it, mounted and set off, faster and faster, heading west, until he flew right off a 600ft cliff into the sea. The news destroyed the Australian team in Tennessee.

The 1980 American victory was another watershed in the sport. The Comet made every other hang glider obsolete. All the foreign teams immediately bought one and brought them home. I came to a deal through Tracy Knauss to send him a powered trike, then just being developed, in return for the best Comet at the meet, that flown by Jeff Burnett.

The trike we developed in Britain turned hang gliders into microlights, and nearly twenty years later I went on to be the first man to fly around the world in a trike-style microlight, the wing a direct descendent from the Solar Wings Typhoon.

I delivered the Comet to Solar Wings, where I was a 25 per cent shareholder, with the plea to copy it as quickly as possible, or face financial wipeout as Comets swept across the hang gliding world. Others in different parts of the world surely did the same. Those that didn't watched their sales plummet.

Early the following year I invited all the British manufacturers, plus La Mouette of France, to a meet in South Wales. Each manufacturer was to choose a team of three, one from the top ten of the League, one from the second ten, one from the third ten, in an effort to equalise pilot skill. They flew against each other in heats of three in marginal conditions, while we tested speed, handling and sink rate. Bob England's Hiway Demon won, with Solar's Typhoon (the clone of the Comet I brought back) second tied with Southdown's Lightning. Comets placed fourth, La Mouette's X-Ray fifth and then Skyhook and Flexiform.

The effect of that meet was to try and stop Comets destroying our manufacturing base. It succeeded.

But that was the last British competition I was involved in. A month later I was fighting for my political life. Two months later I lost that fight. The issue was sponsorship, but other issues played a part.

I will come back to them.

Chapter 8

Powered Flight

In the wild liberation of ideas triggered by the 1971 first Lilienthal meet, powered flying became a discipline of its own. Almost the first impulse was to ask, could engines work with weight-shift machines? If so, where do you put the engine on a real rag-wing? If an ultralight powered flying machine was to be built, with three-axis controls like mainstream aviation, how was it different than just a very light aircraft? And as important in solving one of the questions man has asked since he saw birds, could we take off from flat ground and, by the strength of our own body, fly?

Before Otto Lilienthal, dozens of men had tried man-powered flight, and failed. Leonardo da Vinci's drawings of bird-winged aircraft could never have flown, though a full-scale version of his more obscure hang glider has. The smaller the flying creature, the more frequently wings seem to need to flap. The albatross does much of its ocean travelling by dynamic soaring, flying the interaction of the wind and waves in a way that looks almost like a perpetual motion machine rather than by continuously flapping its wings. It seems a natural progression that man, heavier than the albatross, should have fixed wings and an engine to drive a propeller to achieve forward motion. But could that engine, even with wings, be a man's body, his legs and arms?

Man-powered flight was driven after 1960 by a prize of £50,000 ($75,000) offered by an English businessman, Henry Kremer, through the Royal Aeronautical Society in London. mainstream aviation set about trying to win, with aeronautical college students producing ingenious and delicate machines into which thousands of hours of work were poured. The Kremer Prize stipulated a figure-of-eight course of 1 mile, to prove not just the power of flight, but the ability to control the aircraft in the air. Our television screens carried stories throughout the 1960s, showing occasional attempts by long-winged aircraft in the still air just after dawn, with the pilot pedalling furiously to sustain flights of yards, even hundreds of yards, but no success in capturing the prize. One big problem was the man-powered aircraft were delicate and likely to be damaged; this took hundreds of hours to repair.

One such aircraft, developed by the Hatfield Man-Powered Aircraft Club (HMPAC) was the Puffin, which achieved a straight-line distance of 2,988ft in May 1962, the first time a man-powered aircraft had exceeded 0.5 mile. The pilot was HMPAC's chairman, a professional aerodynamicist called John Wimpenny. The building and research team had forty members, and included distinguished engineers from de Havilland, which made the brilliant Mosquito, probably the best fighter-bomber of the Second World War, largely built of balsa wood. The Puffin itself was also made meticulously from balsa wood, and with the pilot, weighed 265lb on take-off.

The new aviation was spawned from the ethic of the bamboo butterfly, of Sellotape, plastic sheeting and bamboo, all bought for $10. And it was that ethic – 'quick and dirty' – that won the Kremer Prize, and made far greater distances possible for man-powered flyers.

The last time we saw Dr Paul MacCready he was one of Jack Lambie's 'gang' just after the Montgomery meet in southern California in the summer of 1971. MacCready had previously distinguished himself by running off a sand dune with his arms outstretched in frustration at the failure of some of their early wings. Lambie said he flew further with his jump than their wings did then. In 1971, MacCready and Volmer Jensen looked at the mushroom growth of Rogallos after the first Lilienthal meet and said, 'Aw, it's just like jumping on a bicycle with no steering and pushing off and going down a hill. It's interesting but it has no future!' Volmer Jensen went off to stick a petrol engine on his lightweight wing and start one broad stream of invention. But MacCready gathered some of the best of the hang gliding world around him – including Lambie himself, Taras Kiceniuk (who flew the Rogallo wing at the first Lilienthal meet), top competition pilot Sterling Stoll, and a hang glider pilot/cyclist called Bryan Allen – to conquer man-powered flight. Allen was the first successful man-engine.

Like Len Gabriels, MacCready was a model aircraft enthusiast. Born in 1925, he gained a flying licence at 16, and during the Second World War was assigned to US Navy flight training. He took a BSc at Yale in 1947, turned his attention to gliders, and bought a competition machine – called the 'Screaming Weiner'. MacCready took second place in the US Gliding Nationals at the age of 21.

In 1948, 1949 and 1953 MacCready won the US National Gliding Championships, and was a pioneer of high-altitude wave soaring in the US. He later became the first American to win the International Gliding

Championships in France. For a decade, MacCready worked on sailplane technology, soaring techniques and meteorology. He invented the speed ring, widely used by glider pilots to calculate best glide with speed and height. MacCready earned his masters degree and then a PhD in aeronautics, ran a cloud-seeding project and developed an armoured aircraft for flying in rainstorms. After 1970, he ran an independent hi-tech company, which researched virtually anything.

MacCready got the idea for the Gossamer Condor in 1976, more than a decade after British and Japanese attempts at the Kremer Prize. He says he was day-dreaming on holiday when he realised the secret of man-powered flight lay in two bundles on top of his van – hang gliders!

I was thinking about hang glider performance calculations for a magazine article I was working on, when I realised that if you tripled all the dimensions of an efficient hang glider, without increasing its weight, it would only require one third of a horsepower to keep it going.

The real secret of the success of the Condor is that the concept that I had, that worked, was to build it with hang glider-type construction techniques, tubing and wire, *quick and dirty*. You can build a hang glider in a weekend if you're in a rush. The Condor took longer than that, but it's the same philosophy. Don't worry about every little detail of the wing. If there is a wrinkle here or there, that really doesn't make all that much difference.

It was a quick and dirty atmosphere that permitted me to have something that could be built, rebuilt, re-rebuilt, tested, broken, fixed and built again. It allowed us to make maybe a dozen different versions of the vehicle, evolving it to its final form in one year, whereas other groups would have taken twelve years of intensive effort to go through the same evaluation.

The man-powered aircraft in England were very carefully fashioned with great labour, and they have nicely contoured wings. But when the wing breaks and you face another 12 months' work to fix it, you start losing heart. In our case we just had to use theory, common sense, design it, build it, fly it, find out what was working and refine that, modify it, change it, back to the drawing board. It was this combination of theory and experiment that made it work and it is easy with hang glider type construction compared to other types.

The Gossamer Condor won the Kremer Prize for a figure-of-eight flight over 1 mile at Shaftner Airport, California, on 23 August 1977, after just a year's work. The Condor had a wingspan of 97ft, and the flight took about six minutes. Media interest was tremendous, with virtual fist fights between cameramen, and the giant DuPont chemicals company emerged as a sponsor when a second Kremer Prize was offered, £100,000 to cross the English Channel by man-powered flight. It was widely thought it would be another eighteen years between achieving a man-powered flight of 1 mile in perfect California conditions and a flight of 22 miles in the notoriously difficult weather over the stretch of water between England and France. In fact, such was the virility of ideas liberated by the new aviation, it took just twenty-two months.

The Gossamer Condor needed one third of a horsepower (0.33hp) to make its 1.15-mile flight around a figure-of-eight. MacCready said later the Condor was relatively crudely constructed, weighing 70lb, with materials available forty years earlier. The Albatross, which he designed for the English Channel attempt, used some of the Condor's building principles, and again was built quick and dirty, but the material was the latest state of the art produced by DuPont.

All structural tubing on the Gossamer Albatross was home-made from graphite. The carbon fibre/resin was pasted on to aluminium tubing, wrapped around tape and baked in a makeshift coil oven. After proper curing the tape was removed, and the aluminium removed by prolonged immersion in an acid bath. Mylar polyester film only 0.0005in thick covered the wings; film for the whole craft weighed just 3lb. Gone were the piano wires of the Condor, and in came Kevlar aramid fibres. Kevlar had previously been used to reinforce radial tyres, conveyor belts and soft body armour.

The conventional bicycle chain was replaced by a urethane toothed belt. The aerofoil was smoothed out with more low-density expanded polystyrene ribs. Whenever possible, components were either disposed of, or built of polystyrene (like the beautifully shaped airspeed indicator propeller). MacCready said that if a part did not break on crash landing he would replace it with something lighter and weaker.

The Albatross had an air speed indicator, and a sonic altimeter capable of measuring height to within 0.5in. Weight was reduced, ounce by ounce, but before the attempt was made the Albatross was still 6lb overweight, because of all the Sellotape repairs after various 'dings' during practice. Dave Worth, who followed the project in England, was delighted to find lollipop sticks built in to the wing as deflexors!

On 12 June 1979, less than two years after the Condor's flight, Bryan Allen took the Albatross across the English Channel on his first attempt! The flight, about 16ft above the water, took three hours of steady pedalling, from 7.00 to 10.00am. Sixty years earlier Louis Blériot took thirty-seven minutes to cover the same stretch of water in the best that technology then had to offer.

I met Allen at the following year's American Cup. The first question I asked, was, 'How much did you rely on your strength as a cyclist, as against your hang gliding skills?' He replied the hang gliding skills were the most relevant, though he was extraordinarily fit. We spent some time that evening wondering if men could migrate …

Allen's record flight, officially 35.7km, was overtaken by Glenn Tremmi, at 58.7km, and by 1988 there was actually a man-powered flight on a machine similar in appearance to MacCready's hang glider-based Condor, directly drawing on the earliest Western myths of flight. A wing, sponsored by United Technologies, was pedalled from Heraklion, capital of Crete, 74 miles across the sea to Icaria, where Greek myth says Daedalus landed.

In 1980, the novel ideas pumping around the new aviation also moved into sun-powered flight, with the success of the biplane rigid wing Easy Riser. A pilot and builder named Larry Mauro made a 0.5-mile flight, taking off and landing on the same runway, totally under power provided by direct light from the sun. He called his aircraft the 'Solar Riser', with a clear top wing in which 500 photo-electric cells were inserted. The flight lasted thirty seconds, at a speed of 20mph, and an altitude of 30–40ft.

The Solar Riser project cost Mauro, then 40 years old, about $50,000. His aircraft had a 30ft wingspan, weighed 125lb without the pilot, and 290lb with him. The electric motor was said to develop 3hp, with a 41in propeller.

Mauro commented that representatives of mainstream aviation in the US, the FAA, grounded him at an air meet, 'because they didn't really believe what they were seeing!' He claims he did not get the power from the photo-electric cells that manufacturers claimed he would get (this is known as the MLF, the Manufacturer's Lie Factor). But the photo electric cells were shop-bought, not state of the art, and he thought he would get better performance in the future.

MacCready came back into the picture, first with his prototype Solar Penguin, and then with his Solar Challenger. This was also sponsored by DuPont, and flew the English Channel from France, landing at the ex-RAF emergency field at Manston in Kent in July 1981. MacCready would not have it that his aircraft had any practical use, but the number of photo-electric cells jumped from 500 in the sunny USA, to 16,128, even though Mauro and MacCready both claimed 3hp from their electric motors.

So far the best sun-powered flight in history until 1996 was coast-to-coast across the US, flown by former US hang gliding champion Eric Raymond in 1990. His aircraft, called the 'Sunseeker', covered 2,467 miles in thirty-three days, much faster than the first mainstream aircraft to cross the US, Cal Rodgers in 1911, who took fifty days in a Wright biplane. Raymond's aircraft sounds heavy, compared with the Gossamer Albatross, 198lb compared to 57lb, but it did have to stand up to thermals and rough conditions. It had a sink rate of 60fpm, and flew quite slowly, an average of 25mph. Some days, with a following wind, he could get up to 80mph, and once reached 14,000ft.

Eric Raymond spent four years putting the flight together, and used the small electric motor – this one rated at 2hp – for up to eight minutes, with Sanyo photo-electric cells, before the power faded and the cells recharged. He used that time to climb into thermals, and essentially thermalled his way, west to east, across the US. On his best day, 11 August 1990, he flew 245 miles to set a new solar distance record.

That is one branch, the greenest area of powered flight, opened up by new aviation thinking. It was never really open to the mainstream, though there has been a lot of cross-thinking, especially in the US. In Britain, by contrast, there seems to have been virtually no cross-thinking between the Mainstream and new aviation, which accounted for why we did not win the various imaginative Kremer prizes. Henry Kremer is dead now, but there is a need for that sort of prize money, perhaps from the National Lottery, to encourage long-distance, unpowered, cross-country flight, unsupported on the ground, and lasting for weeks, covering thousands of miles ...

As soon as hang gliding started people wanted to know how to stick a good old-fashioned petrol engine to the developing wings. Two streams of thought opened up. The first, in the United States, worked with former three-axis control hang gliders like the VJ-23, the Easy-Rider and dozens of others. These aircraft had a hang gliding origin, were originally capable of foot launching, and the people building them were part of the ultra-light aircraft movement. But aside from their light weight and their early capability for foot launching, they were mainstream aviation writ small. They had rudders, ailerons, elevators, some even flaps, all features you find on a Boeing 747.

Sticking engines on these hang gliders was really a question of whether you wanted to pull the aircraft or push it through the air, technically known as 'tractor' or 'pusher'. The questions asked had already been answered in mainstream aviation. The only interesting new development was, could we get the weight down far enough to foot launch? In the VJ-23's case, the answer was to stick a very small 9hp engine on a frame atop the wing, and in this, Englishman David Cook made the first powered hang glider flight across the English Channel. In Cook's account of his journey, which took great courage, you can hear the authentic hollow voice of the minority within the new aviation constantly trying to drag us back into the mainstream, as merely smaller members of it:

On Tuesday, May 9th, 1978, the VJ-23, donned in splendid sponsor's colouring, was rigged on a flat shingle beach, and the McCulloch 101B engine fitted and warmed up. Fuel capacity was 10 litres (2.2 imperial gallons, 2.64 US gallons) and the two 5-litre tanks fitted into the D-section of the wing. I had run endurance tests, and 35 minutes/gallon consumption was determined. A total running time of 77 minutes should be available. The wind was Force 5 (Fresh, 19–24mph) from the north and I was to fly to the southeast. Drift angles were calculated.

At 10.40am with five miles visibility, the chase boat was three miles out and radio'd back that they were hitting 28–30 knots (35mph). The VJ-23 lifted off near Walmer Castle, Deal, and took up the chase to the boat. I settled for 100 feet of altitude (about 400 feet lower than Blériot in 1909) and within 6–7 miles I had caught up with the 'African Queen'. We eased around south of the Goodwin Sands, where in places I could see through the water to the bottom. It was a chilling thought that over 30,000 sailors had lost their lives on those Sands. Visibility was closing in and I could see less than one mile ahead of me, although the chase boat was clear enough below. After about 20 minutes or so the 'African Queen' suddenly stopped dead, and I figured it had some small problem so I elected to circle until it was fixed. After five minutes, away we went again (at least I can claim a record for the most 360s in the English Channel, I thought). I felt a bit like God sitting up there, now at 300 feet (gained since the waiting about), watching the 'African Queen', deciding whether to go in front or astern of the supertankers. Passing over these monsters was less God-like or serene. They are longer than I was high, and I recall looking down between my feet and seeing nothing but tanker! The turbulence caused by them was frightening, but I made it.

The shipping up-wind was also causing much turbulence. The Channel is not a nice place. I could not look down without seeing a shipwreck, sometimes more than a dozen at any one time. The water wells up on a wreck and makes it appear strange. I tried not to look too much.

After one hour of flying and with the McCulloch screaming merrily away, I thought that we should soon see the coast. The wind was now about Force 6 (Strong, up to 31mph) and northeast; I could tell from the waves and my compass reading. Below, the 'African Queen' suddenly stopped again. I was left with the agonising decision of whether to go on or do the 360 bit again. I had no idea where I was, or how far off the coast, but thought I must be close. I flew on as far as I could with the 'African Queen' still within my sight, and then waited. I was cold, the air temperature was only 10 degrees C, and there was no sign of France.

The problem with the 'African Queen' was that they were travelling too fast for the conditions. There was about a 4-foot chop on the sea, and the boat was airborne almost as much as myself. She was hitting waves so hard that oil was forced through the distributor on to the points of the 140hp Mercruiser power unit. After a few minutes of frantic work on the boat we were away again. I figured I had just over 8 minutes of fuel left.

At an hour and 10 minutes I saw the coast of France through the foggy haze. Due to our course and drift angle it was to my right ... and back! I banked very quickly to starboard and thundered in a long power dive at the coast about 3½ miles away. The speed was tremendous; it was downwind and my groundspeed as I passed over a Calais–Dover ferry at right angles was about 60 mph. Getting this close and with so little fuel left, I was charged with urgency. I had been totally dispassionate about the whole venture, and had planned the whole thing as if I was to go into the water. Now that I was this close to success I found myself really fired up. I used up 200 feet in the power dive and crossed the shore around 150 feet high. Banking around northwards, I eased the throttle back and made a normal five-step foot landing, 1 hour and 15 minutes after leaving England (on paper, that was with just a minute of fuel left).

The warm sand and sun and sudden quiet slowly sank into me, and I realised I had the taste of success around and within me.

I did not think we were going to get there at all, and it was to my great surprise when we did. Sod's Law intervenes on these things.

The real significance to aviation of this flight is that it was done with less power than the Wright Brothers had when they first flew, and it was done on one quarter of the power that Blériot had when he made the 1909 crossing.

(One of my sponsors, Duckhams Oil, had quite a connection with the original flight. Alexander Duckham, their founder, was a great friend of Blériot. They did not sponsor him on the Channel flight, but did sponsor him on various world altitude record attempts. It was fitting that I had landed within one mile of Blériot-Plage, although at the time I had no idea where I was).

I haven't any more plans for further ventures – you can't fly the Atlantic in a hang glider, can you?

The author had a crack at the Atlantic in a weight-shift trike in 2001, the year of the 9/11 terrorist attack on the New York World Trade Center, but failed on the last take-off in Newfoundland. I wrote about it in *Chasing Ghosts*. The ghosts were Alcock and Brown, and the American Charles Lindbergh.

David Cook wrote:

I still have different projects in various stages of completion. We are building a new rigid. Now, we have the knowledge to test it gently under power, rather than continually running down slopes to see if it will fly. I am trying to get rid of the trailer to see if it can be car-toppable. I want it so that it can be launched under power from flat ground, flown to 2,000 feet and thermalled. This is where all the advantages of a rigid will come in – low sink and a high L/D (glide angle). This one that we are developing should have a glide angle of 22-1, according to Neil Moran who does the calculations.

I think you will always get hill flyers. The performance of flexwings (rogallo hang gliders) is now adequate, probably for all time. I cannot see them getting much better. I could be wrong, but I think flexwings are holding up the development of hang gliders. They are OK for the pilot who flies for enjoyment, but if you want to fly 100 miles in this country we are going to need something much better in flexwings or the rigids we have.

If I could produce a rigid which would beat all the gliders in the British Hang Gliding League, everyone would want one and the rigid vs flexwing argument would disappear overnight. In the end, all competition pilots will end up flying rigids, as well as the people who want to go places. Most of the technology has been screwed out of the flexwing. You might get a few quirks like reducing drag on the tips, but it won't give us great bounds like the Aussies showed us in 1976. At the moment, pilots are sacrificing a lot of performance for the sake of being able to fold a kite up and carry it on the shoulder.

If 50 people in the League flew VJs, I have no doubt that some of them would be a lot better than I am, and we would really see something happen with rigids. Weight-shift hang gliders are unnatural anyway. No bird weight-shifts, does it?

Those words were written in 1978, barely at the beginning of the immense improvements of performance in flexwings, the Rogallo hang gliders. They could not have been more wrong-headed. David Cook owned the only VJ-23 in the country, and could not find a single other person to join him on the crusade for its improvement, yet he was absolutely certain he was right and the thousands of flying flexwing pilots were wrong. It did not seem to occur to him that if any improvement was made, it would only take the VJ-23 closer to mainstream aviation, where none of us wanted to go.

(For the record, the first 100-mile hang glider flight in Britain was achieved four years later, on a flexwing. Within sixteen years, an aircraft called a paraglider, a steerable parachute that you can pack up in two minutes by stuffing it into a rucksack, also flew 100 miles in the UK. And yes, the Atlantic is possible by powered hang glider, as a number of men have proved, a Dutchman called Eppo Harbrink-Numan over the North Atlantic in 1990, and a Frenchman, Guy Delage, over the South Atlantic in December, 1991. Both men did it on flexwings. I did it myself in 1998, on my closing stages of being the first man to fly a microlight – a powered hang glider – around the world, and to make the first microlight crossing of the Atlantic west to east, via the Arctic Circle.)

Yet David Cook's obsession with rigids led to his building one the world's most sophisticated microlights, the CFM Shadow (CFM – Cook's Flying Machine). The Shadow owed a lot, in the hi-tech materials he used, to Paul MacCready's work, but to a mainstream pilot it looks weird. It is essentially a large rigid wing with a two-man, in-line crew pod underneath, and an engine driving a pusher propeller. The boom to the tail is about 8in in diameter, and the tail is 'reversed', with the rudder underneath the elevators and two stabilisers. It has a tricycle undercarriage – a nose wheel – but without the pilot, the aircraft rests on its tail and look appealingly vulnerable. Cook used to offer anyone £1 for every ounce in weight they could safely suggest removing from the Shadow.

It was in a CFM Shadow in 1986–87 that Eve Jackson, a 30-year-old Englishwoman, completed the first microlight flight from England to Australia. She took fifteen months, and flew her aircraft, nicknamed 'Gerty', only when conditions at take-off and landing were ideal; she had many adventures. She was shot at in the air over Yugoslavia, twice had her undercarriage collapse in rough landings, suffered an engine seizure over India, the loss of power in one piston (there were only two pistons anyway) flying down the Burmese coast, and her propeller was smashed on an Indonesian island when she failed to secure a canopy in the passenger compartment and something fell out and hit the prop. On the tarmac at Darwin Airport in northern Australia, after the final sea crossing, she threw the heavy dinghy on to the ground that she had carried as a life-saver all the way from England. When she pulled the release to inflate it, nothing happened! Her flight succeeded despite a severe shortage of money, having left England with £500 and a credit card, and when completed she was heavily in debt. But the award of the lucrative Segrave Trophy helped clear some of her debts. Eve was also awarded a gold medal by the Royal Aero Club, and a sword of honour from GAPAN, the Guild of Air Pilots and Air Navigators.

It was a superb flight, against the odds and conventional thinking, but it was not the first long-distance flight in a rigid microlight, as the new category of aircraft came to be called (ULM in France, Ultralight in the US). On 4 May 1987, a French-built ULM Mistral made history when it was flown to the geographic North Pole by Nicolas Hulot. Between September 1984 and March 1987, another Frenchman, Patrice Franceschi, flew a single-seater Sirocco around the world, except that whenever he came to the oceans, he dismantled his ULM and put it on a ship to take him to the next major land mass. The actual distance flown was 27,960 miles, which took about 700 flying hours. By contrast, Eve Jackson flew all the way to Australia in her Shadow, including hundreds of miles over the sea.

As I did, in my own CFM Shadow, the *Dalgety Flyer*, flying London to Sydney in fifty-nine days in 1987–88. This was for nine years the longest, fastest microlight flight in history. Mine was an official Australian bicentenary event, and I was chasing the ghost of Ross Smith, the first man to fly to Australia in 1919. He flew London to Darwin in a Vickers Vimy in twenty-eight days, but took ninety-six days in all to make it to Sydney. I took fifty-one days to Darwin, but only fifty-nine in all to Sydney. Smith had many of his problems crossing Australia; mine occurred before I got there.

I left London in headwinds on 2 December 1987, and struggled across winter-bound Europe and down the Rhône Valley. I was nearly killed twice trying to fly the French Alps in cloud, without blind-flying instruments. But I made it across both the French and Italian Alps in one day, then down the east coast of Italy, island-hopping my way towards Crete. On the small island of Kythira I landed, short of fuel, in strong winds, and was blown upside down while taxiing. This wrecked the *Dalgety Flyer*, but my mechanic, Mike Atkinson, a fellow League hang glider pilot travelling to Australia with a first-class ticket and fifty stopovers (and waiting for me in Athens) turned up, laughed wildly, and glued the whole lot together in five days with three tins of Araldite and a handful of fibreglass and tubing. Dave Cook was flown out to help and advise us, and test-fly the result.

Driven strongly by the need to race Ross Smith's ghost, and to get to Australia in time for the bicentenary, I had to keep racing in very unsuitable weather (Mike Atkinson reckoned that, of the thirty-six flying days I took to get to Sydney, only ten of them had been flyable; airliners were grounded, I discovered later, on one of the days I flew). Leaving Kythira in low cloud, rain and with funk misting up my canopy, I flew to Crete, 140 miles across the sea, and then the long 400-mile journey to Alexandria and Cairo in Egypt.

Three days later, trying to get to Amman in Jordan with a tank half full of unsuitable jet fuel loaded on at Aqaba, my engine stopped at 5,000ft over the Dead Sea Valley as I was entering some 6,000ft mountains. I landed on a road a mile from the Israeli border, 1,200ft below sea level. Again, Mike Atkinson came to tell me what was wrong, and fix it. Jordan's King Hussein summoned me to an audience, and became patron of the flight, helping me cross the Saudi desert to Dhahran following an oil pipeline, where three years later the first Gulf War was fought.

Crossing the Persian Gulf on Christmas Day 1987, in the middle of the Iran-Iraq War and trying to get to Abu Dhabi, I had a fuel blockage and the engine stopped 32 miles from land. I ditched in the sea, but with Mike's help, rescued the aircraft after six hours in the water, rebuilt it and flew on six days later. Crossing to Pakistan over the mouth of the Persian Gulf, and trying to avoid Iran, I was driven back by a rainstorm and had to return over 150 miles of sea to Muscat. A few days later, over India, still in a tearing hurry but without maps – the Indian government had changed my route after I left London and had no maps available – I had to land on a road with a fuel blockage. The Indian Air Force put me up that night, as I circled, forlorn and frightened, over Allahabad; I went through three days of insanity, haunted by a ferocious Djinn. I believe this was caused by fatigue, vertigo, claustrophobia and plain old-fashioned funk; it caused me to want to jump out of the *Dalgety Flyer* at 5,000ft. It was only by the greatest effort that I did not actually jump. (I understand some solo yachtsmen go through the same problem; I called it 'the panics').

Flying down the coast of Malaysia, one of my earthing leads snapped, reducing the two-cylinder 447cc Rotax engine to just one cylinder, and I landed on a track across a wet paddy field. Mike turned up the following day to fix my machine, but I landed on more roads in Malaysia than runways, because of monsoons. The Malaysian Air Force was particularly efficient in finding me, although one helicopter pilot nearly blew me out of the sky by flying over me with his downdraught in the same way the legendary Bob Wills was killed.

Most of the islands of Indonesia were unflyable in January after eleven o'clock in the morning, because of bucketing monsoon rains, so I took off early each day and flew out to sea, looking at the rain-soaked land and hoping my engine would not stop. In this fashion, I made it to Timor, finally looking as if it was possible to get to Australia on time.

Crossing the shark-infested Timor Sea – it was called 'the White Knuckle Route' in the 1930s – I found an oil rig being towed east, talked to a helicopter pilot circling over the rig, and he gave me the crucial course correction to take me to his base, a tiny island off the coast of Australia called Troughton. It was the only possible place in range for me to land. I got to Darwin the following day, and then raced across Australia, spent the bicentenary in Brisbane, and arrived in Sydney after a couple more adventures, including breaking the nose wheel leg in a landing on a golf course.

An Australian historian at the Powerhouse Museum in Sydney compared my flight to that by Ray Parer and John McIntosh in 1920, over roughly the same route, though those two 'hooligan' flyers took 208 days to get to Darwin. The *Dalgety Flyer* itself is now in Sydney Airport and under the patronage of the Powerhouse Museum. A more detailed account of that flight can be found in a book I wrote afterwards (*The Dalgety Flyer*, published by Bloomsbury) and condensed by the *Reader's Digest* in July 1991. The fullest story of the flight can be found on Kindle, including the full story of how and why I resigned as TV-am's financial correspondent, where I had three daily live slots talking about finance.

There is a satisfying synchronicity here, for it was the staid old *Reader's Digest* that so boosted the new aviation back in 1971 with its article on 'the flyingest flying there is' about the first Lilienthal meet.

Two other long microlight flights were made in CFM Shadows, one by James Edmonds from London to Beijing that fell short of actually crossing the whole of China because of bureaucracy, and the other from London to Delhi by an Indian billionaire, Vijaypat Singhania, in 1988. Vijaypat's journey took enormous courage and dedication, because of the commercial and cultural pressures he came under. He did the flight for India. Vijaypat took Mike Atkinson as his mechanic and Eve Jackson to work out the routes. He wanted to beat my time of thirty-four days to India, and did so handsomely, doing it in twenty-one days, though his engine was slightly bigger and he flew in the long daylight hours of summer, not the short hours of winter. Vijaypat was suitably lauded in India for making the flight, and made an air vice marshal in the Indian Air Force. I was the ghost writer of his book on the journey, *An Angel in My Cockpit*.

But though our engines were small, and we complied with the 390kg weight limit of a microlight (450kg in Europe), the Shadow and the Sirocco are really dead ends in the new aviation. The better a rigid microlight gets, the closer it comes to mainstream flight. The central area of development, where all the really exciting ideas are still occurring, is in weight-shift aircraft and now paragliders, one at least foot launched, both in the central stream of the new aviation.

In the first attempts to apply power to Rogallos, the engine was not attached to the wing, but strapped to the back of the pilot! The propeller worked inside a cage to contain the danger, and the pilot flew seated. He ran off a hill or level ground, his throttle control often being a large peg clenched in his teeth, for both hands were occupied keeping the control bar off the ground. Once in the air and climbing, the pilot could either hold the peg, squeezing it for power, or change to a hand throttle on the control bar.

The performance of early Rogallo wings made all this a pretty dangerous affair, and there are obvious problems in landing. If you land on your feet and you cannot stand up, the control bar digs in, and you whack your head on the keel with all the weight of the engine behind you. A potential neck-breaker. If you put wheels on the control bar, as student hang glider pilots now do, then lift your feet on landing, you bound along the ground with the engine and propeller bouncing on your back. This configuration was quite soon abandoned, though when paragliders came along, all the research into pilot-mounted engines was dusted off again and not wasted.

We then went through a stage where we stuck engines on various parts of the Rogallo until someone was killed, when we moved the engine elsewhere. I have seen engines stuck above the wing with a long shaft to the back and a propeller, attached to the back of the keel, attached to the cross-booms, and the whole unit above and just behind the pilot (including the propeller!) with a bottom guard to stop the pilot getting injured by the flying blades.

I can only vaguely remember doing this, but for a while in early 1978 I seem to have been chairman of the BHGA's powered hang gliding committee, and produced the first definitive report on power, in which there was no real inkling of the way it actually went. I find that we outlined a powered hang glider as being capable of foot launching and landing, with a maximum fuel load of 3 gallons, and a maximum empty weight of just 70kg. The thinking then was that we were still hang glider pilots, and power was just to get us up in the air to where the thermals were, and no more.

The most detailed early experiments in Britain were carried out on a powered Midas E hang glider, made by Chargus, owned by Murray Rose, with Simon Wootton the pilot. Like the very early days of mainstream aviation, every development was a question of suck it and see. Putting an engine on a hang glider meant someone had to test it to see if it would fly. One of those helping was Dave Simpson, an aeronautical engineer whom I later featured in *Wings!* because he asked his future wife Kay for her hand in marriage 500ft above Dunstable Downs, soaring two-up in a hang glider (what would David have done if Kay had said no?). Simpson described the first flight of the powered Midas:

> The engine was a 90cc two-stroke racing McCulloch, de-tuned
> for reliability and life, and using a flexible drive shaft direct to
> the 24 inch propeller under the keel at the tail. After rigging
> the kite, we took her to the top of Dunstable School's nursery
> slopes near Aylesbury in Bucks. Conditions were ideal, a 12
> mph wind blowing straight up the hill. The gradient we chose
> was about 1 in 7; if the first take-off attempt had to be altered
> for any reason, Simon could glide down the slope and land at

the bottom. Taking off on the flat leaves no margin of height to regain speed in the event of a mishap. We were lucky we took this precaution.

With the engine warmed up and everything checked and double-checked, Murray and I stood in the front quarters, holding a wing wire and a nose wire in each hand. Simon checked out his prone harness, and we all started running. Shortly after Simon had dropped into prone, he needed to make a slight correction into wind; his hand left the throttle and the engine dropped to idle, and then cut out. He flew down to the bottom of the slope with Murray racing behind, arms outstretched, legs a blur.

'Glides OK,' said Simon, laconically.

'What (wheeze) happened?' said Murray.

It is obvious that power needed to be on from the start, so we took her back to the top and tried again.

Launch this time was perfect and the glider pulled out and away from the hill at an incredible rate. After five minutes it had made 800 feet, and everyone on the ground was leaping around with delight like Wilbur and Orville must have done. Simon tried a left 360, then a right, ran the engine at different throttle settings to check that the thrust did not affect pitch trim. From the ground it was impossible to hear the engine from more than 400 feet.

After fifteen minutes Simon shut off the engine and glided down to enable himself to leap up and down like everyone else. The landing, into about 5 mph of wind at the bottom, was straightforward and clean.

The next test had to be a flat ground take-off, and this is where the fun began. Simon found that take-offs into winds of 3 or 4 mph were possible with the right techniques (ie, run like stink), but in completely still air, take-offs were very difficult (his term is 'marginal'). The basic problem was revealed in an interesting way. When looking at the thin film of oil deposited on the propeller from the exhaust, there was a line at about ⅔ chord where the film had built up. This suggested that the prop was stalled or part-stalled at low air speeds, and that a finer pitch prop would 'bite' at a lower speed and facilitate nil-wind launches. Another prop was made and tried, and the results were much more promising. Its performance at the air show at Shoreham silenced the crowd and dumbfounded the commentator.

The quality of innocence in David Simpson's research has gone completely from mainstream aviation. Before anything is tried there, it goes through so many exhaustive unrisky computer tests first that flights are really a confirmation of theory. Quick and dirty is the way Paul MacCready described the way research is done in hang gliding, and part of that quality has been carried over delightfully into the powered field.

The most popular of the wing-mounted engines was called the 'Soarmaster', where the engine was mounted above the pilot's head and under the wing, to one side or other of the control bar. It drove a long shaft that stuck out the back, to which was fixed a propeller. The throttle arrangement varied, but certainly the one I flew had two throttles, the big peg that you bit and then spat out once airborne, and the hand throttle on the bottom of the control bar.

Hundreds of Soarmaster-type kits were sold, and some brilliant flying was done on them. They were marketed as a way of getting a pilot up to the clouds where he could catch thermals, and turn off the engine to enjoy them. If he needed power again, he pull-started the engine in the air and away he went, looking for more natural lift. But for years, there was not a lot of this type of free flying done, and almost as soon as they were felt to work, pilots started doing distances on them, keeping power on all the time.

Using a Soarmaster-type unit built by Steve Hunt, Gerry Breen flew 202 miles from South Wales to Norfolk, impressing among others the Americans, who had claimed 160 miles to be a great distance on such a rig. Breen, a supremely gifted natural pilot on any type of aircraft, Mainstream or new aviation, did a lot of flying on the Soarmaster, but lost two of his toes when, inevitably, he had a hard landing and stuck his feet into the propeller. He went on to be first across the English Channel on a powered rag-wing in a flight from London to Paris in 1979. The hang gliding pioneer Len Gabriels chased after and nearly caught him, using the same type of machine. Len was stopped by French police for bureaucratic reasons about 40 miles south of Le Touquet. Publicity on the flight was virtually nil; I chased him by helicopter, but we made the journey on the same day Lord Mountbatten was murdered by Irish terrorists while on holiday in Ireland.

I had hoped myself to be the first to fly a powered hang glider from London to Paris, but my spectacular 250ft fall on Len's machine the previous 13 November (at 3.15pm, as I remember well, having given up cigarette smoking ever since) put me off the whole idea of powered flight for six years. It was the sail of the wing into which I fell that Len used on his flight to Paris, sewn back together and with a new aluminium frame. Len's flight was paid for with sponsorship from Blue Bird Toffees secured by my little company Flight Promotions. Gerry Breen's sponsor was British Airways!

One Soarmaster adventure had deep political consequences, and is a significant indication of the spread of thinking provoked by the new aviation. In October 1987 two young Arabs launched an air raid on Israel, using Soarmaster-equipped hang gliders and carrying automatic weapons. They flew low over the border; one failed to make it cleanly and landed in a minefield, where he perished. The other landed safely near an Israeli military camp, where he shot six soldiers dead before being killed himself. The incident is widely thought to have triggered off the Palestinian *Intifada* about a month later.

The two Arab pilots were probably taught to fly hang gliders by Jim Bowyer, an Englishman who later ran the British Hang Gliding League, but who, when younger, brought hang gliding to many countries in the Middle East. Bowyer only taught them to fly, of course, not to launch doomed air attacks in hang gliders.

One of the driving forces behind powered hang gliding in Britain was Australian-born Steve Hunt, joint owner of Hiway Hang Gliders, based in Brighton until moving disastrously to South Wales with Welsh Development grant money in 1981 (disastrous because it cut Hiway off from the bubbling ideas and top pilots in the Southern Club). Hunt, full of energy and enthusiasm, managed to separate the powered hang gliding club from the BHGA (by ten votes to nine; I spoke against the split and voted against, and felt that BHGA chairman Roy Hill's was the deciding vote on the split). The powered enthusiasts wanted to be free to go where their experiments took them, while I thought the links with hang gliding were too strong to break. The new organisation, the British Microlight Aircraft Association (BMAA), came into being on 18 November 1980, with Steve Hunt as chairman, and a committee of four, including the wonderfully unlikely figure of David Kirke, founder of the Dangerous Sports Club (soon in trouble for a completely mad attempt, ultimately successful, flying a microlight from London to Paris. Kirke's first initiative on this flight included a sudden encounter with a tree).

There were fifty-five powered hang gliders in Britain at the time of the BMAA's formation, divided as follows: fifteen powered foot-launch flexwings, five wheel-launched flexwings, four Catto wheel-launched CA15s, two powered Fledglings, one powered VJ-23 (David Cook's), four powered Mitchell Wings, ten Electra-Flyer Eagles, eight wheeled

Fledglings (called Pterodactyls), four Weedhoppers, one Hummer and one Hiway Special. The Catto, Fledglings, VJ-23, Mitchell Wings, Eagles, Pterodactyls, Weedhoppers and Hummer were all American wings, so like hang gliding itself, we were going to the Americans to kick-start in power. But like the rest of Europe, we took a much different route. The consensus at the time was that we would take the route of which David Cook was an exponent, with power on rigid wings. Some did, but most didn't.

The most important development in powered hang gliding, and where we split from the Americans, occurred in 1980 with the introduction of the trike. The idea, had we known it, was around in the mid-1960s in some of the US Army's experiments with Rogallo wings. When I met Francis Rogallo at the US Masters of Hang Gliding in 1985, he showed me and Bill Moyes some of the amazing film of 30-year-old army experiments, including a crude trike flown by the first man on the moon, Neil Armstrong. I could not believe how many of the developments we had sweated over and lost lives discovering were already in being all those years earlier.

The modern trike seemed to have originated in France and was introduced to England in early 1980 by Frank Tarjanyi of Hiway Hang Gliding, in a classic new aviation way, according to one of his employees, Gordon Faulkner:

> Now I am aware that some of you regard the new trike phenomenon as an ugly festering carbuncle thrusting its way out of the pure body of hang gliding; but then again maybe there are a few more who see it as a real neat little breakthrough that has given us the first easy-to-fly, reasonably safe, power option for flexwings.
>
> Whatever your opinion, the fact remains that if you own or can purchase a suitable flexwing, the Trike will convert it into a powered aircraft, possessing an extremely enjoyable utility quite beyond that of your original wing. So I reckon it is about time someone said, 'Well done, Frank!'
>
> To be strictly accurate, the seed was sown in Frank's mind by Gerry Breen, who showed him a picture in the French hang gliding magazine, *Vol Libre*, of a tricycle device attached to a flexwing. The first I knew of it was when Frank arrived at my place in a more manic state than usual, with a few scribbled drawings in a textbook. He was extremely taken with the trike idea...

He already owned a rogallo-wing Superscorpion II, which he thought would be a suitable wing. And as the Hiway scrap/offcuts bin was reasonably well-stocked with assorted tubes and stuff, there didn't seem to be any reason not to get the project started.

At this time Steve Hunt was engrossed with developing a 3-axis control rigid prototype and he was only vaguely interested in the trike idea.

He offered Frank an experimental propeller which, I believe, was intended for the 3-axis aircraft. This definitely helped a great deal and saved a lot of work.

Various cheap and available engines were considered and ruled out for the usual reasons. The McCullough 101 direct drive unit gathering dust in a corner of the factory gave Frank a few bouts of incipient larceny, tempered by doubts about this unit's suitability. Then the Valmet 160 engine surfaced through a contact of Steve's.

Over the next two weeks or so the device took shape. It was evening and weekend work, often midnight oil stuff with a few niggly problems to solve. Frank winds himself up a bit sometimes so the project cost him restless nights. A reduction gear was worked out for the Valmet/prop combination and machined up. Wheels were taken from the stores (as fitted to Hiway Harrier trainer bottom bars), and axles to suit were turned up on the lathe. Front forks were fabricated and a foot throttle linkage was fitted to them. Manifold and silencer were welded up from sheet steel and tube. All the other non-scrap components were totalled up, and Frank agreed a fair price with Hiway for the whole package, including the Valmet and experimental prop. At about the same time a plastic seated chair disappeared from the canteen. Its dismembered steel skeleton was later unearthed behind a milling machine.

John Ievers, Steve Hunt's partner in Hiway, and Geoff Shine, Hiway's factory manager, were watching progress with increasing interest. It was beginning to look less like another powered pipe dream as each day passed. Frank worked the last two days on it in company time, so I suppose you could say that it was at this point that it became an official Hiway development programme.

The wing-to-trike coupling was worked out finally, and the initial decision to allow control inputs in two axes only, with no facility for yawing the trike relative to the keel, has since proven to be a sound one.

One day, in the afternoon murk of Sirhowy Field, some three weeks after the project's germination, the 'device' began its first taxiing trials. Thrust was a shade low at about 78lb static, which, together with the soggy ground conditions prevented the aircraft reaching takeoff speed. The fact that Frank was blinded by sprayed mud from the open front wheel didn't help much either!

After a lengthy discussion covering most of the technical factors, the solution seemed to be to drag it up to higher ground, out of the swamp. This would also provide a downhill takeoff run to supplement the lowish thrust. Apart from Frank, those present were John Ievers, Geoff Shine, Nick Whittam, Barbara Tarjanyi, Will Bonner and myself.

A fair amount of tension was building up. The trike wasn't a silly mud-buggy, or a nuts and bolts project any more. It was a potentially lethal flying machine. There was no doubt it would leave the ground from its new starting point. But how would it fly?

Its approximate behaviour in the air was theoretically predictable to a point, but there were a few shadowy areas in the calculations. Remember that this was the very first time the trike concept had been put into practice in this country. Certainly, no one present had ever seen one, apart from the photograph in Vol Libre.

Frank was a shade tight-lipped as he strapped in. Barbara was frightened.

After a takeoff run of about 70 feet the wing began flying. The trike lifted off rear wheels first, the front wheel remaining on the ground for a few moments, causing a control problem. But Frank climbed straight ahead towards the factory. The aircraft appeared stable. Conditions were misty, with a visibility of perhaps ¾ of a mile, with little or no wind. I was relieved when the pilot began his first turn before we lost sight of him.

He stayed up for about 5 minutes, completing several turns in each direction, fly-pasts and throttle variation tests. Control appeared smooth and co-ordinated. It looked fine, apart from the trike's slightly nose wheel-down attitude, which was due to too great an angle between the base and the upright members of the airframe. The wing was at a high angle of attack but this had been expected.

Frank set up a power-off approach to a slightly uphill landing on the shoulder of the slope. Again, the too-low nose wheel caused a problem by touching down first. This was aggravated by the uphill landing.

There followed much questioning and congratulations. Nice one, son!

Frank's enquiry, 'Who's next?' received a brief, but pregnant silence. John Ievers said he would try it.

Again, the tricky rotation, followed by a short but interesting flight for John, who sensibly went for a flat-ground landing. Then Frank flew for another 15 minutes in deteriorating visibility.

Geoff Shine flew it next, but he is a bit heavy for the then-available thrust and, after a difficult takeoff, he scored the first mid-air 'nasty' when the fuel line broke free and began dowsing the back of his flying suit with petrol. With a hot engine six inches away, this opened the door to some nightmare possibilities, so Geoff's landing was not as gentle as it might have been!

The result was a bent lateral member and a bent upright on the trike airframe, plus some useful information on the aircraft's overall resistance to a very heavy landing over a ditch with a 16½ stone (264lb) pilot on board. A modification to cure the nosewheel problem was a touch overdue anyway, so it was probably just as well.

The following morning the repaired and modified toy was flown again by Frank, then myself, Chris Johnson, John Ievers, Geoff Shine (after carefully inspecting the new chewing gum fuel line fixings), Nick Whittam and B.J. Harrison, each an employee (or Bwana) of Hiway. Opinions were generally favourable, the low thrust being a very obvious shortcoming that would need to be worked on. After the machine had been flown for a couple of hours or so, almost non-stop, the news spread to nearby Crickhowell and the Welsh Hang Gliding Centre. Gerry Breen was away at the time but Jim Bowyer, Keith Cowan and a few more came trucking over and joined in the growing mood of delight and elated enthusiasm surrounding Sirhowy Field. Not to mention the mild aerobatics which, in retrospect, I guess were not without hazard since the aircraft was getting some heavy treatment and was beginning to show up minor defects that would require modification.

But the Trike had arrived. It worked. One of my thoughts at the time was that, although the aircraft looked very much like a hang glider, it very obviously wasn't one any more.

Apart from doing some spanner-jockeying for Frank, my contribution to the project was that of test dummy. The principle being that if anyone as grossly incompetent as myself can get away with flying it, then it can't be all bad!

Now they pay me to assemble the things!

John Ievers turned up at the manufacturers' meeting where we were trying to encourage resistance to the UP Comet in January 1981. Our thinking then was, bolt the trike to our regular wing and fly away. They were seen then as single-seaters, and perhaps it was not as unsafe to use ordinary hang gliders as I now think it is. We learned we had to beef up the wings employed on trikes, and soon ceased to use our hang gliders at all, buying a complete unit with a specialised wing. Otherwise our taut hang gliders ended up as soggy over-stretched bags.

At the manufacturers' meet, Ievers demonstrated how brilliant the trike was by bungeeing a folded-up hang glider to the keel of the wing of his trike, and flying the lot up to the top of Hay Bluff, landing on top. This was much better than our normal way to the top, carrying the wing up 600ft on our shoulders. We wanted to use him as a taxi service for the rest of the day, but he wanted to sell us all trikes.

In the end, sometime later, lots of us bought a trike as a whole unit. Two early customers were then League pilots, and their experience when they had one delivered recalls the madcap early days of mainstream aviation. Richard Iddon wrote about the experience, calling his piece 'The First Day':

After waiting three months or so, my cousin John Bridge and myself finally took delivery of our 'Sky Trike' one wet Saturday in September, and spent the evening adapting our hang gliders to take the unit. We completed the conversion by 10.15pm and went home, where John found his missus all dressed up and waiting. In our excitement, he had forgotten that he had arranged to go out!

As I was working from 10am on Sunday morning, we decided to go out at first light to try the unit out, providing the weather was OK. I rose at 6.15am to find the sky clagged in and a steady drizzle falling. Ignoring this, I rushed off to the nearest all-night garage for a gallon of juice, and proceeded to drag John out of bed just as dawn was breaking. With the aid of some loud Anglo-Saxon expletives he persuaded me to go home and back to bed.

'It's only raining a bit,' I complained.

By 11am the weather had cleared up and the sun was shining. John turned up at my shop complete with glider and trike, and I decided that my staff could run the business without me 'just for half an hour', even though we were rather busy. I had negotiated the use of a four-acre field immediately behind my house for taking off, so we rigged John's glider there, connected up the power unit, topped up with two-stroke juice, and were ready to begin. We were both eager to be first but wanted to be second, so we tossed up. John won (or lost?). He strapped in, I fired up the motor and he was away up the field.

The rain had been falling heavily for most of the night and the field was not very well drained, and often frequented by a herd of cows. John ploughed along with the throttle locked full open, and teeth gritted, raising great splashes of water, mud and cow dung, with me in hot pursuit shouting encouragement. Three quarters of the way down the field and still on deck he shut down the power and turned to taxi back. What a transformation! Attired in his Sunday best, complete with recently acquired ski jacket, he had a six-inch wide brown stripe from the top of his helmet down to his waist, which had been thrown up by the front wheel. He looked like a zebra, and I nearly fell over laughing.

After cutting a piece of plywood and wiring it on as a 'mudguard', it was my turn. I repeated John's run along the field with muck and bullets flying in all directions, but thankfully without the zebra stripe to show for it, and with the hedge looming up I, too, had to shut down without lifting off. What were we doing wrong? I tried the other way along the field and with a tentative push out the front wheel began to lift, but the hedge was too close to clear so another 'abort' was called for.

John's turn once again. This time halfway down the field he lifted all three wheels clear for a moment. Still the damned hedge was too close but he had been airborne for two seconds. What an achievement! The first man to fly. Eat your hearts out, Wright brothers. 'Push out more,' he said, so I did. Halfway down the field I gave a hefty push and was suddenly flying. 'Can I make it over the hedge this time?' I thought. 'No, maybe … Yes,' and then at the last moment, 'No!' I cut the power and pulled the bar in, hit the deck and using my heels to plough two deep furrows for the last ten yards, stopped with the nose of the glider shot over that infernal hedge.

John's turn. This time he achieved a good clean lift-off and was climbing away nicely when he suddenly veered off towards my house, and at the same time hit a patch of sink. Panic stations! He cut the power but there was not much field left to land in between him and the house, so he pulled the bar in sharply and hit the ground hard. At this point the left wheel flew off into the air, the kite dipped to one side and slewed around in a 360 on a broken axle.

I suppose I should have been annoyed or at least disappointed but all I could do was laugh until my sides ached. We did fix the unit and next day found a larger field with lower hedges and had a couple of hours' good flying, so everything ended OK, but we have not stopped laughing at our experiences that first day. It has given us the classic answer when anyone asks us about our machine.

'Sky Trikes? Oh yeah, we had one of those, but the wheel fell off.'

Trikes were sturdy, easy to fly, and the skills needed were hang glider pilot's skills, so that was all right. We did not need to learn very much new, except not to take the power off in a climb too close to the ground. Otherwise, trikes opened up flatland flying, and people began throwing them around until a few deaths calmed them down. Looping them sounds impossible, and for some pilots it was the last thing they ever did, but Geoff Ball at Mainair got the hang of it in a weight-shift microlight and with a passenger on board, could do six loops in a row.

Races started: the Norfolk Air Race, the Round Britain, rallies across Europe, altitude records, distance flights in a straight line, triangles, World Championships. In Europe, especially France and Britain, the trike mushroomed, three times as many in France as Britain, but the development was almost exactly the opposite to what was happening in the US. There, with 14,000 microlight pilots, rigid wings were the order of the day, three-axis controls, few weight-shift machines. Ultralights, as the Americans called them, came in all shapes and sizes, but were ultra-light aircraft, unusually weird, but which in appearance would not have been out of place in a 1930s air show. The Americans took to building classic mainstream aircraft like the Mustang and Spitfire, but in an ultralight version.

Australia split. The Thruster, a three-axis machine, was developed for use in the Outback, a sturdy, soft-sail aircraft that could land virtually anywhere, pilot and passenger absolutely open to the elements, used to round up sheep or cattle on farms that were measured in hundreds of square miles. But the weight-shift trike also developed through Moyes and the Duncan brothers – Ricky Duncan was world hang gliding champion in 1988 – and specialised in towing hang gliders into the air. That left hang gliders as machines without power, still pure wings, but towing technique also answered the rather bogus question power pioneers had asked in sticking engines on in the first place: 'Surely this is the best way for us to get to the thermals?' In fact, much more imaginative ways of adding power to flexwings have been developed, but they have not mushroomed the way trikes did.

Trikes were my way back into powered flying. I owned a 25 per cent part of a hang glider company, Solar Wings, taken over by a bigger one in 1984 with money from the Australian billionaire Kerry Packer, and part of the price of buying me out was that I took the company trike. My plummeting crash in 1978, which featured in a children's comic called *The Crunch*, and which I could now see whenever I wanted because I had moved into television and had the means to find the original BBC film of my fall, reminded me of what went wrong and how painful it was.

But now I had my own trike perhaps I could recover my nerve? I kept the trike in the garage, and I couldn't find out how to start it. One night the American Cup pilot John Fack came around, and between us we got the engine going. Unfortunately, the throttle stuck open, there were no brakes anyway and we shot from one end of the garage, not very far, to the other end, ending with a crunching noise as the propeller broke. Solar Wings fell about laughing and sent me a new one.

I made my first trike flight on New Year's Day in 1985, all alone on Ashton Court, open parkland near the city of Bristol. It had taken me three months to work through my nerves and get the wing rigged, the trike attached and the engine running. At 3pm on a clear still-air day, there was nothing left but to get in and fly, or admit that I was too frightened. Who was I going to admit this to? Myself and no one else, for I had no one else in front of whom I could be brave, or cowardly.

The flight itself must have been very funny to watch. I clipped in, pull-started the engine, turned into the slight breeze, and put my foot on the throttle. We shot off, gathering speed, but I got frightened and took my foot off the throttle. Then I resolved to go for it and we leapt into the air, but periodic attacks of nerves meant that I climbed in a series of steps, hanging on to the bar and petrified until I reached 500ft, and realised I had to turn or I would be over the city of Bristol. A turn to the right took a great deal out of me, slow and flat and tentative, all the time expecting the wing to fold up and plummet to the ground. The whole ten minutes in the air was like this, but gradually losing some of my fear, and four or five brain cells congratulating me on being in flight. The landing, into wind, was easy, and I made another flight just before darkness, in which I wasn't nearly so frightened. That was my first flight on the step to flying a microlight to Australia, and later, in 1998, to make the first microlight flight around the world.

Three months later, still short of hours to get my licence, Judy Leden and I flew two separate Pegasus XLS trikes from Manchester to London, exactly seventy-five years after the first great air race in 1910 in Britain between France's Louis Paulhan and England's Claude Graham-White. Conditions were horrible, winds so strong that hang gliding competitions were being cancelled. I ran out of fuel at 3,000ft over the Midlands town of Stafford and had to find a field to land. I was so fixated on getting back into the air again and catching Judy that, having found petrol and refuelled, it was only when I rose into the air again to be blown backwards in the high wind that I realised it was too dark to fly (shades of my first day hang gliding eleven years earlier). My landing in a field surrounded by a river and power lines can only be called 'interesting'. By the sheerest chance, a neighbour of the only microlight pilot in the area saw me descend, and he came and shouted in the dark until he found and rescued me, helping me get to Louis Paulhan's hotel in Litchfield, where Judy had already booked in overnight. I did no damage and we completed the flight the following day.

There were a number of brilliant flights on trikes. Gerry Breen came down from John O'Groats on one, with rubber bags of petrol slung on either side of him in addition to the main tanks. He was twelve and a half hours in the air, flew 550 miles, his future wife in the back seat snoring gently through the middle of the day as Gerry hacked it through two opposing air systems. The wind turned against him and he could not make Land's End, and so that arduous flight counted for nothing.

Neil Hardiman, a young Englishman who is now an Australian, and who organised my microlight flight to Australia, set out to fly a flexwing microlight around Australia, emulating a feat by Charles Kingsford Smith back in 1927. Neil used one of the Duncan brothers' trikes, a really tough machine, and spent 189 days on the journey (of which, he says, he only had to pay for his accommodation on five nights). He was wrecked in a forced landing on a beach right up near Cape York, the most northern point in Australia, and spent thirty-six hours listening to his Walkman and sitting in a tent next to his wreckage, surrounded by crocodiles and wild pigs, before being able to contact a passing aircraft. The pilot diverted a barge on to Neil's beach, they carted him and the wreckage to Cairns, and in between all the wild parties, Neil rebuilt his aircraft and set off across the north coast of Australia.

One of his more dangerous moments came when he fell among a tough deep-water fishing crew. They were all women, and Neil, a good-looking man, had to make his excuses and leave as soon as was decent.

South of Perth in Western Australia, and over-confident, Neil landed badly and wrecked his machine again. Taking the sail off, he hitch-hiked 3,000 miles with it under his arm all the way to Sydney to get it sewn up and repaired, said hello and goodbye to his fiancée Robyn, and hitch-hiked 3,000 miles back to rebuild the frame and stick the sail back on again. Most of the rest of the flight along the rough south coast of Australia, he completed in a series of legs at the height of 12,000ft.

Of course, a mainstream pilot could have made the same flight, and back in 1927, did, but none could have repaired their machines as Neil did to get back in the air again, and few modern-day mainstream pilots could rebuild their wing.

Another superb trike flight involved the Dutchman Eppo Harbrink-Numan. He flew the North Atlantic in 1990 on a British-built Raven wing, but the trike unit in which he sat was a flying fuel tank, which would have given me the cold robies. Interestingly, given the prevailing westerly winds, he chose to go east to west, via Scotland and the Faroe Islands to Iceland. I think he chose not to go the other way because the Canadians might have banned him even taking off, as they banned the first powered-hang glider to try the Atlantic back in 1980, piloted by a Californian with the improbable name of Eagle Sarmont.

Eppo ran into problems with the Icelanders, who would not let him continue from Reykjavik to Kulusuk in Greenland in his trike, despite passionate entreaties. Eppo left his aircraft there and went back to Holland, reappearing the following year with a chase plane to fly with him. This time the Icelanders, reluctantly, let him go, and he made it safely to the east side of Greenland. I wish I could tell you how he crossed the 12,000ft of ice, and 350 miles of Greenland, but Eppo wrote only that he took off, and some hours later landed on the west coast of Greenland! He later made it to New York.

The South Atlantic was crossed in December 1991 by a Frenchman, Guy Delage, 41 years old, married, two children, and the man who later swam the Atlantic! Delage trained for months for the epic microlight flight, emulating the great French pioneer pilot Jean Mermoz, who did the same 'jump' across 2,350km of water in one flight back in 1933. Delage did it in twenty-six hours in a weight-shift machine, carrying 350 litres of fuel, and surviving a storm within the infamous Pot au Noir, which he said drove him so low he hit a flying fish leaping out of the sea.

In 1990, a German pilot called Zoltan Ovari flew from Europe to Australia, on a British-built weight-shift Raven wing, taking about fifty flying hours longer than me. He had a lot of problems, being impounded in Burma. In 1997–98 an Englishman, Colin Bodill, flying a flexwing, took forty-nine days to fly from London to Sydney, ten days faster than me, establishing a new speed record. Two years later he also beat my time when he made the second flight around the world in a microlight, again in a weight-shift, the Mainair Blade 912.

But the first and one of the greatest of the weight-shift microlight flights was undertaken by an old Etonian Englishman, Richard Meredith-Hardy, known as RMH. It was terrific because it was so early in our history, more than 6,000 miles when other pilots would boast of 50-mile flights. Richard went on to become world microlight champion, and twice European champion, but his flight from London to Cape Town in 1985, on a trike that seems so dated to us now, was worthy to be matched to any of the mainstream flights across Africa in the 1920s.

RHM was pursued across Africa by Nikki Lindsay-Smith, now his wife, in a huge truck (known as the Rolly) full of spare parts, which ran into more problems than her airborne husband did. Richard was first to fly a trike across the Alps, and first to cross the Mediterranean in a flight of eight hours across water, with a single two-stroke 447cc engine, unaccompanied, to Egypt. Their journey across Africa through war-torn Sudan and down through Uganda, Kenya, Tanzania, Zambia and Zimbabwe to South Africa was an epic. It included an attempt by RHM to fly over Kilimanjaro, the highest mountain in Africa at 19,340ft; he could 'only' get to 18,100ft before he had to abandon his attempt, short of fuel and having no oxygen at all. The whole flight was made without a penny of sponsorship, and there was an air about the journey that would have been recognised by some of the earlier gentlemen explorers of Africa.

In 2004, nine years outside my remit, RMH was the first man to fly a trike over Everest, 29,036ft high. He was towing an Italian hang glider pilot at the time, Angelo d'Arrigo, but the tow line broke at 27,000ft. RMH took photographs, film and a GPS tracker to illustrate his Everest flight, while Angelo claimed to have soared over the summit – allegedly.

Weight-shift microlights have become workhorses for expeditions, crossing Iceland for example, or on the higher reaches of Everest. They have come a long way, in speed, safety and reliability, since the early days of powered hang gliding. In Britain, microlights make up 20 per cent of the register of powered aircraft, though there is still a system on many British mainstream airfields that will not let microlights land. Various excuses are given, that we are not fast enough, that we make too much noise, but at bottom we are still seen as an alien being in the air and cause uneasiness to mainstream flyers. It is a similar feeling to that felt by glider pilots in 1975 on the Long Mynd to hang glider pilots, and of course, there is truth in it. We are alien to them, in the sense that there is still so much we have to find out about our own form of flying, while they have learned most of what there is to know about theirs.

In France, by contrast, almost every conventional airfield has two circuits for air traffic, one at 1,000ft for mainstream aircraft, the other at 500ft for ULMs. To give one example of what flying a ULM is like there, I flew into Biarritz Airport with my son James snoring in the back, and was told to circle over the main runway while a Boeing 737 landed, before being allowed to follow it in! Biarritz ATC only thought it was amusing that I had landed there (and not a bore, as, say, Lydd Airport on the south coast of England would have done). After the computer calculated what was owed on the aircraft's weight, they charged me a landing fee of a derisory £1.87. Microlights are more welcome in France than in any other country I know (except, for some reason, in Calais).

On the other hand, Heathrow, the busiest international airport in the world, let me lead twenty-two other microlights to take-off there on 25 August 1994 to celebrate the seventy-fifth anniversary of the world's first international air service between London and Paris. The manager of Heathrow ATC, a wonderful man called Richard Taylor, stood in the pouring rain for more than an hour while we debated whether to fly, and he waved us all off when we did. When the French ATC at Le Bourget in

Paris, our eventual goal, became nervous at the rotten weather conditions and were minded not to let us land, Richard flew to Paris by airliner and spent three passionate hours persuading them otherwise. The romantic soul is not completely missing in mainstream aviation.

Sixteen microlights made it through the following day to Paris, despite the appalling weather. One that did not, piloted by Dave Simpson, the man who described the first flight of the powered Midas E, had engine failure one minute out of Heathrow and landed in a nearby field. He was greeted by a vicar and a lady doctor, who said they could cope with any of his problems except the mechanical one. Another six microlight pilots did not complete the journey because they found the flying a bit arduous and dropped out voluntarily (and regretted it afterwards). The sixteen of us who got through, guided by Richard Meredith-Hardy on the same old trike he had flown to Cape Town, saw clouds lift magically to reveal the Eiffel Tower. As *The Times* reporter Julia Llewellyn-Smith said (crammed into the back of one of the trikes with her legs around her pilot Tony Hughes: 'We will never forget the experience.')

Something of the flavour of what a long-distance flight in a microlight is like may be gained from an extract from my journal covering my microlight flight to Australia in 1987–88, flying a three-axis CFM Shadow built by the same David Cook who flew the powered VJ-23 across the Channel. My flight was to celebrate the Australian bicentenary, and I was chasing the ghost of Ross Smith, who first made that flight in 1919 – Smith had been Lawrence of Arabia's personal pilot – but I had run into a number of problems.

A strong headwind held me up when I left London on 2 December, and I struggled across Europe via the French and Italian Alps, and down the east coast of Italy to the Greek islands. A week later, short of fuel and forced to land on the island of Kythira, strong cross winds flipped me upside down, wrecking the aircraft. My friend Mike Atkinson, a former paratrooper and hang gliding League pilot, was shadowing my flight with a first-class air ticket to Australia, and carrying a spare engine as hand baggage. He turned up on Kythira the following day, looked at the wreckage, laughed wildly, and began gluing it together again.

On 15 December, he gave me the OK to carry on, and I flew to Crete, then Alexandria and Cairo and on towards Amman in Jordan. But at Aqaba, I was given jet fuel instead of petrol, and my engine stopped running next to the Dead Sea when I was at 5,000ft, trying to cross some 6,000ft mountains. I landed on a road about 1 mile from the Israeli border, and furiously denied accusations that I was an Israeli spy. Then Mike turned up again by helicopter, diagnosed the problem, fixed it, and I flew into Amman the following day to come under the patronage of King Hussein of Jordan.

This eased my journey across the 1,100 miles of the Saudi Desert, which needed easing because poor fuel kept causing partial engine failures, which I wrote on my maps as HFs – heart failures – and twice, BHFs, big heart failures. It was hardly a relief to get to the huge airfield at Dhahran in Saudi, on the edge of the Persian Gulf, on Christmas Eve 1987, because I had to plan a five-hour flight across the sea the following day in the middle of the Iran-Iraq War. As it happened, it was to be a more interesting Christmas Day than I wanted:

The wind had changed direction from the previous day, swinging more to the south, which was a worry. But it was a light wind and I had easily enough fuel to cross the Persian Gulf. I had been routed by air traffic control north of Bahrain and then southeast across the most heavily policed stretch of water in the world to a small emirate called Abu Dhabi. Eve Jackson, the first person to fly a microlight from London to Sydney, but who took fifteen months doing it, had told me in England that Abu Dhabi was an oasis of Europeans within the Arab world. She had been greatly helped there by an outfit called Emirates Air Service. Mike and I decided we would take half a day off there while he changed the engine. It was the only half-day off we planned on the whole flight, the rule being, if I could fly to the next airfield before darkness then I did.

We packed equipment into the back of the *Dalgety Flyer*, including my small travelling bag and the 5-gallon 2-stroke mixing tank, empty of course. There were three fuel tanks on the Flyer, the standard 5-gallon tank at the back, a 7-gallon slipper tank underneath and a 16-gallon main tank in the passenger compartment. Both the 5-gallon and the main tank fed into the slipper tank, which in turn supplied the engine. The main tank was not tied down and whatever we did with the luggage may have moved it. The effect, as I discovered less than four hours after take-off, was to kink the fuel pipe and effectively cut off half my fuel.

Take off was at 7.15 and I climbed to 2,000 feet heading east. Crossing the coast the engine lost power but I managed to refrain from telling ATC, and after about 15 seconds power came back again. It was probably water in the fuel system. The Flyer almost developed a daily cough before settling down to run sweetly the rest of the day. I hoped it wouldn't happen again and flew out over the sea. When I looked up the sky was clear blue with no clouds in sight, but looking down at the calm sea there was a mist in the air and visibility was not brilliant.

For three hours the flight was uneventful. All the air traffic controllers were either British or American, and Bahrain ATC stayed in touch until I was out of radio range. I followed a compass course and looked for any of the warships that were stationed in the Gulf. The Americans had put out a NOTAM – a warning – not to fly too near their ships and to stay tuned to the emergency frequency to pick up their messages. I had hoped, when the flight was being planned, to find a US Navy aircraft carrier and get permission to land on it and pick up the captain's signature for Australia's Birthday Book. But I saw no warships, only tankers, and passed too far to the north to see any islands.

At about 1015 Dhahran time I noticed that the fuel gauge on the 5-gallon tank read empty, and when I switched to the 7-gallon slipper tank it was reading less than half full. I was not as terror-struck by this information as I might have been because I distrusted my fuel gauges ever since Kythira and I knew I had a lot more fuel than the gauges showed. But when Abu Dhabi came into radio range – I heard them calling for me, which was comforting – I told them I might have a problem. They could see me on their radar screens and told me I was 50 miles out and I flew on. I felt that the gauges were wrong but if they weren't there was nothing I could do about it. I hoped the gauges were wrong.

They weren't.

Thirty-two miles away from Abu Dhabi Airport at just after 11 o'clock Dhahran time, the engine stopped. I was at 2,000 feet heading southeast and could see a tanker heading north in front of me. In the stillness I could hear the air rushing past the cockpit and my heart pounding deeply. I called Abu Dhabi and in a shaky voice said, 'My engine's stopped, I'm going in.' They were calm, and I could hear them vectoring aircraft towards me. For the first thousand feet of descent, I was frightened.

David Cook, who had designed my CFM Shadow, had discussed with me the possibility of going into the sea. It was, I thought, an academic discussion, because – ho ho – it won't happen to me. He said I had to wear shoulder straps as well as a lap strap because when the aircraft hit the water I would be thrown forward and smash my face against the instrument panel. I thought it was better to go in with a lap strap only because if the aircraft was turned upside down I wanted to bash the canopy open, undo the lap strap and dive away. Shoulder straps could trap me. When the engine stopped I was wearing only a lap strap and tried half-heartedly to get into the shoulder straps. It was too difficult in the confined space and I gave up and thought about how to fly her on to the water.

I was wearing the same lifejacket I had used when trying to cross the English Channel by hang glider 10 years earlier. Then, when I fell short, I had made the mistake of blowing up the lifejacket before I hit the water, a mistake because I was nearly trapped underneath by the wing and unable to dive because of the lifejacket's buoyancy. I made the same mistake in the *Dalgety Flyer* and inflated it.

At about a thousand feet, still a couple of minutes away from getting wet, I became fatalistic. Inshallah, I said, it is the Will of God. I didn't believe that in the Muslim sense but just that what was happening was happening and I had to make the best of it. I turned the Flyer into wind and watched the tanker. It gave no indication, then or at any time later, that I had been seen. I saw the sea was calm and was relieved in a detached way. A small piece of me was also relieved the flight was now over and I wouldn't have to put up with being afraid for much longer. I had no belief the aircraft would fly again and just wanted to get out of her safely.

At 500 feet I radioed, 'What a way to spend Christmas,' but I think I was too low to be heard and anyway ATC were calmly sending aircraft my way and probably had no time for frivolities. Close to the water I tried putting my spare radio in the back in the vain hope it would not get wet. I pulled the flaps down. David Cook had said I shouldn't use the flaps because of the torque they would create on the wings damaged in Kythira, but, what the hell. She flew very slowly over the surface of the sea and I held her off and held her off.

Just before we hit I radioed, 'This is it!'

The canopy sprang in at me and I tasted a mouthful of salt water. Then water poured off me and I could see again and the canopy was gone and I was sitting in the cockpit with the sea lapping around my waist. My cameras had gone straight to the bottom of the Gulf 60 feet below. Bits of paper floated around in the cockpit. I undid my lap-strap and stood up in the cockpit and looked around. The sea was flat calm and the tanker cruised northwards as if nothing had happened. About half a mile away an Arab dhow was sailing south.

Money, I thought, I must get my credit cards and money out of the back or I will be helpless. I reached into the back cockpit and pulled out the travelling bag and put it on top of the wing. I pulled out the dinghy but thought it would be melodramatic to blow it up immediately as I was in no danger of sinking so I put it, uninflated, on the wing as well. The empty 5-gallon mixing tank was jammed by water pressure in the roof of the wing and I left it there. I saw a plastic bag floating on the water and thought, the Dalgety Birthday Book! Without it my whole flight was worthless, all those signatures and addresses without which I could not write the book of the flight. I dived and swam for it and brought it back to line up on the top of the wing. The seat cushion floated away and I let it go. I waited.

After five minutes a twin-engine aircraft flew overhead and started circling. I waved and the pilot waved back. The Arab dhow had passed by but then stopped in the water and turned. I watched it fearfully. I did not want them to rescue me because I didn't know what would happen if they did. Could they claim me as salvage? They stood off about 200 yards and watched. I carried on waiting but after a while looked at the Flyer. She is undamaged, I thought. The wings are in place and there does not appear to be anything broken. The instruments were awash and the beautiful radio sets were ruined, and probably the engine too. But Mike had a spare engine and if he put it on, why should she not fly again? It was not a strong thought but it was there.

Twenty-five minutes after I hit the water I heard a helicopter and a Bell 212 came out of the south and circled low over me. The pilot, a Canadian called Bill Kipke, hovered six inches above the Flyer's wing while I handed the observer all my luggage. His name was Calum Fryer, also Canadian and both based at an oil rig called Zacum West. Calum lowered a rescue harness and I somehow grasped it and climbed into the helicopter.

'Can you take my aircraft too?' I shouted, 'She is very light.'

'No,' he shouted back, 'it's really dangerous for helicopters to carry aircraft. Their wings could fly up and hit our main rotor!'

We circled the Flyer lying flat in the water. I was rescued but I felt numb. The dhow had turned away from my aircraft but had not gone away. Bill Kipke opened the throttles and we climbed away and the Flyer and the dhow got smaller in the water. I clutched the Birthday Book to my wet jacket and thought about very little.

They took me to the oil rig where I had a cup of tea and talked to the air traffic controller there. I called London and told the PR man for Dalgety, Simon Newlyn, the details about going in the water. I said I was going to try and get her out and get her to fly again. It was very early in the morning in London and Newlyn started to phone media contacts. I phoned my wife Fiona to let her know I was OK, and she should not be alarmed, whatever stories she heard, but I was going to continue the flight. She reassured my children, James and Jade, who did not need that reassurance very much because I had worked the previous five years in television, and everyone knows that whatever bad happens to television people, it is not real. That is certainly how they felt, although James, then 12, did ask Fiona, 'If Daddy doesn't come back, are you going to take to drink?'

I could hear from another phone the tinny sounds of aviation authorities trying frantically to find out what had gone wrong and to get their teeth into me but I was becoming more and more convinced that we could rescue the Flyer, if only I could discover how.

I was aware, because I knew my aviation history, that an Englishman (though he was really a New Zealander) called Francis Chichester, later Sir Francis, had fallen into the sea next to Norfolk Island on his flight between New Zealand and Australia in 1931. Chichester had pulled his aircraft out of the

191

water, and over the next three months he had rebuilt it from scratch. If he could do it, I thought, why could I not do the same thing? He had to wait for spare parts to be shipped by sea from England, on voyages lasting six to eight weeks. I could get my spare parts by air in less than twenty-four hours.

Bill Kipke and Calum Fryer continued their Christmas lunch while I was on the phone, and I had a second cup of tea. Afterwards they helicoptered me to Abu Dhabi, landing at the air force base in Bateen, right on the coast. I dumped my wet luggage and soggy maps and jacket on a trolley and trailed irritably into ATC. It took me a little while to notice a young Arab dressed all in white from head to toe like Lawrence of Arabia. He was quiet with a gentle smile and all the others in the room deferred to him, despite his youth.

'My name is First Lieutenant Rachid Abbad,' he told me, 'and you are under the patronage of Sheikh Mohammed bin Zayed.'

I had no idea who Sheikh Mohammed bin Zayed was and I did not actually understand what Rachid was saying. I was so wrapped up in my grief at losing the aircraft and the faint hope of rescuing her and I badly wanted my friend Mike Atkinson. But Rachid told me that Sheikh Mohammed was the Armed Forces Minister for Abu Dhabi and he was at that time hawking in Pakistan. The Sheikh had learned that I was under the patronage of King Hussein – a direct descendent of the Prophet Mohammed through the Prophet's daughter, Fatima – and said if I was under the King's patronage I must be given whatever I wanted to allow the flight to continue. The Sheikh appointed Rachid as his agent.

'Can you find me Mike Atkinson?' I said, with little hope that he even knew what I was talking about.

'No problem,' he said.

I had heard this comment a number of times in the Middle East, and it usually meant exactly the opposite. But Rachid showed me out to a gleaming new Mercedes 300 and we got in and drove a few hundred yards and there was Mike!

He had seen me off in Dhahran that morning and caught a scheduled flight to Abu Dhabi. When he arrived he was met by a Royal Jordanian Airlines agent who told him the Flyer had crashed into the sea but that I was safe. He told Mike

I was being taken to Bateen Airport and Mike took a taxi and was driven there. The air force guard wouldn't let him beyond the boundary gate and Mike had put the spare engine on the ground and was walking around in frantic circles. He was thinking, 'Should I go to Australia (where his wife was waiting to meet him) before my ticket is cancelled? Or do I fly back to England?'

I got out of Rachid's car and told him I thought my microlight would fly again if we put the spare engine on. There was, I said, no structural damage and as long as the seawater did not make the joints come apart she could fly. But most aircraft which go into the water are as much damaged by retrieval as by hitting the water. Mike got into Rachid's car and we went back to the operations room.

'Now, what else would you like?' Rachid asked gently.

'Can you tell the two ships that are going out to the Flyer not to touch her but to wait until we get out there?' I said.

'And can you get us a helicopter?' said Mike.

'No problem,' he said again, but it was a problem for a while. Rachid had amazing power for a young lieutenant; I heard later he was the son of a Sultan, whatever that means, but he would not tell me. He mustered an Egyptian Army Major who was a helicopter pilot but who was reluctant to take us out. The Major thought we wanted him to lift the Flyer out of the water and that, if she was damaged, we would sue him for that damage. When we heard this we laughed and assured him we didn't want him to lift the Flyer.

'We're not Americans,' I said, 'we're Englishmen, and we don't sue.'

'Just take us there and throw us in and leave us if you like,' said Mike. 'We'll use the ships to rescue the aircraft.'

'Ah,' said the Major, 'if that's all, then no problem.'

While we were conducting these delicate negotiations the four phones inside the operations room rang constantly. Mike was trying to use one to contact the ships on the way to the aircraft by radio-telephone, but every time we picked the phone up an English voice said, 'Can I speak to Brian Milton?' Christmas Day is traditionally a bad day for stories and the duty journalists in London on all the great newspapers and television stations were probably dozing. Then Newlyn broke the story that the *Dalgety Flyer* was in the sea but we proposed to take her out and fly again. It was a lovely Christmas Day story, just the right amount of English eccentricity to it, and the phones started to jump.

I did an interview with *The Times* and it made the front page the following day. But as more demands came in for interviews, Mike and I came under time pressure. Mike got through to the ships and half-sent his message not to touch the aircraft, but we were not sure they would wait for us and we wanted to get away quickly. Trailing half-finished interviews, we left the operations room and were taken by the Major and Rachid to a huge Puma helicopter. Mike had the ITN camera but it was, gently but firmly, taken from us for 'security reasons' while we were on the military base. Rachid joined us in the helicopter and we took off and turned out to sea.

At about that time the Iranians started an attack on two tankers to the north of where the Flyer was lying in the water (they killed seven people). The helicopter had a full search-and-rescue crew on board, who smiled at us through all their equipment. Mike and I each wore trousers and a Dalgety T-shirt, leaving shoes and socks on board with Rachid. Mike had a handful of tools including a hacksaw blade and an old screwdriver. He had been thinking about how to lift the Flyer out of the water but did not tell me his plans. I watched the Egyptian Major follow the beam of a radio VOR over the sea and strained to catch the first glimpse of the Flyer.

When we found her she was lying nose-up, deep in the calm water. The leading edges of the wings and my cockpit were clear of the sea but the rest was submerged. About 50 yards away was a flat ship with two cranes, and behind that a tug. A small rubber dinghy had put out from the ship and was slowly circling the Flyer.

I shouted to the Major not to get too close to my aircraft, as his down wash would destroy it. Rachid looked excited and as if he was really enjoying himself. I sat by the open hatchway and Mike told me repeatedly not to jump. He said the only person able to judge when to go was a jumpmaster and without one I would probably jump when the helicopter was too high and knock myself unconscious. I waited. Mike said later I looked very apprehensive. Neither of us thought about sharks.

Finally the jumpmaster put his thumbs up and, 200 yards away from the Flyer and 15 feet off the water, I jumped. I had always wanted to do that, jump into the sea from a helicopter to rescue something, and I felt fulfilled doing it then. The water was warm and tasted of oil and I surfaced in time to see Mike jump after me. We started swimming and watched the helicopter make a dramatic wheeling turn – news of the Iranian tanker attack was coming through and they were needed – and turn away toward Abu Dhabi. I led Mike towards the Flyer and either swam or lay there treading water and laughing madly. Mike grinned wolfishly as he made his stately progress towards the Flyer. It was for both of us the best moment of the whole flight.

The dinghy pulled towards us and in the bow, inevitably, was an Englishman. I made introductions from the water.

'Hello, I'm Brian Milton and this is my friend Mike Atkinson,' I said between mouthfuls of seawater.

He shouted back: 'My name's Charlie Rogerson and I'm a diver on that ship.'

Charlie came from Manchester. I thanked him for not touching the Flyer and he threw a rope and towed us both to the aircraft. Her tail was deep in the water. I took off my life jacket and swam down and attached it to the tail and inflated it. The tail slowly rose to the surface. Mike asked Charlie again for a towing rope and attached it to the Flyer's nose wheel. Charlie towed us slowly to the ship and laid us along side.

'Charlie,' I called out, 'I am a journalist. Please get a camera and take whatever shots you can of us taking the Flyer out of the water.'

Charlie left the dinghy and went off for a camera. Mike climbed into the cockpit of the aircraft and started cutting, bashing and karate chopping a big hole in the top of the wing. I clung on to the right strut and watched in horror. He threw away bits and pieces and when the hole was 15 inches square he started to thread a rope under the intersection point between fuselage and wing. This was, he decided, the only place to lift the aircraft and whatever damage was done could be repaired later. He could not thread the rope through however, and tore the radio aerial out of the cockpit roof and bent it to make a hook.

'Is that absolutely necessary?' I asked from the water. 'Will it work again?'

Mike grunted and ignored me, continuing to push and at last threaded the rope through and made a loop. He called for a crane and a hook descended and the Flyer was pulled a couple of feet out of the water. We dived to dismantle the wings, first the right wing and then the left. That meant diving to undo the linkages between the cockpit and ailerons and flaps, then the struts linked to the bottom of the cabin, and then the two big pins that hold the wing on. We stuffed all the bolts and pins into our soggy pockets. The wings floated easily and we pushed them around to waiting hands from the crew.

The NMS401 was an oilrig support vessel, flat shaped, with two cranes and a central superstructure. Her crew, mostly Christians from the Philippines, had been in the Persian Gulf for a month and had run out of beer. It was Christmas Day and if they could rescue us, we were the reason they were going into Abu Dhabi to replenish their beer stocks. We were very popular. Fifty hands reached down to lift each wing gently on to the deck. The crane lifted the body of the Flyer and deposited her dripping on the deck. Mike and I climbed out of the water, after our ninety-minute struggle.

Mike looked her over carefully, feeling the wings in particular. We felt anything else on the aircraft was repairable except the wings. In the six hours she lay in the water the waves had moved the elevator on the tail-plane so much that the Morse cable, which controlled it, was broken. That was the only structural damage.

'You're right, she will fly again,' Mike said.

We were shown to a cabin and a shower and given clean dry clothes. We had forgotten it was Christmas Day in the battle to get the Flyer out of the water, and thought anyway that no one celebrated Christmas in the Persian Gulf because it is not a Muslim feast. But the captain of the ship was a Lebanese Christian called Ibrahim Youssef Makhoul (known as Michel) and he and Charlie Rogerson were sitting down to a big turkey dinner with Christmas pudding to follow.

Mike and I joined them and in the heat of the Persian Gulf we had the most extraordinary Christmas dinner we had ever had.

That evening with the moon soft and yellow and the sea calm and dappled in moonlight, we steamed for Abu Dhabi. The big deck lights were turned on and Mike filled a 50-gallon drum with diesel fuel and began throwing in engine parts to preserve them after being in the salt water. I hosed down the wings and fuselage with fresh water, a process we continued for the next five days to remove all the corrosive salt from the airframe. We lifted out the radios and instruments and sprayed them with WD40 but they were beyond hope.

Dismantling the fuel system and taking out the tanks, I wanted to know what had gone wrong. I knew how much fuel there was at the start of the flight but I was deeply fearful I had miscalculated and was out of petrol when the engine stopped. Both the 5-gallon standard tank and the 7-gallon slipper tank were full of seawater, but when we emptied the main 16-gallon tank we found it was half full of fuel.

'There you are,' said Mike. 'You were in the air four hours and the two empty tanks hold twelve gallons. At three gallons an hour that accounts for those tanks. There must have been a blockage to stop fuel coming from the main tank.'

We made a careful examination of the main tank but could find no obvious source for the blockage. It could only have been a kinked pipe caused by movement of the tank on the back seat. We had only just completed the strip-down by 11 o'clock in the evening when we docked, and there was Rachid and his values of Arab hospitality to meet us in his beautiful Mercedes.

'Leave her on board tonight,' he said, 'and come back tomorrow. I will make arrangements tomorrow to get her to the airfield!'

We were driven to pick up our luggage and then on to the 4-star Airport Hotel where we checked in. We had a meal in the restaurant and some much-needed beer and then unpacked. I took all my wet money, more than two thousand dollars in $20, $10 and $1 bills, and separated each note and laid them out to dry. I did the same with about $2,500 worth of sopping traveller's cheques. Mike separated all the wet maps, some of which were very tatty, and laid those out to dry. When we had finished the room looked like a counterfeiter's paradise.

I was hyped up with energy and adrenaline. It was 2 o'clock before I went to bed. It was the best Christmas of my life.

In the event, Mike and I got the *Dalgety Flyer* repaired within five days and, after a number of other bizarre adventures, I flew her on to Australia. I arrived in Sydney fifty-nine days after I had set out from London; for nine years this was the longest, fastest microlight flight in history. The *Dalgety Flyer* is now on display in an adjunct to the prestigious Powerhouse Museum in Sydney.

Another Australian compliment was passed to me by the 'Father of Hang Gliding' Bill Moyes, who said he would have given odds of fifty to one against me succeeding.

My flight was contemptuously dismissed by my peers in Britain. Norman Burr, editor of the official British microlight magazine *Flightline*, labelled it 'the world's longest ego trip'. A year after my flight ended, nine months after I had returned to England, I had received not one invitation from a British microlight club to talk about it. I was invited, though, to speak about it by Squadron Leader Tony Iveson DFC of 617 'Dambuster' Squadron on the forty-fourth anniversary of this elite squadron sinking of the fearsome German battleship *Tirpitz* on 12 November 1944. Tony had been on all three *Tirpitz* operations, and twenty-one years later he and I went on to write *Lancaster – The Biography* together.

Why the diametrically opposing views? The values of different generations, I suppose. The best values of the mainstream trumped the worst values of the new aviation.

I want to write just a short note on my microlight flight around the world in 1998 – two years outside my remit – which started off with a companion and co-pilot, Keith Reynolds. It ended with me coming back alone. I had set the flight up in conscious imitation of the first aerial circumnavigation of the earth by an eight-man US Army team called 'the World Cruise'. Flying four single-engined Douglas World Cruiser aircraft, they took off from Seattle, Washington State, in 1924, and went west ('the wrong way' – BM) via Alaska, the Aleutian Islands, Japan, China, Singapore, Malaysia, Burma, India, the Middle East, Italy, France, England, Scotland, Iceland, Greenland and Labrador back to the US. The journey took 175 days, more than twice as long as the mythical Phileas Fogg in *Around the World in Eighty Days*, but only sixty-six days were spent flying. Two of the four aircraft made it all the way around (no one was killed when the other two force-landed, one in Alaska, the other heading for Iceland fell into the North Atlantic), with a flight time of 351 hours at a speed of 85mph. The engines had been changed five times, and their wings twice at pre-arranged spots. Every time they came to seas, they exchanged wheels for floats.

I did the flight in 120 days, flying on 71 of the days, with 405 flying hours. My major delays were caused by bureaucrats, in China, Japan, Russia and even Denmark. The book I wrote about the flight, *Global Flyer*, is to be made into a Hollywood film. Hugh Bonneville, the star of *Downton Abbey*, will play me.

In the second volume of the history of the new aviation – entitled *Wild Adventures of the New Aviators* – I describe some of the characters attracted to this new form of flight – flying a forest fire, how one top pilot was charged with 104,000 counts of assault with a deadly weapon because he flew over America's annual Rose Bowl. There are chapters on how big-distance flights developed; the entry of women into the new aviation; flying with the birds, including eagles; the early roots of paragliding; how competitions developed to test cross-country flying; how and why deaths have occurred; why isn't hang gliding and paragliding an Olympic sport; and bivouac flying, including the story of the beau ideal, Didier Favre, and his 1,000-mile flight in a hang glider.

Sources

W   *Wings*, the BHGA magazine that I edited for a year
XC   *Cross Country* magazine, then mainly edited by Sherry Thevenot
FL   *Flightline*, the magazine of the British Microlight Aircraft Association
HG   *Hang Gliding*, the magazine of the USHGA

Features from various miscellaneous magazines

Reference Coding

Wings: W576.15 an article published on p.15 of the May 1976 edition.

Cross Country: SO94 was published in the September-October edition in 1994.

Flightline: FL3/486.8 is an article published in the March-April 1986 edition on p.8.

Hang Gliding: HG991 was published on September 1991.

1. Alvin Russell, My Best Friend

W576.15 Mynd Magic (Alvyn Russell)
W576.30 Poem, Pilot's Creed, Mike Collis
W976.18/19 Alvin Russell's report on training
W177.4 Alvin Russell memorial

2. History of Aviation to Lilienthal in 1896

HG991.36 Backgrounder on Lilienthal
XCSP89.20/21 Detail, Cayley's coachman in 1852!

XCAU89.32 da Vinci's flying machine 'a turkey' claims media
XCJJ94.48/50 Leonardo da Vinci's glider flies in UK, Michael Pidcock

3. Roots of Hang Gliding to the first Lilienthal meet

XCSU90.5 Francis Rogallo on origin of rog wings, John Dickenson!
XCFM92.10/11 More details on Francis Rogallo
W1077.21 Jeannie Knight interview Bill Moyes
W480.17/18 ROOTs, including good material on J. Lambie
W884.8/9 Interview Bill Moyes
HG477.36/37, 42, 44 Interview with Jack Lambie on roots
HG378.20/23 Interview, part 1, Volmer Jensen
HG680.14/15 Nostalgia about building wings with bamboo and plastic
HG1084.38/40 Three-page interview with Bill Moyes
HG991.19 History of early HG and USHGA
HG991.29 Jack Lambie on Richard Miller (looks like a Beat poet!)
XCJJ93.47/49 Mark Woodhams profiles John Dickenson
HG181.18/21 History of HG, including Dave Kilbourne soaring
Water Skier, June 1972, p.21: Bill Bennett's jump into Death Valley
XCSO94 Part 1 of Bill Liscomb's early days 1971–72
XCON94.52/53 Part 2 (need Part 1) Bill Liscomb's early days, '71–72
XCDJ94/5.42/44 Part 3 of Liscomb's early days at Torrey

4. Early British Years

W1284.6, 18 Profile Len Gabriels
UKFP874.3 B. Wood's duration record (food story)
UKFP874.10 Bob Makay's brilliant poem
W275.10 Bob Makay's lament for 'Mad Carew' (nee Kipling)
UKFB874.11 Foundation of the BHGA
W4 & 575 Accounts of 1975 Kössen
W575.5 Brian Wood's Kössen tumble
W675.10 Tony Fuell's 'A Spring Day' with Gary Glitter
W176.20 Nick Regan, flying in autumn 1972
W177.8 Row over South Africa
W575.18 Bob Mackay's 'Too many of us now' poem

5. Learning How to Fly Cross-Country

W980.5 Tony Fuell attacks Selsey thinking in editorial
W1080.8 Mike Collis replies to Tony Fuell over Selsey
W775.6 Graham Hobson's 'them thermals'
W576.14 Wave Lift (Maritos and Hobson)
W976.16/17 Hiway ad, Calvert's first XC flight in England
W1076.19 A mile high over Snowdon, Maritos & Hobson
W677.22/23 Nigel Milnes' 22-mile XC, 2nd real XC in UK
W777.2 First ad for electronic vario
W777.10/11 Johnny Carr's three superb XCs, path-finders
W877.20, George Worthington flies 95 miles in Mitchell Wing
W877.20 Jim McDougal flies 13 miles in Scotland
W1077.9 Calvert on 14-, 16-, 18-mile XCs
W1077.17 Jerry Katz of USA flies 103 miles in flexwing
W1077.18 Bob Bailey flies 24 miles for new UK record
WN579.13 Nigel Miles, Jerome Fack & 'Bob' fly 34 miles, UK rec
WN579.13 Early flash news that Bailey flew 50 miles
WN679.10/11 Robert Bailey's classic 50-mile account
W780.24/25 'Pork' on the Owens Valley Classic (good on nostalgia)
W880.17 Cockroft at 20,750 in Owens sans oxygen
W880.25/26 & 32 J. Hudson on the Bishop Animals
W980.6, Calvert does 79.3 miles, new Euro record
W581.16/17 John Stirk's new distance record

6. Hang Gliding and Sailplanes

Flying Scot, Spring 1976, pp.19–22, spirited comparison of HG and G
W1077.23 Instructive cartoon on G & HG
W480.18/19 First Brothers in Law (BiL), the Long Mynd
W580 2nd BiL (Sutton Bank)
W680 3rd BiL (Frocester)
W780.10/11 4th BiL (Bishop in Fife)
W880.12/13 5th BiL (Dunstable)
W880.17 Account by glider pilot of HGs (We're all mad)
W1180.20/21 The BGA replies to BiL articles
W281.5 Editorial on shocking BiL affairs at Dunstable

XCSP89.8/9 Comparison, pros and cons, gliding and HG
XCDJ92/3.32 Intelligent plea by glider pilot to link with HG

7. Competitions – How they Evolved

W476.16 Ken's Birdman competition
W876.33 Milton proposal to start League
W378.12 Milton's written challenge from Tracey Knauss about AmCup
W1178.15/23 First American Cup
HG877.10 Jerry Katz break 100 miles barrier in Owens, Pacific Gull
HG578.20/23 Debate on Owens Valley, safe or not?
HG781.1416 Jim Lee flies 168 miles
W281.11/19 Apres AmCup manufacturers meet, lots of comment

8. Powered Flight

W778.20/21 Dave Cook, flies Channel, silly comments on Rogallos
W880.6 First attempt at the Atlantic
W980.7 Atlantic Birdman grounded
W181.22/23 John Long as James Bond
WN679.14/15 Gossamer Albatross flight across Channel
W780.8 Sun-powered flight, on Easy Riser
W881.14 Solar Challenger flies the Channel
XCSP88.25 Daedalus Project, 74-mile man-powered flight
XCFM91.42 Eric Raymond flies C to C America by sun power
W877.14 Details on first powered Midas flight
W1077.19 Power HG conference
W1177.15 Power back-pack
W178.12/13 Len Gabriels on powered hang gliding
W978.12/13 Early birth pangs of powered hang gliding
W1178.12 My accident on BBC *Nationwide*
WN579.6 & 17/19 Breen flies 202 miles on a powered Scorpion
W180.23 Formation of the BMAA
W480.27 First Flight Line, including stats on M/Ls
W880.15 2nd Wellsbourne Power Meet
W880.16 Frankie Tarjanyi's trike XC

W980.8 Ashley Doubtfire on Land's End to John O' Groats
W980.16/17 Dave Garrison account of Land's End to John O' Groats
W980.22/23 Recreation of 1910 Ferguson flight in Newcastle
W1180.9 D. Kirke makes it to Paris by microlight
W1180.12/13 The first sky trike
W1280.12 The first Norfolk Air Race (by trikes)
W181.21 Richard Iddon 'Wheel fell orf' on sky trikes
W787.20/21 Gerry Breen's 550 m trike flight from John O'Groats
XCWI88.14/16 My flight to Oz, 1987/88
XCWI88.16 Eve Jackson's recognition
W189. Neil Hardiman half way around Oz. Vijay an AM!
W289.20/21 Part One of Neil's Oz flight
XCSU89.41 Dreadful French M/L accident rates
XCAU89.24/25 World distance records, a summary
XCAU89.29 Motorised cocoon, more details
XCAU89.40 Trans-Sahara by trike again
XCAU89.40 Crossing the Med by powered paraglider
XCWI89.21 Foot-launched motorised HG record 253k
XCWI89.31/34 2nd Trans-Sahara, an account
XCSU90.40/41 Using a trike to supply water to desert expedition
XCAM91.49 NZ, M/Ls now 18% of registration, also safest A/C
XCFM92.42/43 M/Ls in South America, used on health missions
W584.22/25 Towing by Trike, details report from Dave Simpson
FL3/486.8 News on RHM's Africa flight
FL3/486.27/28 Army tests on microlights
FL3/486.44/46 Accident review for 1985 in M/Ls in UK
FL3/487.30/38 RMH on London-Cape Town by trike